PostgreSQL 11 Server Side Programming Quick Start Guide

Effective database programming and interaction

Luca Ferrari

BIRMINGHAM - MUMBAI

PostgreSQL 11 Server Side Programming Quick Start Guide

Copyright © 2018 Packt Publishing

Commissioning Editor: Amey Varangaonkar
Acquisition Editor: Namrata Patil
Content Development Editor: Mohammed Yusuf Imaratwale
Technical Editor: Shweta Jadhav
Copy Editor: Safis Editing
Project Coordinator: Hardik Bhinde
Proofreader: Safis Editing
Indexer: Pratik Shirodkar
Graphics: Jason Monteiro
Production Coordinator: Jyoti Chauhan

First published: November 2018

Production reference: 1271118

Published by Packt Publishing Ltd.
Livery Place
35 Livery Street
Birmingham
B3 2PB, UK.

ISBN 978-1-78934-222-2

www.packtpub.com

To my beautiful wife, Emanuela; I love her like Santa loves his reindeer.
To my great son, Diego, who has changed our lives on 1283788200.
To my parents, Miriam and Anselmo; my greatest fans since day one.

– Luca Ferrari

`mapt.io`

Mapt is an online digital library that gives you full access to over 5,000 books and videos, as well as industry leading tools to help you plan your personal development and advance your career. For more information, please visit our website.

Why subscribe?

- Spend less time learning and more time coding with practical eBooks and Videos from over 4,000 industry professionals

- Improve your learning with Skill Plans built especially for you

- Get a free eBook or video every month

- Mapt is fully searchable

- Copy and paste, print, and bookmark content

Packt.com

Did you know that Packt offers eBook versions of every book published, with PDF and ePub files available? You can upgrade to the eBook version at `www.packt.com` and as a print book customer, you are entitled to a discount on the eBook copy. Get in touch with us at `customercare@packtpub.com` for more details.

At `www.packt.com`, you can also read a collection of free technical articles, sign up for a range of free newsletters, and receive exclusive discounts and offers on Packt books and eBooks.

Contributors

About the author

Luca has been passionate about computer science since the Commodore 64 era, and today holds a master's degree (with honors) and a PhD from the University of Modena and Reggio Emilia. He has written several research papers, technical articles, and book chapters.

In 2011, he was named Adjunct Professor by the University of Nipissing. An avid Unix user, he is a strong advocate of open source, and in his free time he collaborates with a few projects. He met PostgreSQL back in release 7.3; he was a founder and former president of the **Italian PostgreSQL Community** (**ITPUG**), he talks regularly at technical conferences and events, and delivers professional training. In his teenage years, he was quite a proficient archer. He lives in Italy with his beautiful wife, son, and two (female) cats.

I thank my family for being patient while I was spending so much time in front of my computer. And I thank Olivia and Sofia for constantly purring alongside me while typing.

A big thank you to my best friends, Monica Piccinelli and Claudio Chiossi, for being there to listen to my musings and patiently keep me on track.

Thanks to my friend, Enrico Pirozzi, who believed in me from the very beginning.

The people at Packt have been really professional and collaborative: thank you, all!

And, of course, I really thank the people behind PostgreSQL, for giving us such a big database and community!

About the reviewers

Sheldon Strauch is a 20-year veteran of software consulting at companies such as IBM, Sears, Ernst & Young, and Kraft Foods. He has a bachelor's degree in business administration and leverages his technical skills to improve businesses' self-awareness. His interests include data gathering, management, and mining; maps and mapping; business intelligence; and the application of data analysis for continuous improvement. He is currently focused on the development of end-to-end data management and mining at Enova International, a financial services company located in Chicago. In his spare time, he enjoys the performing arts, particularly music, and traveling with his wife, Marilyn.

Andrew Caya started programming computers in GW-BASIC and QBASIC in the early 90s. Before becoming a PHP developer almost 10 years ago, he did some software development in C, C++, and Perl. He is now a Zend-Certified PHP Engineer and a Zend-Certified Architect. He is also the creator of Linux for PHP, the lead developer of a popular Joomla extension, and a contributor to many open source projects.

He is currently CEO, CTO, and founder of *Foreach Code Factory*, an instructor at *Concordia University*, an author and a technical reviewer for Packt Publishing, and a loving husband and father.

Packt is searching for authors like you

If you're interested in becoming an author for Packt, please visit `authors.packtpub.com` and apply today. We have worked with thousands of developers and tech professionals, just like you, to help them share their insight with the global tech community. You can make a general application, apply for a specific hot topic that we are recruiting an author for, or submit your own idea.

Table of Contents

Preface

This book will guide you through the development of code inside PostgreSQL 11, the world's most advanced open source database.

PostgreSQL has grown a lot from being a relation database to a whole ecosystem, and has a very rich feature set, a professional and supportive community, and delivers a high quality rock-solid DBMS with outstanding documentation. Thanks to its features and capabilities, PostgreSQL is every day embraced by more and more professionals and industries, and it is for this reason that it is important to understand what is possible with this great database.

Who this book is for

This book is intended for developers and database administrators who already know a few of the basic concepts about relational databases, SQL statements, and transactions. Because the installation and configuration of PostgreSQL is out of the scope of this book, readers should already be familiar with how to run and interact with PostgreSQL.

In this book, we are going to learn about the main features that PostgreSQL provides in order to ease the development of code on the database side, as well as how to use code to implement business rules and keep data under control and consistent. As it is focused on the development side, this book does not cover other topics related to the database, such as tuning, query optimization, privileges, or replication.

What this book covers

This book aims to teach the reader how powerful server-side programming can be in PostgreSQL. At the same time, we are going to learn how fun can it be to implement even complex tasks directly in the database engine. This book is structured as follows:

Chapter 1, *PostgreSQL Server-side Programming*, presents the idea behind server-side programming and the relationship with PostgreSQL.

Chapter 2, *Statement Tricks: UPSERTs, RETURNING, and CTEs*, explains some of the powerful features of handling SQL statements that are supported by PostgreSQL, such as obtaining automatically computed data, resolving insert conflicts, and performing looping and joins.

Chapter 3, *The PL/pgSQL Language*, discusses the default language that can be used to implement code in PostgreSQL. This is an imperative, SQL-like language.

Chapter 4, *Stored Procedures*, teaches you how to store pieces of code in the server in order to execute them and re-use them later.

Chapter 5, *PL/Perl and PL/Java*, provides insights into how to use Perl and Java within the PostgreSQL server to implement stored procedures and run code.

Chapter 6, *Triggers*, explains how to run code that can react to data change events and data definition change events.

Chapter 7, *Rules and the Query Rewriting System*, explains how PostgreSQL can be used to transform statements into other forms.

Chapter 8, *Extensions*, teaches you how to organize your code in a way that PostgreSQL can handle and manage, as well as how to deal with updates.

Chapter 9, *Intra-Process Communication and Background Workers*, looks at how to interact with processes (database connections) and how to plug your own processes into the server.

Chapter 10, *Custom Data Types*, shows how it is possible to extend the already rich PostgreSQL data type to implement your own type with specific business logic.

To get the most out of this book

In order to test and run the code examples you will need a working instance of PostgreSQL 11 or greater. In particular, it is required that you have a working client (such as *psql*), a user account, and a database you can work on.

In order to test Perl examples you will need a recent installation of Perl 5, and a Java 8 JDK to compile and run Java examples.

Any other specific requirements will be detailed in the chapters.

Download the example code files

You can download the example code files for this book from your account at www.packt.com. If you purchased this book elsewhere, you can visit www.packt.com/support and register to have the files emailed directly to you.

You can download the code files by following these steps:

1. Log in or register at `www.packt.com`.
2. Select the **SUPPORT** tab.
3. Click on **Code Downloads & Errata**.
4. Enter the name of the book in the **Search** box and follow the onscreen instructions.

Once the file is downloaded, please make sure that you unzip or extract the folder using the latest version of:

- WinRAR/7-Zip for Windows
- Zipeg/iZip/UnRarX for Mac
- 7-Zip/PeaZip for Linux

The code bundle for the book is also hosted on GitHub at `https://github.com/PacktPublishing/PostgreSQL-11-Quick-Start-Guide`. In case there's an update to the code, it will be updated on the existing GitHub repository.

We also have other code bundles from our rich catalog of books and videos available at `https://github.com/PacktPublishing/`. Check them out!

Conventions used

There are a number of text conventions used throughout this book.

`CodeInText`: Indicates code words in text, database table names, folder names, filenames, file extensions, pathnames, dummy URLs, user input, and Twitter handles. Here is an example: "Mount the downloaded `WebStorm-10*.dmg` disk image file as another disk in your system."

A block of code is set as follows:

```
ImgRes* new_ImgRes() {
  ImgRes* new_object = (ImgRes*) palloc( sizeof( ImgRes ) );
  new_object->h_px = 300;
  new_object->v_px = 300;
  new_object->dpi  = 96;
  return new_object;
}

char* to_string( ImgRes* object ){
```

```
return psprintf( TEXT_PATTERN,
                    object->h_px,  object->v_px,  object->dpi );
}
```

Any command-line input or output is written as follows:

```
testdb=> CREATE TYPE t_media_file_type
AS ENUM ( 'audio', 'image', 'text' );
```

Bold: Indicates a new term, an important word, or words that you see onscreen. For example, words in menus or dialog boxes appear in the text like this. Here is an example: "Select **System info** from the **Administration** panel."

Warnings or important notes appear like this.

Tips and tricks appear like this.

Get in touch

Feedback from our readers is always welcome.

General feedback: If you have questions about any aspect of this book, mention the book title in the subject of your message and email us at customercare@packtpub.com.

Errata: Although we have taken every care to ensure the accuracy of our content, mistakes do happen. If you have found a mistake in this book, we would be grateful if you would report this to us. Please visit www.packt.com/submit-errata, selecting your book, clicking on the Errata Submission Form link, and entering the details.

Piracy: If you come across any illegal copies of our works in any form on the Internet, we would be grateful if you would provide us with the location address or website name. Please contact us at copyright@packt.com with a link to the material.

If you are interested in becoming an author: If there is a topic that you have expertise in and you are interested in either writing or contributing to a book, please visit authors.packtpub.com.

Reviews

Please leave a review. Once you have read and used this book, why not leave a review on the site that you purchased it from? Potential readers can then see and use your unbiased opinion to make purchase decisions, we at Packt can understand what you think about our products, and our authors can see your feedback on their book. Thank you!

For more information about Packt, please visit `packt.com`.

1
PostgreSQL Server-side Programming

The motto of PostgreSQL is widely known: *the most advanced open source database in the world*. PostgreSQL is a rock-solid, scalable, and safe enterprise-level relational database that is gaining increasing popularity thanks to its wide variety of features and its stability. It is developed and maintained by a team of database experts, but it is open source, which means it is not a commercial product; it belongs to everyone and everyone can contribute to it. Moreover, thanks to its permissive BSD-style license, it can be released as a custom product, allowing both the marketplace and business opportunities to grow.

The latest release of this database is PostgreSQL 11. This version includes a number of new features on both the core side, such as replication and partitioning, and the in-database development side, such as procedures and improved support for event triggers. Developing within PostgreSQL is fun and easy, as it provides a rich infrastructure for developers to integrate the business logic within the database itself. We can implement this logic in a large set of available languages, including Perl, Python, Java, and Ruby, breaking the restriction of having to carry out all database-related activity in SQL.

This book focuses on the development side of interacting with PostgreSQL, which means embedding the code into the database in order to automate tasks, keep data more coherent by enforcing rules, mangling data, and transforming it. Throughout this book, we will look at two "external" languages: Perl and Java. Choosing which external languages to use was not easy, since PostgreSQL supports a large number of them, but the important concept is that, you, the developer, are free to choose the language you prefer in order to implement server-side programming with PostgreSQL. Of course, as you can imagine and as we will see over the course of the book, this does not mean that any language is appropriate for any task. Languages behave differently because they have different sets of features, different cultures, different ecosystems and libraries, and different support for different tools. Therefore, even though PostgreSQL allows us freedom with regard to the language we use, it is important that we bear in mind that different situations might require different languages.

Why is my favorite language not listed?

PostgreSQL supports a lot of *foreign* languages, which can be either scripting languages or not. As you can imagine, explaining all the details of every language is outside the scope of this book. However, in order to demonstrate the differences between the *native* PostgreSQL language (which is often called PL/pgSQL) and foreign languages, we chose to show a well-integrated scripting language, Perl, and a compiled one, Java. The same concepts, advantages, and drawbacks of these two languages can be applied to other languages.

Some examples will be implemented using the C language, which is the language that PostgreSQL itself is implemented in. For this reason, it has better support in PostgreSQL. However, it is possible to almost totally avoid developing in the C language and to opt instead for friendlier and easier languages.

In this chapter, we will take a look at the following topics:

- What server-side programming is
- An introduction to the languages that will be used in the rest of the book to implement examples
- How the book is organized and which topics will be covered in each chapter
- How to read and understand the code examples

What is server-side programming?

Server-side programming is a term used to indicate the development (or programming) of features (such as code) within the server directly, or, in other words, on the server side. It is the opposite of **client-side programming**, which is where a technological stack accesses the database, manipulates the data, and enforces rules. Server-side programming allows developers to embed business logic directly into the server (such as PostgreSQL), so that it is the duty of the server to run code to enforce constraints and keep the data secure and coherent. Moreover, since server-side programming embeds code in the server, it helps to implement automation.

One advantage of server-side programming is that the code runs locally to the data it uses; no network connection or external resources are required to access the underlying data. This usually means that the code that is embedded into the server runs faster than the client-side code, which requires the user to connect to the database in order to gain access to the data that is stored.

This also means that the client application can exploit embedded code, since it is centralized to the server, without any regard to the technological stack that the client is using. This often speeds up the implementation of applications, since no distributed or external dependencies are required, other than the ones needed by the server itself.

Last but not least, server-side programming allows the code to be stored into the database itself. This means that this code is managed like any other database object and can be backed up and restored with the usual database-backup tools. This is not quite true for the languages that come in a compiled form, such as Java, but having code stored within the database simplifies a lot of the management involved in migrating and upgrading the code regardless. Of course, server-side programming should not be thought of as a comprehensive solution to every problem. If it is used incorrectly, the code stored within the server can make it consume too many resources, including memory and temporary files (and also I/O bandwidth), resulting in the users' data being served at a lower speed. It is therefore really important to exploit server-side programming only in situations in which it makes sense to do so and when it can simplify the management of the data and the code.

How to get help

PostgreSQL is well known for its extensive and accurate documentation. Moreover, the PostgreSQL community is very responsive and collaborative with regard to welcoming and helping new users. Typically, help is provided by the community via both **Internet Relay Chat** (**IRC**) channels and mailing lists. Related projects often have their own IRC channels and mailing lists as well.

However, having channels through which we can ask for help does not mean that every question we ask will be answered. Bear in mind that the people behind the mailing lists or the IRC channels are often volunteering their own time. Therefore, before sending a question, be sure to have done your homework by reading the documentation and providing as much information as possible so that other people can replicate and test out your particular problem. This usually means providing a clear indicating of the version of PostgreSQL that you are running, the type and version of the OS that you are using, and a compact and complete SQL example to replicate your scenario. If you do this, you will be astonished at how quickly and accurately the community can help.

The example database

This book aims to be a practical guide. For this reason, in the following chapters, you will see several code examples. Instead of building ad-hoc examples for every feature, the book references a small database from a real-world application, in order to show how you can improve your own database with the features covered.

The example database, named `testdb`, is inspired by an asset-management software that stores file metadata and related tags. A **file** is something that is stored on a disk and is identified by properties such as a name, a hash (of its content), and a size on the disk. Each file can be categorized with **tags**, which are labels that are attached to the file itself.

Listing 1 shows the SQL code that generates the structure of the `file` table, which has the following columns:

- `pk` is a surrogate key that is automatically generated by a sequence
- `f_name` represents the file name on the disk
- `f_size` represents the size of the file on the disk
- `f_type` is a textual representation of the file type (for example, **MP3** for a music file)
- `f_hash` represents a hash of the content of the file

We might want to prevent the addition of two files with the same content hash. In this case, the `f_hash` column works as a unique key. Another optional constraint is related to file size; since every file on a disk has a size greater or equal to zero (bytes), it is possible to force the `f_size` column to store only non-negative values. Similarly, the name of the file cannot be unspecified. More constraints can be added; we will cover some of these in the following chapters.

```
CREATE TABLE IF NOT EXISTS files (
    pk int GENERATED ALWAYS AS IDENTITY,
    f_name text NOT NULL,
    f_size numeric(15,4) DEFAULT 0,
    f_hash text NOT NULL DEFAULT 'N/A',
    f_type text DEFAULT 'txt',
    ts timestamp DEFAULT now(),
    PRIMARY KEY ( pk ),
    UNIQUE ( f_hash ),
    CHECK ( f_size >= 0 )
);
```

Listing 1: Code to create the files table

Listing 2 shows the structure of the `tags` table:

- `pk` is a surrogate key that is automatically generated by a sequence.
- `t_name` is the tag name.
- `t_child_of` is a self-reference to the tuple of another tag. Tags can be nested into each other to build a hierarchy of tags. As an example, let's say the `photos` tag contains the `family` and `trips` tags; these are children of the `photos` tag. The same tag can appear in different hierarchies, but cannot appear twice in the same position of the same hierarchy. For this reason, a unique constraint over the tag name and its relationship is enforced.

```
CREATE TABLE IF NOT EXISTS tags(
    pk int GENERATED ALWAYS AS IDENTITY,
    t_name text NOT NULL,
    t_child_of int,
    PRIMARY KEY ( pk ),
    FOREIGN KEY ( t_child_of )      REFERENCES tags( pk ),
    UNIQUE( t_name, t_child_of )
);
```

Listing 2: SQL code to generate the tags table structure

Since a file can have multiple tags, a join table has been used to instantiate a many-to-many relationship. Listing 3 shows a join table, which is named `j_files_tags`. This simply stores a relationship between the tuple of a file and the tuple of a tag, allowing only one association between a file and a tag.

```
CREATE TABLE IF NOT EXISTS j_files_tags (
    pk int GENERATED ALWAYS AS IDENTITY,
    f_pk int,
    t_pk int,
    PRIMARY KEY ( pk ),
    UNIQUE( f_pk, t_pk ),
    FOREIGN KEY ( f_pk ) REFERENCES files( pk ) ON DELETE CASCADE,
    FOREIGN KEY ( t_pk ) REFERENCES tags( pk )  ON DELETE CASCADE
);
```

Listing 3: SQL code to create a join table to match files and tag tables data

There are also some other tables that are used to demonstrate particular scenarios. The first is named `archive_files`, and has the same structure as the `files` table. The other is named `playlist`, and represents a very minimalistic music playlist with filenames and a simple structure, as shown in listing 4:

```
CREATE TABLE IF NOT EXISTS playlist (
        pk int GENERATED ALWAYS AS IDENTITY,
        p_name text NOT NULL,
        PRIMARY KEY ( pk )
);
```

Listing 4: SQL code to generate the playlist table

We can either construct these tables by hand or by using one of the scripts provided with the book code snippets from the code repository, located at `https://github.com/PacktPublishing/PostgreSQL-11-Quick-Start-Guide`. In this case, the tables will also be populated with some test data that we can use to show the results of queries that we will be running in the following chapters.

 As you can see, each table column has a prefix letter that identifies the table to which it belongs. For example, `f_name` has a prefix, `f`, that reminds the files table it belongs to. This can help us to discriminate the columns of a table when they are joined or when a complex query is built. Throughout the examples in this book, the same concept will be applied to different objects. For example, a function will have a name starting with an `f`, a procedure with a `p`, a trigger with `tr`, and so on. While this is not a commonly-used best practice, it can help us to understand the type of an object and its context from its name.

All the examples shown in this book have been tested and run on PostgreSQL 11 on FreeBSD. They should work seamlessly on any other PostgreSQL 11 installation. All the code has been run through the official `psql` command line client, even if it is possible to run them with other supported clients (such as pgAdmin4).

Most of the code snippets can be executed as a normal database user. This is emphasized in the code by the `psql` default prompt, which is as follows:

```
testdb=>
```

If the code must be run from a database administrator, otherwise known as a superuser, the prompt will change accordingly, as follows:

```
testdb=#
```

As well as this, the examples in which superuser privileges are required will be clearly indicated.

Each time we execute a statement via `psql`, we get a reply that confirms the execution of the statement. If we execute `SELECT *`, the reply we receive will be a list of tuples. If we execute other statements, we will get a *tag* that represents the execution of the statement. This is demonstrated in the following examples:

```
testdb=> INSERT INTO playlist VALUES( ... );
INSERT
testdb=> LISTEN my_channel;
LISTEN
testdb=> CREATE FUNCTION foo() RETURNS VOID AS $$ BEGIN END $$ LANGUAGE
plpgsql;
CREATE FUNCTION
```

So that we can focus on the important parts of a code snippet, we will remove the output reply of each statement execution if it is not important. The preceding listing can therefore be represented in a more concise way, as follows:

```
testdb=> INSERT INTO playlist VALUES( ... );
testdb=> LISTEN my_channel;
testdb=> CREATE FUNCTION foo() RETURNS VOID AS $$ BEGIN END $$ LANGUAGE
plpgsql;
```

In this way, you will see only the commands and the statements that you have to insert into the server connection.

The source code of the examples in this book

All the source code of the book is available as individual files with the downloadable source code. Almost every file name includes the number of the chapter it belongs to and a suffix that indicates the type of file. In most cases, this will be `sql`, which denotes the SQL script. Files with the `output` extension are not runnable code; instead, these are the output of commands. As an example, the `Chapter3_Listing01.sql` file is the first listing script from Chapter 3, *The PL/pgSQL Language*, while `Chapter3_Listing01.output` is the textual result of the execution of the former file. Both are shown with the listing number 3.

Please note that the code formatting in the source files and the code snippets of the book are not exactly the same due to typographical constraints.

Summary

PostgreSQL is a powerful and feature-rich enterprise-level database. It allows database administrators and application developers to store code directly in the server and execute code whenever it is required, allowing us to use a server-side-programming approach. The advantage of having code that is executed by the server itself is that it runs nearer the data, it is under the control of the server, and it is centralized, which means that every connection that accesses the data will execute the same code.

Developing in PostgreSQL is fun and powerful, thanks to its rich and modular platform.

Statement Tricks: UPSERTs, RETURNING, and CTEs

2

Before taking a closer look at server-side programming, it is worth exploring some of the cool features PostgreSQL provides that allow us to enhance statements. Sometimes, developers start working in a rush to solve a specific problem, which often means writing a function, a routine, or a whole program just to inspect some data. The features provided by PostgreSQL alleviate the need to do this.

This chapter will look at some of these features, and will offer hints and tricks so that you can gain as much as possible from ordinary statements. This will not only make any problems simpler to address, but will also improve your database experience.

In particular, in day-to-day database activity, there is often the need to get back auto-generate values (for example, keys, dates, timestamps, and so on), fix insertion conflicts, and even recursing on a flat data set.

So, after reading this chapter, we will have learned the following:

- How to solve tuple insertion conflicts
- How to get back automatically generated tuple data, such as incremental keys or timestamps
- How to write better statements with Common Table Expressions
- How to perform recursion at a statement level using Recursive Common Table Expressions

Inserting, updating, or both?

The UPSERT statement is a way of performing an UPDATE over an INSERT, allowing an INSERT statement to be automatically rewritten as an UPDATE statement under certain conditions. In particular, if the INSERT statement cannot be performed due to a conflict between data that already exists and data that is going to be inserted, the UPSERT statement enables you to override this conflict.

This technique is similar to what many **Object Relational Mappers** (**ORMs**) do when a generic persistence action is performed. The ORM examines the object it has to persist (the data), and if it finds out that an object has never been seen on the database, it executes an INSERT; otherwise, it performs an UPDATE. In this way, the client code (and therefore the developer) never has to consider which database actions have to be performed to persist the data. This is also the case when using the UPSERT statement.

It is important to note that in order for a database to decide if a regular INSERT statement can proceed, or if it has to be converted into an UPDATE, a conflict must exist—otherwise there is no chance of the database understanding if the data already exists. Typically, this conflict happens against a primary key or a unique constraint. This is, effectively, what many ORMs check: if an object already has a primary key, an UPDATE is required. Otherwise, a normal INSERT statement can be issued instead.

In order to better understand how an UPSERT statement works, insert the following data into the files table, as follows:

```
testdb=> INSERT INTO files( f_name, f_hash )
VALUES ( 'chapter1.org', 'f029d04a81c322f158c608596951c105' )
     , ( 'chapter2.org', '14b8f225d4e6462022657d7285bb77ba' );
```

Listing 1: Inserting two entries in the file table

Let's not say that another INSERT statement for the same file content has been issued. In this case, the database has to reject the incoming data because of the unique constraint defined over the f_hash column, as shown in the following listing:

```
testdb=> INSERT INTO files( f_name, f_hash )
VALUES ( 'chapter2-reviewed.org', '14b8f225d4e6462022657d7285bb77ba' );

ERROR: duplicate key value violates unique constraint "files_f_hash_key"
DETAIL: Key (f_hash)=(14b8f225d4e6462022657d7285bb77ba) already exists.
```

Listing 2: Unique constraints in action

In order to allow the database to accept the incoming data and perform an UPDATE to resolve the conflict, we need to specify the ON CONFLICT predicate, as shown in the following:

```
testdb=> INSERT INTO files( f_name, f_hash )
VALUES ( 'chapter2-reviewed.org', '14b8f225d4e6462022657d7285bb77ba' ) ON
CONFLICT ( f_hash ) DO UPDATE SET f_name = EXCLUDED.f_name;
```

Listing 3: UPSERT in action

When the query shown in the preceding *Listing 3* is executed, the system finds a conflict over the unique constraint for the f_hash column. This time, however, there is an ON CONFLICT resolution strategy. The ON CONFLICT (f_hash) DO UPDATE predicate indicates that if a conflict arises from the f_hash column, the database should perform an UPDATE instead of INSERT. In the UPDATE part of the statement, the special alias EXCLUDED represents the tuple that has been rejected due to the conflict. In other words, in the code of *Listing 3*, the database will either perform a regular INSERT statement if the data is not already present, or it will update the f_name of the conflicting tuple.

It is worth noting that the UPDATE predicate can also include a WHERE condition in order to better filter the update to be performed. Since the excluded tuple is aliased as EXCLUDED, the current tuple must be referenced with the table name, as we can see in the following listing. In this case, only tuples with the f_type org can be updated when a conflicting INSERT statement is issued. Other types of files, such as f_type, will simply fail if a unique constraint violation occurs:

```
testdb=> INSERT INTO files( f_name, f_hash )
VALUES ( 'chapter2-reviewed.org', '14b8f225d4e6462022657d7285bb77ba' ) ON
CONFLICT ( f_hash ) DO UPDATE SET f_name = EXCLUDED.f_name WHERE
files.f_type = 'org';
```

Listing 4: Filtering the update within an UPSERT

This is not the only strategy available, of course; it is also possible to simply do nothing at all. Note that doing nothing is different from the default behavior, which is failing on conflicts. When an INSERT statement is instructed to do nothing upon conflict, data is gracefully rejected, no error is reported, and our transaction will not abort. Everything works as if we had never executed the INSERT statement.

As shown in the following listing, all we need to do is to specify DO NOTHING within the ON
CONFLICT part of the statement to ensure the conflicting tuples are gracefully thrown away:

```
testdb=> INSERT INTO files( f_name, f_hash )
VALUES ( 'chapter2-reviewed.org', '14b8f225d4e6462022657d7285bb77ba' ) ON
CONFLICT ( f_hash ) DO NOTHING;
```

Listing 5: Rejecting conflicting data without aborting the current transaction

Getting back modified data with RETURNING

Each write-statement (INSERT, UPDATE, or DELETE) supports an optional RETURNING
predicate that makes the statement return a results set with the manipulated tuples. From a
conceptual point of view, it is as if these INSERT, UPDATE, and DELETE commands are
immediately followed by an automatic SELECT statement.

This feature is very useful. It allows us to get back the exact values of the manipulated
tuples, such as an automatically generated key, a computed timestamp, or other non-
predictable values. It also allows us to pipeline write statements one after another, as you
will see later in this chapter.

Let's take a look at the RETURNING function in action. Imagine that we need to insert some
random data into the files table, as follows:

```
testdb=> INSERT INTO files( f_name, f_hash, f_size )
SELECT 'file_' || v || '.txt', md5( v::text ), v * ( random() * 100 )::int
FROM generate_series(1, 10 ) v;
```

Listing 6: Populating the files table with some random data

The preceding lines generate ten records with a random f_size and f_hash, as well as an
auto-generated value for the pk primary key. We don't know the exact values that are going
to hit, which are the values that are stored in the underlying table. RETURNING helps to
solve this problem by providing us with the tuples inserted by the statement, as shown in
the following listing:

```
testdb=> INSERT INTO files( f_name, f_hash, f_size )
SELECT 'File_' || v || '.txt',
       md5( v::text || random() ), v * ( random() * 111 )::int
FROM generate_series( 1, 10 ) v
RETURNING pk, f_name, f_hash, f_size, ts;
```

```
 pk  |   f_name    |                 f_hash                  |  f_size  |
ts
----+-------------+-----------------------------------------+----------+----------
-------------------
 24 | File_1.txt  | c09206052f182c8a01cd83ee0d4a7a78        |  21.0000 |
2018-10-31 09:37:29.036638
 25 | File_2.txt  | cec37633a67a66f99e4e427df5e40ee0        | 208.0000 |
2018-10-31 09:37:29.036638
 26 | File_3.txt  | afd08c4410e7600931bfcef8c3627cde        | 267.0000 |
2018-10-31 09:37:29.036638
 27 | File_4.txt  | e8e56856ba183212b433151aeb3506cd        | 384.0000 |
2018-10-31 09:37:29.036638
 28 | File_5.txt  | eab791d36b1fa25816d6715e628db02c        | 235.0000 |
2018-10-31 09:37:29.036638
 29 | File_6.txt  | 552ed45e182088346cfd0503f2fef1f8        |  54.0000 |
2018-10-31 09:37:29.036638
 30 | File_7.txt  | 1a89ccc034a8d48b8bc92bf58d18e8bf        | 679.0000 |
2018-10-31 09:37:29.036638
 31 | File_8.txt  | 0fe766ac50617ea7ff6d1cfb3e8060d2        | 400.0000 |
2018-10-31 09:37:29.036638
 32 | File_9.txt  | 063a175cf2b498dab6bf93fb8f76427a        | 648.0000 |
2018-10-31 09:37:29.036638
 33 | File_10.txt | 42c450d54f4fe7e29b245a3d50258f4d        | 770.0000 |
2018-10-31 09:37:29.036638
```

Listing 7: An INSERT that provides a result set

As we can see in the preceding snippet, the RETURNING function accepts the same column list as a regular SELECT command, including the special * symbol, which means the statement will return all available columns. The following listing illustrates how to use the * symbol to get back all the columns of the deleted tuples:

```
testdb=> DELETE FROM files RETURNING *;

 pk | f_name | f_hash |f_type|f_size| ts ----+------------+---------------
-------------------+------+------+------------------------- 1 |
file_1.txt | c4ca4238a0b923820dcc509a6f75849b | | 54 | 2018-06-18
19:49:52.59167 2 | file_2.txt | c81e728d9d4c2f636f067f89cc14862c | | 78 |
2018-06-18 19:49:52.59167 3 | file_3.txt | eccbc87e4b5ce2fe28308fd9f2a7baf3
| | 153 | 2018-06-18 19:49:52.59167 4 | file_4.txt |
a87ff679a2f3e71d9181a67b7542122c | | 280 | 2018-06-18 19:49:52.59167 5 |
file_5.txt | e4da3b7fbbce2345d7772b0674a318d5 | | 160 | 2018-06-18
19:49:52.59167 6 | file_6.txt | 1679091c5a880faf6fb5e6087eb1b2dc | | 234 |
2018-06-18 19:49:52.59167 7 | file_7.txt | 8f14e45fceea167a5a36dedd4bea2543
| | 420 | 2018-06-18 19:49:52.59167 8 | file_8.txt |
c9f0f895fb98ab9159f51fd0297e236d | | 232 | 2018-06-18 19:49:52.59167 9 |
file_9.txt | 45c48cce2e2d7fbdea1afc51c7c6ad26 | | 396 | 2018-06-18
```

```
19:49:52.59167 10 | file_10.txt | d3d9446802a44259755d38e6d163e820 | | 280
| 2018-06-18 19:49:52.59167
```

<small>Listing 8: Getting back all of the deleted tuples</small>

Note that the result provided by the RETURNING function represents the final state of the manipulated tuples. This means that the result set is built after all of the triggers, if any, have been fired.

In order to test the following code snippets, you will need to keep some tuples in the files table. You can execute *Listing 7* to re-populate the table once you have deleted the tuples.

The result set provided by a RETURNING predicate is also available from external client applications. For example, as shown in the following listing, it is possible to iterate over results from a Java client:

```
class returning {
    public static void main( String argv[] ) throws Exception {
        Class.forName( "org.postgresql.Driver" );
        String connectionURL = "jdbc:postgresql://localhost/testdb";
        Properties connectionProperties = new Properties();
        connectionProperties.put( "user", "luca" );
        connectionProperties.put( "password", "secret" );
        Connection conn = DriverManager.getConnection( connectionURL,
        connectionProperties );

        String query = "INSERT INTO files( f_name, f_hash, f_size ) "
            + " SELECT 'file_' || v || '.txt',"
            + " md5( v::text ),"
            + " v * ( random() * 100 )::int"
            + " FROM generate_series(1, 10 ) v "
            + " RETURNING pk, f_name, f_hash, f_size, ts;";

        Statement statement = conn.createStatement();
        ResultSet resultSet = statement.executeQuery( query );
        while ( resultSet.next() )
            System.out.println( String.format( "pk = %d, size = %d,
            hash = %s", resultSet.getLong( "pk" ), resultSet.getInt(
            "f_size" ), resultSet.getString( "f_hash" ) ) );
            resultSet.close();
            statement.close();
    }
}
```

<small>Listing 9: Getting back inserted tuples from a Java client</small>

When the Java code is executed, the output will look as follows:

```
pk = 11, size = 22, hash = c4ca4238a0b923820dcc509a6f75849b
pk = 12, size = 90, hash = c81e728d9d4c2f636f067f89cc14862c
pk = 13, size = 225, hash = eccbc87e4b5ce2fe28308fd9f2a7baf3
pk = 14, size = 368, hash = a87ff679a2f3e71d9181a67b7542122c
pk = 15, size = 460, hash = e4da3b7fbbce2345d7772b0674a318d5
pk = 16, size = 330, hash = 1679091c5a880faf6fb5e6087eb1b2dc
pk = 17, size = 140, hash = 8f14e45fceea167a5a36dedd4bea2543
pk = 18, size = 544, hash = c9f0f895fb98ab9159f51fd0297e236d
pk = 19, size = 801, hash = 45c48cce2e2d7fbdea1afc51c7c6ad26
pk = 20, size = 980, hash = d3d9446802a44259755d38e6d163e820
```

Common Table Expressions (CTEs)

Common Table Expressions (CTEs), also known as *queries*, take advantage of a particular syntax when writing sub-queries that make statements a lot more readable. Readability, however, is not the only reason to use CTEs: their structure also allows for a statement pipeline of sorts, and in their recursive version, they can be used to loop through joins.

Introducing CTEs

Any DML statement (such as SELECT, INSERT, UPDATE, and DELETE) can be enhanced by placing a WITH predicate before the query. Any sub-query appearing in the WITH clause can be thought of as a materialized result set over the data, or as a temporary table that exists throughout the duration of a statement. CTEs have many applications—the primary one being the ability to split a complex query into a set of smaller queries. A CTE can be made up of the following two parts:

- A main query, also known as a top-level statement.
- One or more sub-queries, which materialize data for the duration of a main query. Each sub-query is also known as an auxiliary statement.

Every auxiliary statement has a name that is used to reference it from the main query or other sub-queries. It may also have a list of returned column names. The template of a CTE, therefore, is as follows:

```
WITH
-- sub-queries
sub-query_1 AS ( <query> )
, sub-query_2 AS ( <query> )
```

```
-- main query
<query referencing sub-query_1 and sub-query_2>
```

The following listing shows a very simple CTE that selects all file names from a sub-query that, in turn, select specific hash values:

```
testdb=> WITH get_files_by_hash AS (
     SELECT pk, f_name FROM files WHERE f_hash like 'abc%' )
SELECT f_name FROM get_files_by_hash;
```

Listing 10: An example of a simple CTE

There are a few rules to bear in mind relating to the use of CTEs. The first important rule is that PostgreSQL does not optimize any query outside of a WITH boundary. This means that each auxiliary statement is considered on its own by the optimizer, and that constraints are not pushed outside of sub-query boundaries.

Another important rule is that every auxiliary statement of a CTE is evaluated no more than once. This means that CTEs can be used to wrap complex computations that will be executed once, no matter how many times the result is requested in the main query. If the CTE auxiliary statement is read-only (if it is a SELECT statement, for example), it will be executed only once it is referenced. This means that it is possible to insert a CTE auxiliary statement that has never been executed. Similarly, if the CTE auxiliary statement is writable (if it contains any INSERT, UPDATE, or DELETE statements), it will only be executed once and without any regard to whether the auxiliary statement has been referenced in the main query.

Let's take a look at an example to make this clearer. As you can see in the following listing, the CTE defines two read-only sub-queries, but only get_random_number is referenced across the whole CTE. Therefore, the get_current_time auxiliary statement will never be executed. On the other hand, the delete_files auxiliary statement, as it is writable, will be executed exactly once, even if it is not referenced anywhere:

```
testdb=> WITH get_current_time AS ( SELECT now()::time ) ,
get_random_number AS ( SELECT random() ) ,
delete_files AS ( DELETE FROM files )
SELECT r, s FROM get_random_number r, generate_series( 1, 3 ) s;
```

Listing 11: Writable and read-only CTEs

If you execute the statement in the preceding snippet, the output should be as shown in the following listing. From there, we can clearly see that the random number generated by the get_random_number auxiliary statement is always the same, confirming that the auxiliary statement has been invoked exactly once:

```
        r              | s
----------------------+---
(0.0959695233032107) | 1
(0.0959695233032107) | 2
(0.0959695233032107) | 3
```

Listing 12: Writable and read-only CTEs output

We can also get a better overview of the execution using the EXPLAIN command to get the plan, as shown in the following listing:

```
QUERY PLAN
----------------------------------------------------------------------------
-----
Nested Loop  (cost=18.82..38.84 rows=1000 width=28)
  CTE get_random_number
    -> Result  (cost=0.00..0.01 rows=1 width=8)
  CTE delete_images
    -> Delete on files  (cost=0.00..18.80 rows=880 width=6)
        -> Seq Scan on files  (cost=0.00..18.80 rows=880 width=6)
  -> CTE Scan on get_random_number r  (cost=0.00..0.02 rows=1 width=24)
  -> Function Scan on generate_series s  (cost=0.00..10.00 rows=1000
width=4)
```

Listing 13: Writable and read-only CTEs output plan

Writable CTEs and the RETURNING clause: Pipelining statements

We can combine writable CTEs and the RETURNING clause to create a quick pipeline of SQL statements. As a practical example, let's suppose we need to archive all file entries to another table with the same structure that we will use in a historic archive. We will call this table archive. Since SQL does not allow move statements, a traditional approach would be to perform a two-step transaction, as shown in the following listing, where an INSERT statement is executed and the moved entries are deleted:

```
testdb=> BEGIN;
INSERT INTO archive_files
SELECT * FROM files;
DELETE FROM files;  -- can use also a TRUNCATE
COMMIT;
```

Listing 14: Moving entries with a transaction

With CTEs, we can also attack the problem from another angle; we can define a writable CTE to perform the entry deletion and return all of the deleted records. These records will materialize and can then be pushed into an INSERT statement. Since the CTE will execute as a single whole statement, transaction boundaries will apply to it (in auto-commit mode). This means that the operation with either succeed or fail as a whole. In the latter case, it won't delete any entries from the source table, as shown in the following listing:

```
testdb=> WITH deleting_files AS ( DELETE FROM files RETURNING * )
INSERT INTO archive_files SELECT * FROM deleting_files;
```

Listing 15: Moving entries with a writable CTE

CTEs are also flexible enough to allow for the opposite to happen, as shown in the following listing, where an INSERT statement performs as an auxiliary table and a DELETE statement as the top-level statement:

```
testdb=> WITH inserting_files AS (
INSERT INTO files_archive
SELECT * FROM files RETURNING pk )
DELETE FROM files
WHERE pk IN ( SELECT pk FROM inserting_files );
```

Listing 16: Moving entries with a writable CTE

Recursive CTEs

A recursive CTE is a special construct that allows an auxiliary statement to reference itself and, therefore, join itself onto previously-computed results. This is particularly useful when we need to join a table an unknown number of times, typically to 'explode' a flat tree structure. The traditional solution would involve some kind of iteration, probably by means of a cursor that iterates one tuple at a time over the whole result set. However, with recursive CTEs, we can use a much cleaner and simpler approach.

A recursive CTE is made by an auxiliary statement that is built on top of the following:

- A non-recursive statement, which works as a bootstrap statement and is executed when the auxiliary term is first evaluated
- A recursive statement, which can either reference the bootstrap statement or itself

These two parts are joined together by means of a UNION predicate.

In order to better understand the use case of a recursive CTE, let's consider a tags table, populated as shown in the following listing. As you can see, each tag is related to a possible parent tag; as you can see, the tag music contains the tags rock, hard rock, and pop. The tag hard rock, in turn, contains metallica and foo fighters:

```
testdb=> SELECT t_name, pk, t_child_of FROM tags;

     t_name     | pk |t_child_of
----------------+----+-----------
  holidays      | 10 |
  family        | 12 |
  music         | 13 |
  metallica     | 17 |      16
  foo fighters  | 18 |      16
  rock          | 14 |      13
  pop           | 15 |      13
  hard rock     | 16 |      13
  sicily        | 11 |      10
  2017          | 19 |      11
  2018          | 20 |      11
  2018          | 21 |
```

Listing 17: Tag table example data

So, how can we extract the whole tree structure for every tag? Let's compose a recursive CTE to do this for us. First, we need to declare the auxiliary statement with the RECURSIVE keyword, so that PostgreSQL knows that the CTE will refer itself in the auxiliary statement. Then, we have to write the non-recursive part of the auxiliary statement. In this specific example, the non-recursive part is the extraction of all tags that are not children of other tags, or in other words, the parent tags. The resulting tuples must be combined with each tuple that comes from the non-recursive statement by means of the UNION predicate. This is when t_child_of has a value set to the non-recursive result set, pk. The following listing implements such logic and provides the output of all of the tag names, where each level of the tree has been separated by a > sign. The important part here is that the recursive part of the auxiliary statement (aliased as ct) joins to the non-recursive part (aliased as tt) and that it does this however many times is necessary:

```
testdb=> WITH RECURSIVE tags_tree AS (
   -- non recursive statment
   SELECT t_name, pk
   FROM tags WHERE t_child_of IS NULL

   UNION
   -- recursive statement
   SELECT tt.t_name || ' > ' || ct.t_name, ct.pk
```

```
   FROM tags ct
   JOIN tags_tree tt ON tt.pk = ct.t_child_of
)
SELECT t_name FROM tags_tree ORDER BY t_name;

          t_name
----------------------------------
family
holidays
holidays > sicily
music
music > hard rock
music > hard rock > foo fighters
music > hard rock > metallica
music > pop
music > rock
```

Listing 18: Listing the tags tree

Note that we can also add computed-on-the-fly values, for example a level column that holds the depth of the current level within the tree. This can be useful when searching for tags that appear at different levels within a tree. As you can see in the following example, the 2018 tag can appear as a root tag or a leaf tag, and the recursive CTE extracts only the non-leaf tag hierarchy:

```
testdb=> WITH RECURSIVE tags_tree AS (
   -- non recursive statment
   SELECT t_name, pk, 1 AS level
   FROM tags WHERE t_child_of IS NULL

   UNION
   -- recursive statement
   SELECT tt.t_name || ' > ' || ct.t_name, ct.pk
        , tt.level + 1
   FROM tags ct
   JOIN tags_tree tt ON tt.pk = ct.t_child_of
)
SELECT t_name FROM tags_tree
WHERE t_name like '%2018%' AND level > 1;

          t_name
--------------------------
holidays > sicily > 2018
```

Listing 19: Searching for a deeper tag

When dealing with recursive CTEs, it is important to be aware of infinite loops. These can arise if the recursion part of an auxiliary statement does not end properly. As an example, in the previous code snippet, all we need to do is change the recursive part of the auxiliary statement to reference the column `tt.pk` in the output of the `SELECT` statement, instead of the correct reference to the column `ct.pk`, to make the query loop infinitely by joining each row to itself. As you can see, it is really important to constrain the recursive term in such a way that it can end properly.

Summary

PostgreSQL provides advanced features that allow you to avoid writing a program to solve common problems when dealing with data structures and SQL statements. Thanks to the `RETURNING` predicate, it is possible for you to get back automatically generated data, such as an incremental key. Conflict resolution allows us to perform a kind of 'tuple merging' when dealing with `INSERT` and `UPDATE` statements against the same tuples, but one of its most powerful features is surely the Common Table Expression, which not only allows us to re-write complex queries by splitting them into more readable pieces, but also allows us to perform statement pipelining and recurse over a result set.

Knowing these features will allow you to interact with a PostgreSQL cluster efficiently and solve common problems in your day-to-day use quickly and easily.

In `Chapter 3`, *The PL/pgSQL Language*, we will look at how to implement complex constructs by means of the default procedural language built in in PostgreSQL: PL/pgSQL.

References

- `INSERT` and `ON CONFLICT`—Official PostgreSQL 11 documentation can be found at: `https://www.postgresql.org/docs/11/static/sql-insert.html`
- Common Table Expression—Official PostgreSQL 11 documentation can be found at: `https://www.postgresql.org/docs/11/static/queries-with.html`

3
The PL/pgSQL Language

The PL/pgSQL language is the default PostgreSQL language to implement functions, procedures, and other general SQL-like executable code.

The idea behind PL/pgSQL is to provide a more flexible and rich language to allow for complex computations, conditionals, iterations, and error handling. PL/pgSQL allows us to group several operations, including SQL statements, into code blocks, which are stored and executed on the server side. This has the benefit of reducing the traffic among the client and the backend.

This chapter will cover the following topics:

- What a block of code looks like
- How to execute a block of code with the DO statement
- How to declare, assign, and use variables, as well as how to print messages
- Conditionals, iterations (loops), and special variables
- How to deal with errors and exceptions

An introduction to PL/pgSQL

PL/pgSQL is an imperative SQL-like language that offers several features to write a piece of runnable code. Besides SQL, this is the default language used in PostgreSQL to write functions, procedures, triggers, and **programs** in general.

PostgreSQL has a special statement called DO that accepts a PL/pgSQL piece of code and executes it as an anonymous code block. This is particularly handy to learn features of the language or to execute a code snippet without having to wrap it into a function or a routine. The syntax of the DO statement is quite straightforward and only requires us to specify the block of code to execute:

```
DO <plpgsql code block>;
```

In the rest of the chapter, the DO statement will be used to run PL/pgSQL pieces of code and demonstrate all the main features of the language.

A runnable PL/pgSQL piece of code must contain at least one code block. A PL/pgSQL code block is composed of two main parts:

- A DECLARE section, where you declare (and, if needed, initialize) variables
- A BEGIN/END section, where you write the execution flow

The variable declaration part can be omitted if the code block does not require any variables. Otherwise, any referenced variable must appear within this part. It is worth noting that the BEGIN/END control flow part does not define a transaction boundary; the BEGIN keyword has nothing to do with the one used to open a transaction.

Variables are declared using a name, which must be a valid SQL identifier, have a type and can have a default initial value. When a variable is declared, its initial value defaults to the SQL NULL PL. Otherwise, the variable assumes the specified initial value. In this case, it is also possible to declare the variable as a constant, meaning its value cannot be altered. It is important to note that the initial values are computed and assigned when the code block is effectively executed, not when it is defined. This means that dynamic values are computed when the block executes.

The control flow part includes expressions that end with a semicolon. These can be categorized as one of the following:

- **Recognized expressions**, such as a variable assignment, conditionals, or loops
- **Non-recognized expressions**, which are interpreted as regular **SQL statements**

There is a special statement, NULL, which does nothing at all. It is therefore a placeholder for the branches where no operation is required or implemented.

Each PL/pgSQL code block is managed as a single SQL case-insensitive text string, which you must write with the appropriate quoting. Since the function can contain other quoted strings, determining the right number of ticks can become a nightmare. Luckily, PostgreSQL provides **dollar-quoting**, which is where each string is contained between two identical tags, made by a couple of '$' signs. A dollar-quoted string is handled as if it were written between regular quotation marks, ' , but the content of the string itself is easier and more readable. The content of the tags does not matter, it could even be omitted:

```
$code$    -- opening tag
<plpgsql>
$code$    -- closing tag

$$        -- empty opening tag
<plpgsql>
$$        -- closing tag
```

Thanks to dollar quoting, writing a PL/pgSQL block of code is easy and only requires us to put the block within two dollar quote tags:

```
$code$
DECLARE
    ...
BEGIN
    ...
END
$code$
```

When we develop a piece of code, we should think about its maintenance and readability, so we should add comments. SQL-style comments are allowed within a block of code, including the following:

- A single-line comment that begins with a -- sign
- A multi-line comment that begins with /* and ends with */

As you might imagine, comments are ignored by the executor.

Neither horizontal or vertical spaces are important in this context, so we can choose to indent our code however we like. The language is also case-insensitive, so we can write a block of code in almost any format. It is, however, recommended to write keywords with an uppercase letter and variable names in lowercase. It is advisable to avoid the camel-case notation for names, since this can lead to name clashing because the block code will be treated in a case-insensitive mode.

Let's take a quick look at the RAISE statement. This is used to throw exceptions, such as signal error conditions, and can be used to print out messages while the code block executes. RAISE accepts an optional level of error reporting that corresponds to the log levels (such as WARNING, INFO, or DEBUG). It also accepts a message that can be dynamically built with positional arguments. The format of a RAISE message uses a single '%' sign as a placeholder for the next positional argument, which will be interpolated as a string. The following statement prints out a text message '1 + 2 = 3' at the DEBUG log level:

```
RAISE DEBUG '1 + 2 = %', (1 + 2);
```

We will look at more details about the RAISE statement in the following sections. For now, we can think of RAISE as a possible way to print out messages as the code executes.

It is now time to see plpgsql in action. The quickest way to do this is by means of the DO statement. The code in *Listing 1* shows a simple block of code that declares three variables of different types, where i has no initial value and therefore defaults to NULL, and d and t are assigned to an initial value by means of the DEFAULT keyword. After the variable declaration part, the BEGIN/END section wraps the control flow part and a RAISE statement is used to display the variable values:

```
testdb=> DO
  $code$
    DECLARE
        i int;   -- initial value is NULL
        t text DEFAULT 'Hello World!';
        d date DEFAULT CURRENT_DATE;
    BEGIN
        RAISE INFO 'Variables are: d = [%], t = [%], i = [%]', d, t, i;
    END
  $code$;
OUTPUT:
Variables are: d = [2018-07-11], t = [Hello World!], i = [<NULL>].
```

Listing 1: The very first block of PL/pgSQL code

We can nest PL/pgSQL blocks, but the language provides a single variable namespace, and therefore the inner block masks out variables if it provides a DECLARE part and re-defines the same variable names, as shown in *Listing 2*:

```
testdb=> DO $code$
 DECLARE
  i int  DEFAULT 10;
  t text DEFAULT 'Hello World!';
  j int  DEFAULT 100;
 BEGIN
    RAISE INFO 'Outer block: i = [%] t = [%] j = [%]', i, t, j;
    -- nested block
    DECLARE
      i text DEFAULT 'PostgreSQL is amazing!';
      t int  DEFAULT 20;
      j int  DEFAULT 999;
    BEGIN
    RAISE INFO 'Inner block i = [%] t = [%] j = [%]', i, t, j;
    END;

    RAISE INFO 'Outer block: i = [%] t = [%] j = [%]', i, t, j;
 END; $code$;

INFO: Outer block: i = [10] t = [Hello World!] j = [100]
INFO: Inner block i = [PostgreSQL is amazing!] t = [20] j = [999]
INFO: Outer block: i = [10] t = [Hello World!] j = [100]
```

Listing 2: Nested code block and masked variables

Variables and variable assignment

A variable is a placeholder for a value and is identified by a valid name and a type. Variable types are those that PostgreSQL allows within a table definition, including user-defined types. A variable can either hold a single value or multiple values of the same type in an array. If it holds a single value, such as an integer, it is called a scalar.

A variable can also handle more complex types, such as tuples, which represent table rows or query results. These variables are called records. There are two specific types of record variable: record and rowtype. The record type is a general abstract type that can handle any specific tuple structure, while rowtype can handle well-defined tuple structures and is therefore tied to a specific result set structure. In other words, a record variable can interchangeably hold a tuple coming from the files table or the tags table, while a rowtype variable must be associated with a particular table. As they are complex structures, both the record and rowtype variables must be de-referenced to obtain a single value (such as a column value). This is done using a . symbol followed by the name of the field to be accessed. More details about these two types of variables will be discussed later.

We can assign values to a variable in two ways:

- The := assignment operator (or its equivalent shorter form, =)
- The INTO predicate in conjunction with an SQL statement that returns tuples

The := assignment operator works for an inline single value assignment of either a scalar or complex type. The INTO predicate, on the other hand, can be used to perform multiple assignments in a single statement, such as assigning columns of a row to separate scalar variables. If required, the assigned value can be coerced through a cast to the type of the variable it is assigned to.

The INTO predicate is mainly used in conjunction with the SELECT statement, allowing for the assignment of multiple values or the assignment of values extracted from a query, such as a row. We can also use the INTO predicate with any statement that returns a tuple. These statements are INSERT, UPDATE, or DELETE with the RETURNING clause.

As shown in *Listing 3,* variables are first assigned one at a time via the := operator. Then, a single SELECT INTO statement assigns different values at the i and t variables at the same time:

```
testdb=> DO $code$
   DECLARE
       i int;   -- initial value is NULL
       t text := 'Hello World!';
       d date := CURRENT_DATE;
   BEGIN
       RAISE INFO 'Variables are: d = [%], t = [%], i = [%]', d, t, i;
       -- single assignment
       i := length( t );
       d := now();   -- coerced to 'date'
       -- multiple assignment!
       SELECT 'Happy new ' || EXTRACT( year FROM d ) + 1 || ' year!', i * i
       INTO   t, i;

       RAISE INFO 'Variables now are: d = [%], t = [%], i = [%]', d, t, i;
   END $code$;

INFO:   Variables are: d = [2018-07-12], t = [Hello World!], i = [<NULL>]
INFO:   Variables now are: d = [2018-07-12], t = [Happy new 2019 year!], i =
[144]
```

Listing 3: Variable assignments

Under the hood, the := operator implies the execution of a SELECT statement to assign the value. *Listing 4* shows how to use the INTO predicate with both an INSERT statement and a SELECT statement:

```
testdb=> DO $code$
   DECLARE
       file_name text      := 'TestFile.txt';
       file_size numeric  := 123.56;
       file_pk   int;
       file_ts   timestamp;
   BEGIN
       -- insert a new file and get back the key
       INSERT INTO files( f_name, f_size )
       VALUES ( file_name, file_size )
       RETURNING pk
       INTO file_pk;

       RAISE INFO 'File [%] has been inserted with pk = %', file_name,
file_pk;

       -- query back to get the ts column
       SELECT ts INTO   file_ts
       FROM   files WHERE  pk = file_pk;
       RAISE INFO 'Timestamp is %', file_ts;
   END $code$;

OUTPUT
File [TestFile.txt] has been inserted with pk = 27
Timestamp is 2018-07-12 10:56:17.600594
```

Listing 4: Using the INTO predicate

What happens if there is more than one row that is subject to assignment? This depends on the statement that performs the assignment: in the case of an INSERT, UPDATE, or DELETE statement with a RETURNING clause, an error is thrown. This means that only one tuple at a time can be inserted or modified while being targeted at a variable assignment. In the case of a SELECT statement, it is possible to get more than one row as a result, but only the first tuple is considered as part of the assignment and all subsequent tuples are discarded.

As an alternative, we can use the `INTO STRICT` optional form, which imposes a single row returned from a `SELECT` statement and therefore ensures that exactly one row value is assigned, resulting in an error if more than one row is returned by the query. The code snippet of *Listing 5* works, but throws away all rows except the first one:

```
testdb=> DO $code$
    DECLARE
      file_name text;
      file_size numeric;
    BEGIN
      SELECT f_name, f_size
      INTO   file_name, file_size
      FROM   files WHERE  f_type = 'png'
      ORDER BY f_name;

      RAISE INFO 'The first png file is %', file_name;
    END $code$;

  INFO:  The first png file is picture1.png
```

Listing 5: Discarding all the rows except the first one

The code of *Listing 6*, however, does not work because `STRICT` throws an exception since the query returns more than one row:

```
testdb=> DO $code$
    DECLARE
      file_name text;
      file_size numeric;
    BEGIN
      SELECT f_name, f_size
      INTO STRICT file_name, file_size
      FROM   files WHERE  f_type = 'png'
      ORDER BY f_name;

      RAISE INFO 'The first png file is %', file_name;
    END $code$;

  ERROR:  query returned more than one row
```

Listing 6: INTO STRICT producing an exception

In order to make *Listing 6* work with `STRICT`, the query must be changed to explicitly return a single result. We can do this by means of a `LIMIT` predicate, as shown in *Listing 7*:

```
testdb=> DO $code$
   DECLARE
      file_name text;
      file_size numeric;
   BEGIN
      SELECT f_name, f_size
      INTO STRICT file_name, file_size
      FROM    files WHERE   f_type = 'png'
      ORDER BY f_name
      LIMIT 1; -- to make STRICT happy!

      RAISE INFO 'The first png file is %', file_name;
   END $code$;

INFO:  The first png file is picture1.png
```

Listing 7: INTO STRICT with a good query

Therefore, the `STRICT` optional predicate is a way to let the code executor check for a single result row. We can use it to be sure that the query is not discarding results and therefore assigning values that are possibly wrong to variables.

PL/pgSQL interpolates variables only where a value is expected. We cannot use a variable value to reference an identifier, such as the name of a column. As a consequence, DDL and utility statements (such as `ALTER TABLE`) cannot be executed with variable interpolation. There are a few ways to build dynamic statements where variables interpolate as identifiers, which we will discuss later in this section. With regard to ordinary DML statements, *Listing 8* works as expected, because `file_type` is interpolated in the query:

```
testdb=> DO $code$
   DECLARE
      file_name text;
      file_size numeric;
      size_kb int := 1024;
      size_mb numeric := size_kb * size_kb;
      size_gb numeric := size_mb * size_mb;
      unit text;
   BEGIN
      -- get the max file size
      SELECT max( f_size )
      INTO file_size
      FROM files;
```

```
      IF file_size > size_kb THEN
         file_size := file_size / size_kb;
         unit := 'kB';
      ELSIF file_size > size_mb THEN
         file_size := file_size / size_mb;
         unit := 'MB';
      ELSIF file_size > size_gb THEN
         file_size := file_size / size_gb;
         unit := 'GB';
      ELSE
         unit := 'bytes';
      END IF;
      RAISE INFO 'Biggest file size is % %', file_size, unit;
   END $code$;

OUTPUT
Biggest file size is 520.1000 bytes
```

Listing 8: Variable interpolation example

A problem that can arise when working with variable interpolation in SQL statements is name ambiguity. What happens if the `file_type` variable that is interpolated in *Listing 8* is renamed `f_type` (which is also the name of the table column)? The interpreter aborts the execution because it does not know which `f_type` item the code is referring to, as shown in *Listing 9*:

```
testdb=> DO $code$
 DECLARE
    f_type text := 'png';
    file_size text;
    file_name text;
 BEGIN
   SELECT f_size, f_name
   INTO STRICT file_size, file_name
   FROM    files
   WHERE   f_type = f_type   -- f_type = 'png'
   ORDER BY f_size DESC
   LIMIT 1;
   RAISE INFO 'Biggest % file is %', f_type, file_name;
 END $code$;

ERROR:  column reference "f_type" is ambiguous
```

```
LINE 3:    WHERE  f_type = f_type  -- What is what?
                         ^
DETAIL:  It could refer to either a PL/pgSQL variable or a table column.
```

Listing 9: Variable and identifier name clashing

The interpreter cannot understand if the right-hand f_type refers to the variable or to the column itself, so it aborts the execution. While simply renaming the variable would solve the problem, and, in most cases, is the best thing to do, we can also use the variable_conflict pragma, which can be set to the following:

- error: This is the default behavior. It aborts the execution, as shown in *Listing 9*.
- use_variable: This forces the use of the variable as a value.
- use_column: This forces the use of the column as a value.

It is therefore possible to fix the code snippet in *Listing 9*, transforming it into *Listing 10* and forcing the interpreter to use the right-hand f_type as a variable to interpolate:

```
testdb=> DO $code$ #variable_conflict use_variable
  DECLARE
     f_type text := 'png';
     file_size text;
     file_name text;
  BEGIN
    SELECT f_size, f_name
    INTO STRICT file_size, file_name
    FROM   files
    WHERE  f_type = f_type  -- f_type = 'png'
    ORDER BY f_size DESC
    LIMIT 1;
    RAISE INFO 'Biggest % file is %', f_type, file_name;
  END $code$;

OUTPUT
Biggest .png file is picture2.png.
```

Listing 10: Variable and identifier name clashing: the use_variable pragma

We can also make a variable immutable, so that its value cannot change, using the CONSTANT keyword immediately before the variable type at the time of declaration. A constant variable must be assigned an initial value, or a NULL immutable value will be assigned (but this case does not have many practical uses).

To demonstrate how to use CONSTANT, *Listing 11* shows an incorrect snippet of code: since database_name and page_size are declared immutable, the executor will not allow any of the subsequent re-assignments to those variables:

```
testdb=> DO $code$
 DECLARE
    page_size CONSTANT int := 8;
    database_name CONSTANT text := 'PostgreSQL';
 BEGIN
    RAISE INFO '% page size is % kilobytes by default', database_name,
page_size;

   page_size := page_size * 2;
   RAISE INFO 'but you can change to % kB at compile time', page_size;
   database_name := 'MySQL';
   RAISE INFO 'or switch to % if you are unhappy!', database_name;
 END $code$;

ERROR:  variable "page_size" is declared CONSTANT
LINE 11:    page_size := page_size * 2;

ERROR:  variable "database_name" is declared CONSTANT
LINE 13:    database_name := 'MySQL';
```

Listing 11: Constant variables

A variable can be also aliased, which means that it can have different names at once. An alias is defined with the ALIAS FOR clause, indicating the new name and the target value. Consider *Listing 12*, where a is aliased by b and everything operates on either of the two results:

```
testdb=> DO $code$
 DECLARE
   a int := 10;
   b ALIAS FOR a;
 BEGIN
    RAISE INFO 'a is %, b is %', a ,b;
    -- will impact 'a'
    b := b * 2;
    RAISE INFO 'a is %, b is %', a ,b;
 END $code$;

OUTPUT
a is 10, b is 10
a is 20, b is 20
```

Listing 12: Variable alias

As you can see, creating an alias to a variable simply defines another name that the same variable can be accessed with.

Conditionals

There are two main conditional constructs: IF ... END IF and CASE ... END CASE, which are similar to the Java `switch` construct or the Perl `given` construct. Both constructs evaluate a Boolean condition and execute the branch only if the condition results in a `true` value. Both IF and CASE allow for multiple branches with different condition evaluations—ELSIF and WHEN respectively—and both allow for a `catch-all` branch named ELSE.

Listing 13 shows how to use an IF statement. First, we extract the maximum file size from the `files` table and check it against the predefined file sizes to print out a human readable file size with the measurement unit:

```
testdb=> DO $code$
  DECLARE
    file_name text;
    file_size numeric;
    size_kb int := 1024;
    size_mb numeric := size_kb * size_kb;
    size_gb numeric := size_mb * size_mb;
    unit text;
  BEGIN
    -- get the max file size
    SELECT max( f_size )
    INTO file_size
    FROM files;

    IF file_size > size_kb THEN
       file_size := file_size / size_kb;
       unit := 'kB';
    ELSIF file_size > size_mb THEN
       file_size := file_size / size_mb;
       unit := 'MB';
    ELSIF file_size > size_gb THEN
       file_size := file_size / size_gb;
       unit := 'GB';
    ELSE
       unit := 'bytes';
```

```
END IF;
    RAISE INFO 'Biggest file size is % %', file_size, unit;
  END $code$;
```

Listing 13: Multiple branches IF example

Listing 14 shows the very same execution flow with a CASE statement. As you can see, translating an IF to a CASE statement mainly involves re-writing any ELSIF predicates to WHEN predicates:

```
testdb=> DO $code$
  DECLARE
    file_name text;
    file_size numeric;
    size_kb int := 1024;
    size_mb numeric := size_kb * size_kb;
    size_gb numeric := size_mb * size_mb;
    unit text;
  BEGIN
     -- get the max file size
     SELECT max( f_size )
     INTO file_size
     FROM files;

     CASE
     WHEN file_size > size_kb THEN
        file_size := file_size / size_kb;
        unit := 'kB';
     WHEN file_size > size_mb THEN
        file_size := file_size / size_mb;
        unit := 'MB';
     WHEN file_size > size_gb THEN
        file_size := file_size / size_gb;
        unit := 'GB';
     ELSE
        unit := 'bytes';
     END CASE;
     RAISE INFO 'Biggest file size is % %', file_size, unit;
  END $code$;
```

Listing 14: Multiple branches CASE example

The CASE example also has another operational form in which equality is imposed. A value is checked for equality against one or more values expressed in one or more WHEN predicates. In *Listing 15*, for example, the file_type variable is checked for equality against different values. Each WHEN predicate can check for multiple values (such as png or jpg):

```
testdb=> DO $code$
   DECLARE
     file_type text;
   BEGIN
     -- get the biggest file type
     SELECT f_type
     INTO STRICT file_type
     FROM files
     ORDER BY f_size DESC
     LIMIT 1;

     CASE file_type
         WHEN 'txt', 'org' THEN RAISE INFO 'Biggest file is a text one';
         WHEN 'png', 'jpg' THEN RAISE INFO 'Biggest file is an image
one';
         WHEN 'mp3' THEN RAISE INFO 'Biggest file is an audio';
         ELSE
             RAISE INFO 'Biggest file is of type %', file_type;
     END CASE;
   END $code$;
```

Listing 15: Equality case example

The same result can be achieved with an IF conditional and the appropriate usage of the AND and OR Boolean operators, as follows:

```
IF file_type = 'org' OR file_type = 'txt' THEN
   ...
ELSIF file_type = 'png' OR file_type = 'jpg' THEN
   ...
END IF;
```

Iterations

Iterations are implemented by means of loops. Each loop body is always wrapped between the LOOP and END LOOP keywords and can be assigned a label. This can be useful for jumping out of an inner loop to an external loop.

The simplest form of loop is the unconditional loop, which is repeated infinitely until an explicit EXIT is invoked. EXIT forces the current loop to stop immediately and can be subject to a Boolean condition specified by a WHEN predicate. As an example, *Listing 16* and *Listing 17* show the same loop that prints out a message four times:

```
testdb=> DO $code$
 DECLARE
   counter int := 0;
 BEGIN
   LOOP
      counter := counter + 1;
      RAISE INFO 'This is the % time I say HELLO!', counter;
      EXIT WHEN counter > 3;
   END LOOP;

   RAISE INFO 'Good bye';
 END $code$;

INFO:  This is the 1 time I say HELLO!
INFO:  This is the 2 time I say HELLO!
INFO:  This is the 3 time I say HELLO!
INFO:  This is the 4 time I say HELLO!
INFO:  Good bye
```

Listing 16: Simple loop example with conditional exit

```
testdb=> DO $code$
 DECLARE
   counter int := 0;
 BEGIN
   LOOP
      counter := counter + 1;
      RAISE INFO 'This is the % time I say HELLO!', counter;
      IF counter > 3 THEN
         EXIT;
      END IF;
   END LOOP;
   RAISE INFO 'Good bye';
 END $code$;
```

Listing 17: Simple loop example with unconditional exit

```
Output:
This is the 1 time I say HELLO!
This is the 2 time I say HELLO!
This is the 3 time I say HELLO!
This is the 4 time I say HELLO!
Good bye
```

It is worth noting that the unconditional LOOP combined with an appropriate EXIT predicate can implement the do...while loop of other programming languages, such as Java:

```
LOOP   -- do {
   counter := counter + 1;
   ...
   EXIT WHEN counter > 10; -- } while ( counter <= 10 );
END LOOP;
```

As already stated, loops can be labeled, which allows EXIT to specify which loop to terminate in a nested loop. Each label is wrapped into two angled brackets and is placed immediately before the LOOP keyword. As an example, *Listing 18* shows two nested loops, one labeled MAIN_LOOP and the other labeled INNER_LOOP. The inner loop can also terminate the outer loop (the main loop) with an EXIT that explicitly specifies the MAIN_LOOP label:

```
testdb=> DO $code$
 DECLARE
   counter       int := 0;
   inner_counter int := 0;
 BEGIN
   <<MAIN_LOOP>>
   LOOP
      counter := counter + 1;
      RAISE INFO 'This is the % time I say HELLO!', counter;
      inner_counter := 0;

      <<INNER_LOOP>>
      LOOP
        inner_counter := inner_counter + 1;
        RAISE INFO 'I do repeat: HELLO!';
        -- exit from this loop
        EXIT WHEN inner_counter >= 2;
        -- terminate also the main loop
        EXIT MAIN_LOOP WHEN inner_counter >= 4;
      END LOOP;
      EXIT WHEN counter >= 10;
   END LOOP;
   RAISE INFO 'Good bye';
```

```
   END $code$;

INFO:   This is the 1 time I say HELLO!
INFO:   I do repeat: HELLO!
INFO:   I do repeat: HELLO!
...
INFO:   This is the 10 time I say HELLO!
INFO:   I do repeat: HELLO!
INFO:   I do repeat: HELLO!
INFO:   Good bye
```

Listing 18: Nested loop with different exits

The counterpart of EXIT is CONTINUE. This allows the loop to restart from the very next iteration and is therefore a handy way to skip a part of code and continue the iteration. The syntax for CONTINUE is the same as EXIT and therefore it accepts an optional WHEN Boolean condition as well as an optional loop label. If no label is specified, the innermost loop is assumed to be the one from which the iteration will restart. *Listing 19* shows an example of mixing EXIT and CONTINUES with nested loops:

```
testdb=> DO $code$
 DECLARE
    counter        int := 0;
    inner_counter int := 0;
 BEGIN
    <<MAIN_LOOP>>
    LOOP
       counter := counter + 1;
       -- skip to the next iteration if counter is a multiple of 3
       CONTINUE WHEN counter % 3 = 0;
       RAISE INFO 'This is the % time I say HELLO!', counter;
       inner_counter := 0;

       <<INNER_LOOP>>
       LOOP
          inner_counter := inner_counter + 1;
          -- restart from the outer loop when inner_counter is a multiple of
2
          CONTINUE MAIN_LOOP WHEN inner_counter % 2 = 0;
          RAISE INFO 'I do repeat: HELLO!';
          -- exit from this loop
          EXIT WHEN inner_counter > 0;
       END LOOP;
       EXIT WHEN counter >= 10;
```

```
END LOOP;
    RAISE INFO 'Good bye';
  END $code$;
```

Listing 19: Nested loop with different Exits and Continues

The simplest form of conditional loop is WHILE. This accepts a Boolean condition to test on each iteration and can be labeled to allow CONTINUE and EXIT to identify exactly which loop to operate on. *Listing 20* shows two nested WHILE loops in action:

```
testdb=>  DO $code$
  DECLARE
    counter       int := 0;
    inner_counter int := 0;
  BEGIN
    <<MAIN_WHILE>>
    WHILE counter < 5 LOOP
          counter := counter + 1;

          RAISE INFO 'This is the % time I say HELLO!', counter;
          inner_counter := counter;

          <<INNER_WHILE>>
          WHILE inner_counter > 0 LOOP
              RAISE INFO 'I do repeat: HELLO!';
              inner_counter := inner_counter - 1;
          END LOOP;
    END LOOP;
    RAISE INFO 'Good bye';
  END $code$;
```

Listing 20: While loops

The FOR loop evaluates expressions to determine the beginning and end of the iteration. The idea is to limit the iteration between a lower and upper integer bound with an iteration variable that gets assigned to every value between the loop boundaries, depending on an increment. The iteration variable declaration can be omitted; in this case, the variable is automatically declared to be of integer type. The lower and upper bounds can either be literal integer values or expressions that are dynamically evaluated and they appear separated by two dots: ...

The integer increment of the iteration variable is specified with the BY keyword followed by the literal value or expression. If the BY keyword is omitted, a literal increment of one unit is assumed. To summarize, the PL/pgSQL FOR loop appears as follows, compared to a Java for cycle:

```
FOR i IN 1 .. 10 BY 1 LOOP
   -- computation here
END LOOP;

// Java style
for ( int i = 1; i < 10; i = i + 1 ){
 // computation here
}
```

Listings 21 shows two equivalent simple FOR loops, where the variable counter starts from the BEGIN expression with a value of 1 and is incremented one unit at time until the end expression is reached, which is a value of 5. Both the begin and end expressions can be computed dynamically:

```
testdb=>  DO $code$
  BEGIN
   FOR counter IN 1 .. 5 LOOP
       RAISE INFO 'This is the % time I say HELLO', counter;
   END LOOP;
  END $code$;
```

Listing 21: Simple FOR loops

The FOR loop can loop backwards when used with the REVERSE keyword, as shown in *Listing 22*:

```
testdb=> DO $code$
 BEGIN
  FOR counter IN EXTRACT( month FROM CURRENT_DATE ) .. 12 LOOP
      RAISE INFO 'The month % I say HELLO', counter;
  END LOOP;

  FOR counter IN REVERSE 5 .. 1 BY 1 LOOP
      RAISE INFO 'This is the % time I say HELLO', counter;
  END LOOP;
 END $code$;
```

Listing 22: A dynamic expression based on backward FOR loops

As with other loops, FOR loops can be labeled and nested and can exploit both EXIT and CONTINUE predicates.

The FOR loop is definitely the most powerful iteration construct. It not only allows for iterations over values, but also over results sets. When iterating on query results, the cycle variable must be a record, a specific row type variable, or, in the case that single variables are extracted out of each tuple, a list of appropriate scalar variables. *Listing 23* and *Listing 24* do the same thing, but *Listing 23* uses a record variable to iterate through results, while in *Listing 24*, single column variables are assigned to each iteration. As you can see, this form of FOR does not allow a BY expression, since it is the query specified after the IN clause that defines which values to use for the next iteration:

```
testdb=> DO $code$
 DECLARE
  current_record record;
 BEGIN
  FOR current_record IN SELECT f_name, f_size
                            FROM files
                            ORDER BY f_name
                            LOOP
      RAISE INFO 'The file % has a size of % bytes', current_record.f_name,
current_record.f_size;
  END LOOP;
 END $code$;
```

Listing 23: A FOR loop over a query result set

```
testdb=> DO $code$
 DECLARE
  file_name text;
  file_size numeric;
 BEGIN
  FOR file_name, file_size IN SELECT f_name, f_size
                                FROM files
                                ORDER BY f_name
                                LOOP
      RAISE INFO 'The file % has a size of % bytes', file_name, file_size;
  END LOOP;
 END $code$;
```

Listing 24: A FOR loop over a query result set using single column variables

There are various other ways of iterating over a result set by means of a FOR loop, such as by using cursors. We will look at these in more detail later on. We also have a FOREACH loop construct that iterates over array elements. The syntax is quite simple, since it only requires us to specify the iteration variable and the array over which to iterate. This is shown in *Listing 25*, where current_person is assigned a single name extracted from the people array at each iteration:

```
testdb=> DO $code$
 DECLARE
   pi CONSTANT real := 3.14;
   greeting_text CONSTANT text := 'Greetings ';
   people text[] := ARRAY[ 'Mr. Green', 'Mr. Red' ];
   current_person text;
 BEGIN
   FOREACH current_person IN ARRAY people LOOP
      RAISE INFO '% %', greeting_text, current_person;
      RAISE INFO 'Did you know that PI is %?', pi;
   END LOOP;
 END $code$;


INFO:  Greetings  Mr. Green
INFO:  Did you know that PI is 3.14?
INFO:  Greetings  Mr. Red
INFO:  Did you know that PI is 3.14?
```

Listing 25: FOREACH over an array values

Unlike the FOR loop, where the iteration variable can be declared in the loop control statement, the FOREACH loop requires the iteration variable to have already been declared in the code before the FOREACH statement is used.

Exceptions and error handling

Every PL/pgSQL code block can include a section for exception handling. Exceptions are errors that arise during the flow of the code block and are of different types. A block can handle these errors in order to recover. The exception handling part of a code block begins with an EXCEPTION keyword and can include different branches, marked with the WHEN keyword, to handle different error types. Error types are coded into the server and are identified by either a mnemonic name, such as unique_violation, to indicate a unique constraint violation, or a numeric SQL State, such as 23505.

By default, WHEN branches refer to error names, while numeric SQL States have to be placed as strings preceded by the SQLSTATE keyword. The OTHERS special error name is used as a general way to catch any kind of error other than user cancelled statements.

If a code block does not provide an EXCEPTION section, or if the EXCEPTION section does not catch the exception thrown, the block execution is aborted. Every time a code block enters its EXCEPTION section, all changes made to the database are rolled back, without any regard to whether or not the EXCEPTION section handles the specific error.

In order to demonstrate the exception handling capabilities, let's consider *Listing 26*. This listing implements a kind of UPSERT; the block tries to perform an INSERT statement and, if the record already exists in the table, the server raises a unique_violation exception. The block then *catches* the exception and *converts* the INSERT statement into an UPDATE of the very same record. If the exception is different from unique_violation, the others branch catches it but does nothing. This means it gracefully ends the control flow:

```
testdb=> DO $code$
  DECLARE
    file_hash text := 'f029d04a81c322f158c608596951c105';
  BEGIN
    -- try to perform the insert
    INSERT INTO files( f_name, f_hash )
    VALUES ( 'foo.txt', file_hash );

  EXCEPTION
      -- did the insert fail due to a unique constraint?
    WHEN unique_violation THEN
          UPDATE files
          SET f_name = 'foo.txt'
          WHERE f_hash = file_hash;
    WHEN others THEN
          -- don't know how to recover from other errors
          NULL;
END $code$;
```

Listing 26: An UPSERT done with exception handling

In order to test the code snippet of *Listing 25*, you need to place an existing file hash into the fila_hash variable. If you deleted and inserted records in the files tables, the hash could be different.

Since every PL/pgSQL code block can have its own EXCEPTION section, it is possible to nest different blocks with different levels of exception handling. For instance, as shown in *Listing 27*, the inner code block handles the `division_by_zero` exception without aborting the outer loop:

```
testdb=> DO $code$
  DECLARE
      a real := 10;
      b real := 10;
      c numeric(3,1);
  BEGIN
      LOOP
        b := b - 5;
        BEGIN
          c := a / b;
          RAISE INFO 'a/b= %', c;
          EXCEPTION
              WHEN division_by_zero THEN
                  RAISE INFO 'b is now zero!';
                  b := -1;
          END;
        EXIT WHEN b <= -5;
      END LOOP;
  END $code$;

INFO:   a/b= 2.0
INFO:   b is now zero!
INFO:   a/b= -1.7
```

Listing 27: Nesting of code blocks to handle exception at different levels

It is possible to throw an exception by means of the RAISE statement with the EXCEPTION level. These exceptions can then either be caught in other code blocks or cause the abortion of the block. As an example, *Listing 28* is a modified version of *Listing 27*, where the LOOP has a separated block that handles the newly thrown exception from the inner block:

```
testdb=> DO $code$
  DECLARE
      a real := 10;
      b real := 10;
      c numeric(3,1);
  BEGIN
      LOOP
        BEGIN
          b := b - 5;
          BEGIN
            c := a / b;
```

```
            RAISE INFO 'a/b= %', c;
            EXCEPTION
                WHEN division_by_zero THEN
                    -- throw another exception
                    RAISE EXCEPTION 'b is now zero!';
                    b := -1; -- this is never executed!
            END;
         EXIT WHEN b <= -5;
        EXCEPTION WHEN others THEN EXIT;
        END;
      END LOOP;
  END $code$;

INFO:  a/b= 2.0
```

Listing 28: Throwing an exception and catching it in the outer block

It is also possible to re-throw an exception once it has been handled. From within an EXCEPTION block, a RAISE statement without any arguments will re-throw the current exception:

```
BEGIN
   ...
EXCEPTION
  WHEN unique_violation THEN
     -- do something
     ...
     -- re-throw unique_violation
     RAISE;
END;
```

Alternatively, RAISE can also accept the error name or the SQL State to throw that specific exception:

```
BEGIN
   ...
EXCEPTION
  WHEN unique_violation THEN
     -- convert an exception into another
     RAISE division_by_zero;
END;
```

It is worth noting that a code block with an EXCEPTION section is much more expensive, in terms of resources, than a block without. Exception handling should therefore only be used when it is really necessary.

The RAISE statement revisited

As shown in previous sections, RAISE can be used to either display a message or to throw an exception. Effectively, the aim of RAISE is to report errors. The fact that it can be used to display messages is just a consequence of reporting errors.

The first important thing to note is that the level at which an error is reported, such as INFO, is shown in the console or within the server logs, depending on the configuration of the show_client_min_messages and log_min_messages variables respectively. When used to report flow messages, RAISE should be used at a DEBUG level, which, by default, is not shown on the client console. Lowering the message level of client_min_messages, as shown in *Listing 29*, makes the message appear:

```
testdb=> SET client_min_messages TO debug;
testdb=> DO $code$
 BEGIN
    RAISE DEBUG 'A debug message';
    RAISE INFO  'An info message';
 END $code$;

DEBUG:  A debug message
INFO:  An info message

testdb=> SET client_min_messages TO info;
testdb=> DO $code$
 BEGIN
    RAISE DEBUG 'A debug message';
    RAISE INFO  'An info message';
 END $code$;

INFO:  An info message
```

Listing 29: RAISE and levels

Since RAISE can log messages to the server log, depending on the log_min_messages variable setting, it is better not to use RAISE to print out sensitive data.

The RAISE statement also allows for a set of *extended* attributes that are specified after the USING clause:

- HINT, which is a suggestion about the reported error.
- DETAIL, which is a detail about the reported error.

- ERRCODE, which is the name or the SQL State numeric value of a specific error.
- MESSAGE, which is usually used when reporting an exception. It is mutually exclusive with the message specified before the USING clause.

As an example, imagine a block of code that tries to perform the insertion of an already existing f_hash in the files table. The exception thrown from such a block of code could have been prepared as follows:

```
testdb=> DO $code$
  BEGIN
    -- do stuff
    ...
    RAISE USING
          ERRCODE = 'unique_violation',
          HINT = 'You should check your unique constraints',
          DETAIL = 'Cannot insert duplicated hash values!',
          MESSAGE = 'Cannot proceed further';
  END $code$;

ERROR:  Cannot proceed further
DETAIL:  Cannot insert duplicated hash values!
HINT:  You should check your unique constraints
```

Listing 30: Fully parameterized RAISE example

Executing dynamic statements

Non-PL/pgSQL statements are sent to the server engine as regular SQL statements. A few examples in the previous sections have already performed some queries within code blocks. It is possible for a code block to construct an SQL statement dynamically to be executed by the server engine. This can be achieved using the EXECUTE statement.

An EXECUTE statement is made of three parts:

- A **mandatory query string,** which represents the SQL statement that will be executed
- An optional INTO (or INTO STRICT) clause, which allows us to store values from the previous statement in variables
- An optional USING clause, which provides positional values for parameter substitution

The query string will not be interpolated, which means that no variable substitution will be performed on it. In order to insert variable values into a query string, we must use special positional placeholders, identified by a $ sign and the position starting from 1: $1, $2, $3, and so on. The first positional argument will be substituted with the first value in the USING list, the second with the second value and so on. It is even possible to specify a whole tuple type, using an asterisk after the positional argument, such as $1.*. In this case, however, the corresponding variable in the USING predicate must be of type rowtype. It is possible to use a record, but this requires a more complex and verbose syntax. As an example, *Listing 31* shows a dynamically built query with parameter substitution and variable assignment:

```
testdb=> DO $code$
 DECLARE
    file_name text;
    file_size numeric;
    query_string text;
    file_type text;
 BEGIN
    file_type := 'txt';
    -- build the query to execute
    query_string := 'SELECT f_name, f_size FROM files WHERE f_type = $1
LIMIT 1';

    -- execute the query
    -- and get back the results
    EXECUTE query_string
    INTO STRICT file_name, file_size
    USING file_type;

    RAISE INFO 'File of type % has name % and size % bytes', file_type,
file_name, file_size;
 END $code$;

INFO:  File of type txt has name TestFile.txt and size 126525.4400
bytesbytes
```

Listing 31: Dynamic statement execution using EXECUTE

Since EXECUTE runs a dynamically created SQL statement, no plan caching is performed against the query string. In other words, the query string does not represent a prepared statement (even if the syntax looks like the one used for prepared statements).

We cannot use positional parameters for the interpolation of identifiers, such as column names. The following code snippet, for example, will not work:

```
EXECUTE 'SELECT $1, $2 FROM $3'
USING 'f_name', 'f_size', 'files';
```

If we need to dynamically interpolate identifiers, the built-in `format()` function can be used. `format()` works in a similar way to `printf(3)`: it accepts a string template and a list of values to substitute in the template. The template strings accepts two possible placeholders:

- `%I` for an identifier (such as a column name or a table name)
- `%L` for a value (such as variable interpolation)

Listing 32 shows a more dynamic way of building and executing a query, where the query string is prepared by `format()` and then passed to `EXECUTE`:

```
testdb=> DO $code$
 DECLARE
    file_name text;
    file_size numeric;
    query_string text;
    file_type text;
 BEGIN
    file_type := 'txt';
    -- build the query to execute
    query_string := format( 'SELECT %I, %I FROM %I WHERE %I = $1 LIMIT 1',
'f_name', 'f_size', 'files', 'f_type' );
    -- execute the query
    -- and get back the results
    EXECUTE query_string
    INTO STRICT file_name, file_size
    USING file_type;

    RAISE INFO 'File of type % has name % and size % bytes', file_type,
file_name, file_size;
 END $code$;

INFO:  File of type txt has name TestFile.txt and size 126525.4400
bytesbytes
```

Listing 32: Dynamic statement execution using EXECUTE and format()

While `format()` is a handy function for building dynamic queries from a template, there are a couple of other functions we can use for an even more dynamic approach:

- `quote_ident()`: This is used to convert an identifier name (such as column or table) into a quoted string (equivalent to `format() %I`)
- `quote_literal()`: This is used to quote a value
- `quote_nullable()`: This is used to quote a value that can be `NULL` (equivalent to `format() %L`)

Just by using `quote_ident()` (which is equivalent to the `%I` placeholder of `format()`), *Listing 32* can be rewritten as follows:

```
testdb=> DO $code$
 DECLARE
   file_name text;
   file_size numeric;
   query_string text;
   file_type text;
 BEGIN
   file_type := 'txt';

   -- build the query to execute
   query_string := 'SELECT '
                   || quote_ident( 'f_name' ) || ',' || quote_ident(
'f_size' )
                   || ' FROM ' || quote_ident( 'files' )
                   || ' WHERE ' || quote_ident( 'f_type' ) || ' = $1 LIMIT
1';

   -- execute the query
   -- and get back the results
   EXECUTE query_string
   INTO STRICT file_name, file_size
   USING file_type;

   RAISE INFO 'File of type % has name % and size % bytes',  file_type,
file_name, file_size;
 END $code$;

INFO:  File of type txt has name TestFile.txt and size 126525.4400 bytes
```

Listing 33: Dynamic statement execution using EXECUTE and quote_ident()

We can also go even further and remove the positional parameters, as shown in *Listing 34*:

```
testdb=> DO $code$
 DECLARE
    file_name text;
    file_size numeric;
    query_string text;
    file_type text;
 BEGIN
    file_type := 'txt';
    -- build the query to execute
    query_string := 'SELECT '
                 || quote_ident ( 'f_name' ) || ',' || quote_ident (
'f_size' )
                 || ' FROM ' || quote_ident ( 'files' )
                 || ' WHERE ' || quote_ident ( 'f_type' )
                 || ' = ' || quote_literal ( file_type )
                 || ' LIMIT 1';

    -- execute the query and get back the results
    EXECUTE query_string
    INTO STRICT file_name, file_size;

    RAISE INFO 'File of type % has name % and size % bytes',
 file_type, file_name, file_size;
 END $code$;

INFO:  File of type txt has name TestFile.txt and size 126525.4400
bytesbytes
```

Listing 34: Dynamic statement execution using EXECUTE, quote_ident(), and quote_literal()

As we have seen, there are different ways of executing dynamic statements. As a general rule, we should avoid concatenating values and identifiers into plain strings, because you must pay attention when quoting literals and values, and in general using such a string could lead to SQL injection. To avoid SQL injection and quote problems, identifiers and values should always be interpolated and substituted via either `format()` or `USING`. If the SQL statement to be executed has a fixed template, where what it changes is only a condition value or an identifier name, it is preferable to use `format()`. On the other hand, if the statement must be built a piece at a time, commit to the `quote_xxx()` set of functions. The resulting query string must be executed via `EXECUTE`.

Throwing away a query result set

Any SQL statement that returns values must put its result into one or more variables by using INTO, for example. This means that invoking other functions that return values, or executing statements that return a result set (such as INSERT, UPDATE or DELETE with RETURNING or SELECT) is not possible until the returned values are stored in variables. This means that even a simple block code such as *Listing 35* will fail because the value returned by the now() function is implicitly discarded:

```
testdb=> DO $code$ BEGIN
  SELECT now();
 END $code$;

ERROR:  query has no destination for result data
```

Listing 35: A throw-away statement that doesn't work

If we have the need to execute a query and throw away its results, the PERFORM statement must be used. This statement can be thought of an alias for SELECT. It is in fact possible to write the query text in the same way, including variable interpolation, just by substituting the SELECT keyword with PERFORM. As an example, *Listing 36* shows a couple of queries that throw away the result without leading to the abortion of the execution:

```
testdb=> DO $code$
 DECLARE
  file_type text := 'png';
 BEGIN
  -- ok
  PERFORM now();
  PERFORM -- SELECT
          f_size, f_name
          FROM files
          WHERE f_type = file_type -- interpolation
          ORDER BY f_size DESC;
  RAISE INFO 'I've survived!';
 END $code$;

INFO:  I've survived!
```

Listing 36: Throwing away results with PERFORM

If the query that must throw away results is a CTE, the whole query must be passed in parentheses as argument to PERFORM, without substituting the SELECT keyword in the top-level statement, as shown in *Listing 37*. However, in this case, the CTE must return a single row from the top-level statement or the execution will be aborted:

```
testdb=> DO $code$
    DECLARE
     file_type text := 'png';
    BEGIN
     PERFORM ( WITH biggest_file_by_type AS (
          SELECT f_name FROM   files
          WHERE  f_type = file_type
          ORDER  BY f_size DESC
          LIMIT 1 ) SELECT f_name
       FROM biggest_file_by_type );

    RAISE INFO 'I've survived!';
    END $code$;

INFO:  I've survived!
```

Listing 37: Throwing away results with PERFORM and CTE

The FOUND Global Variable

When the top-level code block begins, PL/pgSQL declares a global variable named FOUND, which allows for a quick check of the status of the last SQL statement executed. The FOUND variable is of Boolean type and is set to true if the last statement succeeds, or, in other words, if at least one row was processed by the statement. As an example, *Listing 38* shows a very simple check to see if the files table is empty or not. The table is read via PERFORM and, if at least one row is found, the FOUND Boolean variable is implicitly set to true:

```
testdb=> DO $code$
  BEGIN
     PERFORM pk FROM files;
     IF FOUND THEN
        RAISE DEBUG 'The files tables contain some data';
```

```
  END IF;
 END $code$;

DEBUG:  The files tables contain some data
```

Listing 38: A simple use of FOUND

The FOUND variable is defined with a `false` value and is turned to `true` only when:

- SELECT INTO is assigned a row value
- PERFORM throws away at least one tuple
- INSERT, UPDATE, or DELETE affects at least one tuple
- FOR or FOREACH has iterated at least once
- A cursor has found a next tuple.

Please note that the FOUND variable is set after any of these statements have been executed. *Listing 39* shows a possible work-flow to better explain the possible values. As you can see, FOUND begins with a `false` value. Entering the FOR iteration does not change its value, even if one or more tuples have been extracted from the iteration query. The FOUND value will be changed at the end of the statement, which, in this case, is the FOR loop itself. Within the FOR loop, one PERFORM is fails and one succeeds, making the values of FOUND change after each statement. The last PERFORM executed in the loop fails, giving FOUND a `false` value. Once the FOR loop completes, however, the value is changed to `true`, because FOR has iterated at least once:

```
testdb=> DO $code$
 DECLARE
  current_record record;
 BEGIN
  RAISE DEBUG 'In the beginning FOUND = %', FOUND;
  FOR current_record IN SELECT * FROM files LIMIT 3 LOOP
   RAISE DEBUG 'While iterating FOUND = %', FOUND;
   IF current_record.pk % 2 = 0 THEN
     -- this statement will fail
     PERFORM pk FROM files
     WHERE f_hash = 'FAIL' || current_record.f_hash;
     RAISE DEBUG 'After a failing statement FOUND = %', FOUND;
   ELSE
      -- this statement will succeed
      PERFORM pk FROM files
      WHERE f_hash = current_record.f_hash;
      RAISE DEBUG 'After a succeeding statement FOUND = %', FOUND;
   END IF;
  END LOOP;
```

```
  RAISE DEBUG 'Outside the loop FOUND = %', FOUND;
 END $code$;

DEBUG:  In the beginning FOUND = f
DEBUG:  While iterating FOUND = f
DEBUG:  After a failing statement FOUND = f
DEBUG:  While iterating FOUND = f
DEBUG:  After a succeeding statement FOUND = t
DEBUG:  While iterating FOUND = t
DEBUG:  After a failing statement FOUND = f
DEBUG:  Outside the loop FOUND = t
```

Listing 39: FOUND values changes

The FOUND variable is global across nested code blocks. This means a nested block will not redefine FOUND with a `false` value, but will instead keep the outer block value. As you can imagine, FOUND can be masked by an explicit declaration of a variable of the same name, but this will throw away the capability to test the result of an SQL statement that has just been executed.

Summary

PL/pgSQL is the default language used in PostgreSQL to implement runnable pieces of code. It can be used to implement functions, procedures, triggers, and so on. The language allows you to easily interact with the underlying database while providing foundations for iterations, conditionals, and exception handling, or, in short, all the features of a standalone programming language.

Thanks to the DO statement, it is possible to test and run a piece of code as an anonymous block of code. In the next chapters, we will learn how to use the language to implement reusable pieces of code such as functions and procedures.

References

The PL/pgSQL Language and official PostgreSQL 11 documentation is available at: `https://www.postgresql.org/docs/11/static/plpgsql.html`.

4
Stored Procedures

This chapter introduces the main features that allow us to implement Server-Side Programming. Many PostgreSQL features rely on the ability to execute units of code, and, as already discussed, PostgreSQL provides rich support to different languages and execution environments.

In this chapter, we will learn how to write executable code that can be executed directly on the server, how to package it into stored procedures, and how to manage them. In particular, this chapter will focus on the following topics:

- Functions, procedures, and routines
- How to write, modify, and manage a stored procedure
- How to implement a transaction-aware stored procedure

Using functions, procedures, and routines

PostgreSQL 11 provides three main terms to refer to an executable unit of code: functions, procedures, and routines.

A function is what is often called a stored procedure and has always existed in PostgreSQL. A function, generally speaking, is a block of code associated with a mnemonic name. Functions can accept arguments and return a result after they have been executed. Both their arguments and their return values can be either scalar types (such as singles) or complex types (such as tuples). PostgreSQL exploits functions all over the cluster and can be used in queries and statements, to implement trigger behavior and, under particular circumstances, to build indexes.

Functions cannot interact with the transaction layer, which means they execute within the transaction of the invoking statement. Functions can be categorized by their implementation type:

- **Normal functions**: This usually refers to stored procedures
- **Aggregate functions**: These operate on a set of tuples and provide an aggregate single result (such as sum())
- **Window functions**: These perform computations over a set of tuples without reporting a single result (such as rank())

In this chapter, we will learn how to write normal functions, which are the most common ones.

A *procedure* is a new object introduced with PostgreSQL 11. In short, it is a special function that is able to interact with the transaction layer by committing a part of the work. Even if functions and procedures share several properties, procedures are quite different.

A *routine* can be either of the aforementioned two kinds of executable code. There is no object of routine type, rather routine is a shorthand to manage either a function or a procedure by either changing it or dropping it. To a certain extent, a routine is a synonym of either a function or a procedure.

The fact that the ROUTINE keyword can be used as a synonym for both a PROCEDURE or a FUNCTION is due to the fact that both objects are stored into the same system catalog, the pg_proc table. The difference between them is found in the value of the prokind field, which has f for functions and p for procedures.

Functions and procedures share definition attributes and properties, the most interesting of which is the ability to implement the executable code in a lot of different languages. In fact, in PostgreSQL, the syntax of the definition of either a procedure or a function has two parts:

- **Declaration**: This is the definition of the executable code, providing attributes such as the name, the arguments list, and the return types
- **Implementation**: This is the code that will be executed once the function or the procedure is invoked

The declaration is always expressed by an SQL statement, such as CREATE FUNCTION or CREATE PROCEDURE for a function or a procedure respectively. The implementation can be written in any supported language, meaning we can develop code in non-SQL languages such as Java, Perl, Python, and Ruby. The server is in charge of executing the code with the appropriate technology (such as a virtual machine), marshalling parameters, and return values.

Supported languages

While functions and procedures can be written in plain SQL, we are not likely to end up using this in our day-to-day development. More often, we will write functions and procedures in a much richer language with support for iterations, conditionals, and other constructs to provide a better control flow. PostgreSQL comes with a language named PL/pgSQL that enhances plain SQL with control flow predicates, and is often used as the default language for the implementation of functions and procedures.

Nevertheless, as already stated, PostgreSQL supports other external languages as well. In particular, it can handle Perl 5, Python, and TCL code via built-in languages called plperl, plpythonu, and pltcl, as well as the language PostgreSQL is built on, C. Other languages can be installed and used in addition, including Java (by means of pljava), Ruby, and Bash.

 PostgreSQL is written in the C language and, of course, does support it as an external language to build functions and procedures. However, using C is often harder than other languages because it requires a good understanding of PostgreSQL internals.

Usually, all external languages comes in two forms: a *trusted* and an *untrusted* version. The trusted language imposes strict constraints on the execution context, not allowing, for instance, the loading of external resources (such as modules, libraries, or files) or network connectivity (such as socket interaction). On the other hand, untrusted languages allow the code to execute whatever the language allows it to do and, for this reason, can only be managed by database superusers.

Functions

Having explained the main concepts behind the PL/pgSQL language, it is now time to turn code snippets into reusable functions.

A function is an entity uniquely identified by a prototype, which is made up of the following:

- A (mnemonic) name
- An argument list
- A return type

PostgreSQL does allow function overloading, which refers to the ability to define several implementations of the same function with the same name. Overloaded functions must have a different prototype, but cannot have a different return type. This means that overloaded functions differ with regard to their argument list (the type and number of arguments).

Each function's prototype is expressed by the CREATE FUNCTION SQL statement, while the implementation of the function can be any supported code block, with plpgsql being the most common language. The declaration of the function must specify the language its implementation code block is expressed in, so that the executor knows how to run the function.

A typical template for declaring a function is as follows:

```
CREATE FUNCTION foo( arg1,  arg2, ...)
RETURNS int
AS <block of code>
LANGUAGE plpgsql;
```

The function name is specified immediately after the CREATE FUNCTION statement and the argument list is specified in parentheses. The return type value is specified with the RETURNS keyword, and the language in which the function is implemented is specified with the LANGUAGE keyword. The block of code that implements the function is specified after the AS clause, and is usually expressed as a dollar-quoted string. There are more options and properties to declare and define a function, which we will look at later on.

It is interesting to note that CREATE FUNCTION supports the OR REPLACE clause. This makes it very easy to override the current implementation of a function and is therefore a best practice to follow in day-to-day function management.

CREATE OR REPLACE FUNCTION is pretty much equivalent to a DROP and CREATE FUNCTION sequence of commands, but CREATE OR REPLACE FUNCTION will only substitute the original version of the function if the new version does not contain errors and compiles successfully. It is therefore a safer approach because it will not delete the existing function until a new version can be used to replace it.

In order to throw away a function, the DROP FUNCTION statement can be used. The function must be uniquely identified, meaning its name and argument list must be specified. Specifying the return type is not important because overloaded functions cannot change this. If there is only one implementation of the function, meaning there is no overloading applied, it is sufficient to indicate just the function name:

```
      -- only if not overloaded
testdb=> DROP FUNCTION foo;
        -- trash only this among overloaded implementation of foo
testdb=> DROP FUNCTION foo( int, text );
```

A function is invoked via its name by putting arguments (if there are any) in surrounding parentheses. Each time a regular SQL statement holds a function reference, it will invoke it. The simplest form of function invocation is by means of a SELECT statement, as follows:

```
-- invokes the 'now' function  with no arguments
testdb=> SELECT now();
```

It is possible to see all the user-defined functions with the special psql command, \df (**describe function**). If no arguments are passed, then all functions will be shown, otherwise only functions with a name that matches the argument string will be shown:

```
testdb=> \df
                                     List of functions
  Schema |          Name         | Result data type |
  Argument data types            | Type
--------+-----------------------+------------------+----------------------
----------------------------+------
  public | f_dump_function       | SETOF text       | function_name text
  | func
  public | f_fake_files          | SETOF files      | max integer DEFAULT
10                             | func
  public | f_file_by_type        | SETOF files      | file_type text
DEFAULT 'txt'::text             | func
  public | f_files_from_directory | SETOF files     | dir text DEFAULT
'.'::text                       | func
  public | f_files_tuples        | SETOF files      | fake boolean DEFAULT
false, max integer DEFAULT 5 | func
  public | f_human_file_size     | text             | f_size numeric
  | func
```

```
-- get only function with a name starting with 'f_files'
testdb=> \df f_files*
          List of functions
 Schema | Name | Result data type | Argument data types | Type
--------+--------------------------+--------------------+----------------------
----------------------------------+------
 public | f_files_from_directory | SETOF files | dir text DEFAULT '.'::text
 | func
 public | f_files_tuples | SETOF files | fake boolean DEFAULT false, max
integer DEFAULT 5 | funcc
```

In the following sections, each property of a function will be detailed, with examples of increasing difficulty.

Return Types

A function can return a value that can be a scalar value (either a single value, such as an integer, or a tuple-like complex type) or a results set (such as all the tuples from a table). The return type of a function is specified by the RETURNS keyword, followed by the type of the return value. If the return type is a result set, the RETURNS SETOF keyword must be used before the tuple type. If a function does not return any value at all, the void special placeholder must be used as the returned type.

Function argument list

A function declares its argument list by specifying at least one argument type in a comma-separated list wrapped in parentheses following the function name. Each parameter has the following:

- A mandatory SQL type (or a user-defined type)
- An optional name
- An optional default value, which is used when the function is invoked without a value for the parameter
- An optional direction, which is used when the parameter could also be a return value

If the function does not require any arguments, the list will be empty, resulting in a couple of empty parentheses. If no name is specified for an argument, it will be available through the positional aliases $1, $2, and so on. As a simple example, consider *Listing 1*, where three different arguments are specified for f_args. Since they have no name, the function accesses them via the $1, $2, and $3 positionals. The pg_typeof() internal function provides information about the type of each argument:

```
testdb=> CREATE OR REPLACE FUNCTION
f_args( int, float, text )
RETURNS void AS $code$ BEGIN
 RAISE INFO '$1 (type %) = %', pg_typeof( $1 ), $1;
 RAISE INFO '$2 (type %) = %', pg_typeof( $2 ), $2;
 RAISE INFO '$3 (type %) = %', pg_typeof( $3 ), $3;
 END $code$
LANGUAGE plpgsql;

testdb=> SELECT f_args( 10, 1.2, 'hello world' );
INFO:   $1 (type integer) = 10
INFO:   $2 (type double precision) = 1.2
INFO:   $3 (type text) = hello world
```

Listing 1: Function arguments

It is worth noting that the $ positionals are always available and it is possible to mix prototypes where a few parameters get an explicit name and others do not. This is shown in *Listing 2*, where the first and last variables are explicitly named a and b respectively and the middle argument is accessed via the $2 positional:

```
testdb=> CREATE OR REPLACE FUNCTION
f_args( a int,   float, b text )
RETURNS void AS $code$
  BEGIN
    RAISE INFO 'a (type %) = %', pg_typeof( a ), a;
    RAISE INFO '$2(type %) = %', pg_typeof( $2 ), $2;
    RAISE INFO 'b (type %) = %', pg_typeof( b ), b;
   END $code$
LANGUAGE plpgsql;

testdb=> SELECT f_args( 10, 1.2, 'hello world' );
INFO:   a (type integer) = 10
INFO:   $2(type double precision) = 1.2
INFO:   b (type text) = hello world
```

Listing 2: Function arguments with names and $ positional

In practice, this means that giving a name to a variable within the function prototypes results in the following:

```
CREATE OR REPLACE FUNCTION f_args( a int, real, b text )
RETURNS void AS $code$
  DECLARE
      a ALIAS FOR $1;
      b ALIAS FOR $3;
  BEGIN
  ....
```

The preceding is a legal code and is similar to the pattern often used in Perl 5 functions and arguments.

Arguments can have default values, which are values that are used when the function is invoked without a value for a particular argument. Default values are specified within the function prototype using the DEFAULT keyword followed by a legal value for that particular argument. As an example, *Listing 42* defines a default value for each argument and shows how they are used in different invocations.

```
testdb=> CREATE OR REPLACE FUNCTION
f_args( a int DEFAULT 10, float DEFAULT 3.14,
        b text DEFAULT 'Hello Function World!' )
RETURNS void AS $code$
  BEGIN
    RAISE INFO 'a (type %) = %', pg_typeof( a ), a;
    RAISE INFO '$2(type %) = %', pg_typeof( $2 ), $2;
    RAISE INFO 'b (type %) = %', pg_typeof( b ), b;
  END $code$ LANGUAGE plpgsql;

-- all default values
testdb=> SELECT f_args();
INFO:  a (type integer) = 10
INFO:  $2(type double precision) = 3.14
INFO:  b (type text) = Hello Function World!

-- two default values
testdb=> SELECT f_args( 123 );
INFO:  a (type integer) = 123
INFO:  $2(type double precision) = 3.14
INFO:  b (type text) = Hello Function World!

-- no default values
testdb=> SELECT f_args( 123, 1.5, 'Mewl' );
INFO:  a (type integer) = 123
INFO:  $2(type double precision) = 1.5
INFO:  b (type text) = Mewl
```

```
-- DEFAULT does not triggers when a NULL value
-- is passed!
testdb=> SELECT f_args( 123, NULL, NULL );
INFO:   a (type integer) = 123
INFO:   $2(type double precision) = <NULL>
INFO:   b (type text) = <NULL>
```

Listing 3: Default arguments

As the last invocation in *Listing 3* shows, a default value is applied only when no value at all is specified for an argument. This means that passing NULL does not trigger the default value for that argument; rather it assigns NULL to the argument.

An argument can have an optional direction, which can be any of the following:

- IN: This is the default. It means that the value is passed as an argument from the caller to the function
- OUT: This means the argument will be passed from the function to the caller
- INOUT: This means the argument will be first passed from the caller to the function and then back from the function to the caller

There are some rules to follow when using parameter directions:

- Only IN arguments can have DEFAULT values
- OUT arguments cannot be passed to functions
- If there is only one OUT or INOUT argument, the return type of the function must match that argument type; otherwise, a record type must be used

The example in *Listing 4* shows a modification to f_args() so that it has two output arguments. Note that since the return type of the function is now a record, it is possible to manage the function as a table and perform a SELECT FROM. As you can see, the $2 and b arguments are those that are returned by the function execution, but since the $2 argument does not have an explicit name, it is shown as a generic column1 in the result set, while b keeps its original name:

```
testdb=> CREATE OR REPLACE FUNCTION
f_args( a IN int, INOUT float, b OUT text )
RETURNS record AS $code$
  BEGIN
    b := 'The real value was  ' || $2;
    $2 := a * $2;
  END $code$ LANGUAGE plpgsql;
```

```
testdb=> SELECT * FROM f_args( 10, 5 );
 column1 | b
---------+-----------------------
 50 | The real value was 5
```

Listing 4: Parameter direction

If you have created the function of *Listing 3*, you need to remove it with `drop function f_args(int, float, text);` before executing *Listing 4* or PostgreSQL will not understand which specific function you are referring to.

Of course, another way to pass values to the caller is by means of returning the values, as detailed in the next section.

It is the responsibility of the function to check the input values and manage NULL values. However, it is possible to specify STRICT as a function property, which will avoid the execution of a function with a NULL input in its argument list, replacing the return value with a NULL value directly. Consider the simple function shown in *Listing 5*. It accepts two arguments, prints out a message with its argument values, and returns a string that concatenates the values:

```
testdb=> CREATE OR REPLACE FUNCTION
f_nullable( a int, b text )
RETURNS text AS $code$
  BEGIN
    RAISE INFO 'Invoked with [%] and [%]', a, b;
    RETURN a || b;
  END $code$ LANGUAGE plpgsql STRICT;

testdb=> SELECT f_nullable( 10, 'Ten' ) IS NULL;
INFO:  Invoked with [10] and [Ten]
 ?column?
----------
 f
testdb=> SELECT f_nullable( 10, NULL ) IS NULL;
 ?column?
----------
 t
testdb=> SELECT f_nullable( NULL, 'Ten' ) IS NULL;
 ?column?
----------
 t
```

```
testdb=> SELECT f_nullable( NULL, NULL ) IS NULL;
 ?column?
----------
 t
```

Listing 5: A STRICT function example

If the function is invoked with not-null arguments, it is effectively executed (the `RAISE` message is shown). When any of the two arguments are `NULL`, the function is not executed at all (no RAISE message appears) and the output of the function is immediately substituted with a `NULL` value. This option represents a performance boost (the function is not executed at all on `NULL` input) as well as a handy way of clearly marking a `NULL` output on a `NULL` input.

It is possible to declare a function so that it does not know exactly how many parameters it will receive on each invocation. These functions are commonly named variadic. In PL/pgSQL, the last parameter in an argument list can be marked with the `VARIADIC` special keyword, meaning that this argument will consume all extra arguments. There is, however, a constraint: all extra arguments must be of the same type and will be inserted in an array.

Let's consider the function in *Listing 6*. This accepts a single argument called `separator` and a variable list of tag names. As an output, it produces a single string with the hierarchy of the tags. Since it does not know how many tags will be passed to the function, the tags argument is marked as a `VARIADIC text[]` array, and will consume every extra argument. The implementation of the function is straightforward: it iterates over the tags array and concatenates the current tag string, the separator, and the current tag within the array in a giant string, returning it once no more array elements remain:

```
testdb=> CREATE OR REPLACE FUNCTION
f_tags_to_string( separator text, VARIADIC tags text[]  )
RETURNS text AS $code$
  DECLARE
   tag_string text;
   current_tag text;
  BEGIN
   FOREACH current_tag IN ARRAY tags LOOP
      IF tag_string IS NULL THEN
         -- first assignment
         tag_string := current_tag;
         CONTINUE;
      END IF;

      tag_string := format( '%s %s %s', tag_string, separator, current_tag
);
   END LOOP;
```

```
    RETURN tag_string;
    END $code$ LANGUAGE plpgsql;

testdb=> SELECT f_tags_to_string( '>>', 'favourites', 'music', 'rock' );
     f_tags_to_string
-------------------------------
 favourites >> music >> rock

testdb=> SELECT f_tags_to_string( '~', 'work', 'travel', 'conferences',
'rome', '2018' );
            f_tags_to_string
------------------------------------------
 work ~ travel ~ conferences ~ rome ~ 2018
```

Listing 6: A variadic function example

Variadic arguments impose several constraints on the function:

- The array must handle variables of the same type, as shown.
- The variadic argument must be the last one in the function declaration.
- This also implies that the arguments before the variadic one cannot have default values.
- If the function is declared as STRICT (meaning it returns NULL on a NULL input), the argument array is managed as a whole. This means that the whole array must be NULL.
- It is not possible to pass an already built array as a variadic argument unless it is explicitly marked as VARIADIC at the time the function is invoked.

With regard to the latter point, if the f_tags_to_string() function is invoked with an array of tags, the executor will not find any executable function, producing an error:

```
testdb=> SELECT f_tags_to_string( '~', ARRAY[ 'work', 'travel',
'conferences', 'rome', '2018' ] );
ERROR:  function f_tags_to_string(unknown, text[]) does not exist
```

To solve the problem, the VARIADIC keyword must be used at the time the function is invoked:

```
testdb=> SELECT f_tags_to_string( '~',VARIADIC ARRAY[ 'work', 'travel',
'conferences', 'rome', '2018' ] );
            f_tags_to_string
------------------------------------------
 work ~ travel ~ conferences ~ rome ~ 2018
```

Returning values to the caller

A function can either return a single value of the specified type, or a whole result set (called SETOF). In order to return a single value, either a scalar or complex type, a RETURN statement is used. When the control flow reaches a RETURN, it immediately stops the function execution and provides the value to the caller.

It is possible to issue an empty RETURN, which is a statement that simply ends the control flow of the function without returning any particular value.

In order to see how RETURN can work with a scalar type, let's examine the code snipper of *Listing 46*. Here, the function accepts a single argument, f_size, which is supposed to be the size of a file (in bytes). The function compares the file size to constant values and determines a final value and a unit of measurement to express the size in. It then creates a string that contains both the numeric value (rounded to two decimal points) and the unit, and performs a RETURN to provide the computed text to the caller. It is possible to invoke the function on each tuple of the files table to get the results, as shown in *Listing 7*, where the f_size field is passed as an argument to the function, making the latter evaluate the argument on each tuple extracted from the SELECT statement:

```
testdb=> CREATE OR REPLACE FUNCTION
f_human_file_size( f_size numeric )
RETURNS text AS $code$
    DECLARE
        size_kb CONSTANT int    := 1024 * 1024;
        size_mb CONSTANT bigint := size_kb * 1024;
        size_gb CONSTANT bigint := size_mb * 1024;
        unit text := 'bytes';
    BEGIN
      IF f_size > size_gb THEN
         f_size := f_size / size_gb;
         unit   := 'MB';
      ELSEIF f_size > size_mb THEN
         f_size := f_size / size_mb;
         unit   := 'MB';
      ELSEIF f_size > size_kb THEN
         f_size := f_size / size_kb;
         unit   := 'KB';
      ELSE
         unit := 'bytes';
      END IF;
      RETURN round( f_size, 2 ) || unit;
    END $code$ LANGUAGE plpgsql;

  testdb=> SELECT f_name, f_human_file_size( f_size ) FROM files;
```

```
    f_name       | f_human_file_size
-----------------+--------------------
 picture1.png    | 120.80MB
 picture2.png    | 520.10MB
 picture3.png    | 300.00MB
 audio1.mp3      | 157.65MB
 audio2.mp3      | 221.50MB
 chapter2.org    | 22.40KB
 chapter3.org    | 36.40KB
 TestFile.txt    | 123.56KB
 foo.txt         | 10.50KB
```

Listing 7: Function returning a text string

It is possible to return tuples from a function. This can be done in two main ways:

- If the tuples are extracted from a query, use a RETURN QUERY statement, providing the query to be executed
- Use RETURN NEXT if the tuples are appended to the result set one at a time

Consider a function that returns all data in the files table that matches a particular type. The results set is made up of a simple SELECT statement. The function that implements this behavior is shown in *Listing 8*. It accepts a single argument, which is the type of file to search for. Note that the return type of the function is not a single value but instead a result set, so RETURNS SETOF is used to declare it. Since the function is going to return tuples coming from the files table, its return type will be the table itself. In other words, RETURNS SETOF means the function returns tuples with the same structure as the files table. The implementation of the function is straightforward: it performs a simple SELECT statement and returns the entire results set to the caller by means of RETURN QUERY. In other words, this function works a a query wrapper.

Finally, since the function produces a results set of tuples, it can be used where a set of tuples is expected. This means it can be used as a table in the query that runs it.

```
testdb=> CREATE OR REPLACE FUNCTION
f_file_by_type( file_type text DEFAULT 'txt' )
RETURNS SETOF files AS $code$
  BEGIN
    RETURN QUERY
    SELECT * FROM files
    WHERE f_type = file_type
    ORDER BY f_name;
  END $code$ LANGUAGE plpgsql;

testdb=> SELECT f_name, f_size FROM f_file_by_type( 'png' );
```

```
    f_name     |      f_size
---------------+------------------
 picture1.png  | 129708383096.83
 picture2.png  | 558453371016.99
 picture3.png  | 322122916439.53
```

Listing 8: A function that returns tuple from a query

Another way to return tuples is by using the RETURN NEXT statement. This statement produces a function to append a tuple to the output result set. This, to some extent, gives precedence to the caller that can start consuming the tuples, then resumes its execution and appends a new tuple to the result set. Once the function has finished appending tuples, it must perform an empty RETURN. It is also possible to change *Listing 8* into *Listing 9*, where a FOR loop over a query is performed and each tuple is returned to the caller.

```
testdb=> CREATE OR REPLACE FUNCTION
f_file_by_type( file_type text DEFAULT 'txt' )
RETURNS SETOF files AS $code$
    DECLARE
        current_tuple record;
    BEGIN
      FOR current_tuple IN SELECT * FROM files
                           WHERE f_type = file_type
                           ORDER BY f_name
                           LOOP
        -- append this tuple to the result set
        RETURN NEXT current_tuple;
      END LOOP;
      --mandatory when done
      RETURN;
  END $code$ LANGUAGE plpgsql;

testdb=> SELECT f_name, f_size FROM f_file_by_type( 'png' );
    f_name     |      f_size
---------------+------------------
 picture1.png  | 129708383096.83
 picture2.png  | 558453371016.99
 picture3.png  | 322122916439.53
```

Listing 9: A function that returns tuples one at a time

Using RETURN NEXT is suggested when there is a very large result set, so that it can be built and consumed a piece at a time, such as by a result paginator. Alternatively, suppose we have a need to populate the files table with fake data.

It is possible to build a function that generates tuples on the fly, as shown in *Listing 10*:

```
testdb=> CREATE OR REPLACE FUNCTION
f_fake_files( max int DEFAULT 10 )
RETURNS SETOF files AS $code$
    DECLARE
        current_tuple files%rowtype;
    BEGIN
        IF max <= 0 THEN
            RAISE EXCEPTION 'Specify a positive limit for tuple generation';
        END IF;
        FOR i IN 1 .. max LOOP
            current_tuple.pk = nextval( 'files_pk_seq' );
            current_tuple.f_name := initcap( 'file_' || i );
            current_tuple.f_size := random() * 1024 * 1024;
            CASE i % 3
                WHEN 0 THEN current_tuple.f_type := 'txt';
                WHEN 1 THEN current_tuple.f_type := 'png';
                WHEN 2 THEN current_tuple.f_type := 'mp3';
            END CASE;
            current_tuple.f_hash := md5( current_tuple.f_name );
            current_tuple.ts     := now();
            RAISE DEBUG '%) % generated', i, current_tuple.pk;
            RETURN NEXT current_tuple;
        END LOOP;
        RETURN;
    END $code$ LANGUAGE plpgsql;

testdb=> SET client_min_messages TO debug;
testdb=> SELECT * FROM f_fake_files( 3 );

DEBUG:  1) 42 generated
DEBUG:  2) 43 generated
DEBUG:  3) 44 generated
pk | f_name |   f_size   |               f_hash               | f_type |
ts
----+--------+------------+------------------------------------+--------+----
------------------------
 42 | File_1 |   979597.23 | 8ba5c586d44c70ca777c0f66b5243b40 | png    |
2018-07-16 16:18:27.782463
 43 | File_2 | 7134489.49 | f08d556d964b7a7b9374d96c6c2ca8ec | mp3    |
2018-07-16 16:18:27.782463
 44 | File_3 |   258768.02 | aac47180851be5de7f5b19fa7afa91b7 | txt    |
2018-07-16 16:18:27.782463
```

Listing 10: Generating fake tuples via a function

The function shown in *Listing 10* returns a set of tuples like the files table ones, the same as in the preceding example. However, to handle the tuple it is constructing, the function declares a `current_tuple` variable of `files%rowtype` type. Row type variables are always of the special type <table>, followed by `%rowtype`. In this case, `current_tuple` is a tuple with the same data structure as a row from the files table. It is worth noting that a `rowtype` variable has the same structure as a table tuple, but not the same defaults and constraints. The function performs a `FOR` loop starting from 1 and limited to the maximum integer argument in order to generate the maximum number of tuples.

Within the `FOR` loop, the `current_tuple` fields are initialized with randomly generated values. Each field of the tuple is de-referenced with the dot operator (such as `current_tuple.f_name`) and each field is assigned an appropriate value. Note that some fields are set to the return value of another function, such as the `pk` field, which is set to the return value of `nextval()` against the same sequence of the files table. Once the tuple has been fully built, `RETURN NEXT` is executed to append the tuple to the output result set that yields the function execution. Once the tuple has been appended to the result set, the function resumes from the `FOR` cycle and initializes another tuple to append the results set. Once the `FOR` loop ends, a regular `RETURN` marks the result set as complete and ends the execution of the function.

In the result set of *Listing 10*, there is another important thing to note: the `ts` timestamp is the same for every tuple. This is due to the fact that the function is executed in a single-statement transaction (`SELECT`) and the time is set at the beginning of the transaction. If you need to get a different time value each time the function is evaluated, it is required to substitute the `now()` function call to `clock_timestamp()`.

As you can see in *Listing 11*, it is possible to use more than one function within the same statement, concatenating the results of a function as arguments of another function and more complex scenarios:

```
testdb=> SELECT f_name, f_human_file_size( f_size ) FROM f_fake_files( 3 );
 f_name | f_human_file_size
--------+--------------------
 File_1 | 146713.36bytes
 File_2 | 590618.06bytes
 File_3 | 1.38KB
```

Listing 11: Using more than one function within the same statement

Let's now consider *Listing 12*, which accepts a Boolean parameter that indicates the function to either create fake tuples or return existing ones from the `files` table. The function achieves its aim by issuing either a RETURN QUERY, to provide existing tuples from the database, or a RETURN NEXT to dynamically generate tuples:

```
testdb=> CREATE OR REPLACE FUNCTION
f_files_tuples( fake bool DEFAULT false, max int DEFAULT 5 )
RETURNS SETOF files AS $code$
  DECLARE
    current_tuple files%rowtype;
  BEGIN
    IF fake THEN
      FOR i IN 1 .. max LOOP
          current_tuple.pk = nextval( 'files_pk_seq' );
          current_tuple.f_name := initcap( 'file_' || i );
          current_tuple.f_size := random() * 1024 * 1024;
          CASE i % 3
              WHEN 0 THEN current_tuple.f_type := 'txt';
              WHEN 1 THEN current_tuple.f_type := 'png';
              WHEN 2 THEN current_tuple.f_type := 'mp3';
          END CASE;
          current_tuple.f_hash := md5( current_tuple.f_name );
          current_tuple.ts     := now();
          RETURN NEXT current_tuple;
      END LOOP;
      RETURN;
    ELSE
      RETURN QUERY
      SELECT * FROM files ORDER BY random() LIMIT max;
    END IF;
  END $code$ LANGUAGE plpgsql;

testdb=> SELECT * FROM f_files_tuples( false, 2 )
      UNION
          SELECT * FROM f_files_tuples( true, 2 )
      ORDER BY f_name;

 pk |    f_name    |    f_size     |               f_hash              |
 f_type |            ts
----+--------------+---------------+-----------------------------------+--
-------+---------------------------
 61 | File_1       |    1705244.13 | 8ba5c586d44c70ca777c0f66b5243b40 |
png    | 2018-07-16 17:15:48.571018
 62 | File_2       |    2520174.21 | f08d556d964b7a7b9374d96c6c2ca8ec |
mp3    | 2018-07-16 17:15:48.571018
 18 | chapter2.org |   23488405.98 | 14b8f225d4e6462022657d7285bb77ba |
org    | 2018-07-12 10:56:15.239616
```

```
 21 | picture2.png | 558453371016.99 | 323412345666462022657daa85bb77a2 |
png     | 2018-07-12 10:56:15.239616
```

Listing 12: A function that either creates or return existing tuples

Another way to return tuples out of a function is by using RETURN TABLE. The idea behind this is that the function declares a table-like structure to output, including column names and types. The names effectively work as OUT arguments to the function and are therefore variables that are visible within the code block. When the function needs to append a new record to the returning result set, it does so with an empty RETURN NEXT statement. All the values of the named arguments will be used to build the returning tuple. To make this clearer, consider *Listing 13*, which provides a function to generate fake files tuples, similar to that shown in *Listing 10*. The difference in this case is that the returned result set is shrunk down to only three columns, called pk, file_name, and file_type, within the RETURNS TABLE clause. This clause defines the three variables that are then assigned within the FOR loop. RETURN NEXT outputs these variable values and appends a new tuple to the result set. Note that neither the table files (or its structure) or a record variable have been used to achieve the final result set.

```
testdb=> CREATE OR REPLACE FUNCTION
f_fake_small_files( max int DEFAULT 10 )
RETURNS TABLE ( pk int, file_name text, file_type text )
AS $code$
  BEGIN
    IF max <= 0 THEN
       RAISE EXCEPTION 'Specify a positive limit for tuple generation';
    END IF;
    FOR i IN 1 .. max LOOP
        pk = nextval( 'files_pk_seq' );
        file_name := initcap( 'file_' || i );
        CASE i % 3
            WHEN 0 THEN file_type := 'txt';
            WHEN 1 THEN file_type := 'png';
            WHEN 2 THEN file_type := 'mp3';
        END CASE;
        RETURN NEXT;
    END LOOP;
    RETURN;
  END $code$ LANGUAGE plpgsql;

testdb=> SELECT * FROM f_fake_small_files( 5 );
 pk  | file_name | file_type
-----+-----------+-----------
 148 | File_1    | png
 149 | File_2    | mp3
 150 | File_3    | txt
```

```
151 | File_4   | png
152 | File_5   | mp3
```

Listing 13: A function that returns a table

From a purely syntactic point of view, the function of *Listing 13* is equivalent to the one in *Listing 14*, which explicitly uses a few OUT parameters and RETURNS SETOF to achieve the same result:

```
testdb=> CREATE OR REPLACE FUNCTION
f_fake_small_files( max int DEFAULT 10, pk OUT int,
                    file_name OUT text,
                    file_type OUT text )
RETURNS SETOF record AS $code$
    BEGIN
        IF max <= 0 THEN
            RAISE EXCEPTION 'Specify a positive limit for tuple generation';
        END IF;
        FOR i IN 1 .. max LOOP
            pk = nextval( 'files_pk_seq' );
            file_name := initcap( 'file_' || i );
            CASE i % 3
                WHEN 0 THEN file_type := 'txt';
                WHEN 1 THEN file_type := 'png';
                WHEN 2 THEN file_type := 'mp3';
            END CASE;
            RETURN NEXT;
        END LOOP;
        RETURN;
    END $code$ LANGUAGE plpgsql;

testdb=> SELECT * FROM f_fake_small_files( 5 );
 pk  | file_name | file_type
-----+-----------+-----------
 148 | File_1    | png
 149 | File_2    | mp3
 150 | File_3    | txt
 151 | File_4    | png
 152 | File_5    | mp3
```

Listing 14: A function that returns a result set with OUT parameters

It is also possible to build a more complex function that scans a directory in order to build up a set of records that correspond to the files found in that directory. A possible simple implementation of such a function is shown in *Listing 15*, but before digging into the code of the function, bear in mind that this kind of function must be run as database superuser. The reason for this is that the function exploits other PostgreSQL functions, such as `pg_ls_dir()`, that require superuser privileges in order to inspect the filesystem. While it is possible to grant execution permissions to a normal user, the `pg_ls_dir()` function will only take into account relative path, resulting therefore in a partial limitation in its capabilities. To overtake the problem, and for sake of simplicity, let's assume the function will be executed by a database superuser.

```
testdb=# CREATE OR REPLACE FUNCTION
f_files_from_directory( dir text DEFAULT '.' )
RETURNS SETOF files AS $code$
  DECLARE
    current_tuple files%rowtype;
    current_file  text;
    name_parts    text[];
    is_dir        bool;
  BEGIN
    RAISE DEBUG 'Reading files into %', dir;
    FOR current_file IN SELECT pg_ls_dir( dir ) LOOP
        RAISE DEBUG 'Building tuple for entry [%]', current_file;
        current_tuple.f_name := current_file;
        -- absolute file name
        current_file := dir || '/' || current_file;
        -- use the real file size and moditification time
        SELECT size, modification, isdir
        FROM   pg_stat_file( current_file )
        INTO   current_tuple.f_size, current_tuple.ts, is_dir;
        -- do not manage directories
        CONTINUE WHEN is_dir;
        -- initialize tuple primary key
        current_tuple.pk = nextval( 'files_pk_seq' );
        -- try to get the type of the file from its extension
        name_parts := string_to_array( current_tuple.f_name, '.' );
        IF array_length( name_parts, 1 ) > 1 THEN
           current_tuple.f_type := name_parts[ array_length( name_parts, 1
) ];
        ELSE
           current_tuple.f_type := 'txt';
        END IF;
        -- read the content of the file (not binary!) and compute an hash
         current_tuple.f_hash := md5( pg_read_file( current_file ) );
        RETURN NEXT current_tuple;
    END LOOP;
```

```
    RETURN;
END $code$ LANGUAGE plpgsql;
```

Listing 15: A function that scans the local filesystem to produce tuples

The function in *Listing 15* accepts the `dir` argument, which represents the directory in which to search for files. The `pg_ls_dir()` is used to obtain a set of file names in that directory. Then, those files are cycled in a `FOR` loop, in which each relative file name is assigned to the `current_file` variable. Since `pg_ls_dir()` does not output only the files but also the subdirectories, `current_file` may also hold the name of a subdirectory. Another utility function, `pg_stat_file()`, provides information about the metadata of the files, such as its size, its modification timestamp, as well as whether the current entry is a regular file or a directory. After having kept the relative file name in the `current_tuple.f_name` field, `SELECT INTO` is performed against `pg_stat_file()` to get the metadata. Since the directories are not managed, `CONTINUE` is issued if the `is_dir` local variable is set to a true value. In this case, the `FOR` loop restarts from the next directory entry (the next file name). On the other hand, if `CONTINUE` is not issued (so if the current entry is a file), more `current_tuple` fields are initialized with data extracted from the `pg_stat_file()` function call.

It is then time to decide the file type. To keep things simple, the type is determined by the last extension of the file name (for example, `foo.txt` will result in a file type `.txt`). First of all, the file name is split into a string array by the `string_to_array()` function, where each part of the array is the string behind a `'.'` separator. The resulting array is assigned to a `name_parts` variable. For example, a file with the name `foo.bar.txt` is transformed into an array with `{'foo', 'bar', 'txt'}`. If the `name_parts` array has more than one element, the last element is the extension and therefore determines the type of the file, otherwise the file type defaults to a `.txt` one. The last field that must be properly initialized is `f_hash`. In order to compute the hash of the file, its whole content is read via `pg_read_file()` and the `md5()` hash is computed. This function chain works for the content of text files. At this point, the whole tuple has been properly initialized and the function can append it to the result set with `RETURN NEXT`. Once no more files on the disk are left, the `FOR` loop ends and the function does an empty `RETURN` to finish the result set.

Listing 16 shows a possible invocation of the function and its results. The result set of the function can be used to populate the files table via an INSERT statement:

```
testdb=# SELECT * FROM
files_from_directory( '/home/luca/git/fluca1978-pg-utils/examples/cte' );
 pk  |           f_name            | f_size  |           f_hash
 | f_type |          ts
-----+----------------------------+---------+------------------------
-------+--------+--------------------
 124 | family_tree.sql            | 1879.00 |
cc948a6e78a1581e350958c71093927d | sql    | 2018-05-31 16:17:19
 125 | family_tree_recursive_cte.sql |  400.00 |
42a149f41d3c78241160ea473154e4b5 | sql    | 2018-05-31 16:17:19
 126 | file_system_cte.sql        | 1424.00 |
acc41b140745747e7647de742868d768 | sql    | 2018-05-31 16:17:19
 127 | star_wars_family_tree_cte.sql | 2937.00 |
3e2bf991e553ae86e6f1ca2aa525b597 | sql    | 2018-05-31 16:17:19
```

Listing 16: Filesystem inspecting results

Security

The f_files_from_directory() function shown in *Listing 15* must be executed as a superuser in order to work. This is due to the fact that the function body exploits other internal functions to read the local filesystem, which is considered dangerous and therefore restricted to database administrators.

While we have the possibility of explicitly granting permission to other users, what is required in this case is to be able to execute the function as a superuser. Functions can achieve this by means of the SECURITY option. This can be one of the following:

- INVOKER: This is the default value. It means that the function will run with the privileges of the user that invoked it
- DEFINER: This means that the function will always run with the privileges of the user that has defined it

In other words, using a Unix analogy, the SECURITY DEFINER option is similar to the setuid(2) option for Unix executables.

Given this, we can declare the function of *Listing 15* with the SECURITY
DEFINER option from a database administrator, as shown in *Listing 17*. The function will
always be executed as a superuser from any other user:

```
testdb=# CREATE OR REPLACE FUNCTION
f_files_from_directory( dir text DEFAULT '.' )
RETURNS SETOF files AS $code$
   ...
  $code$ LANGUAGE plpgsql SECURITY DEFINER;

testdb=> SELECT current_user;
 current_user
--------------
 luca
testdb=> SELECT * FROM
f_files_from_directory( '/home/luca/git/fluca1978-pg-utils/examples/cte' );
 pk  |           f_name          | f_size  |           f_hash
 | f_type |         ts
-----+---------------------------+---------+---------------------------
-------+--------+--------------------
 136 | family_tree.sql           | 1879.00 |
cc948a6e78a1581e350958c71093927d | sql    | 2018-05-31 16:17:19
 137 | family_tree_recursive_cte.sql |  400.00 |
42a149f41d3c78241160ea473154e4b5 | sql    | 2018-05-31 16:17:19
 138 | file_system_cte.sql       | 1424.00 |
acc41b140745747e7647de742868d768 | sql    | 2018-05-31 16:17:19
 139 | star_wars_family_tree_cte.sql | 2937.00 |
3e2bf991e553ae86e6f1ca2aa525b597 | sql    | 2018-05-31 16:17:19
```

Listing 17: Transforming the function as a "setuid" one

It is interesting to note that the privilege escalation propagates to all the function execution
flow, so there is no additional need to grant any other permission to functions such as
pg_ls_dir(), which would not normally work as expected for a non-administrator user.

Immutability

What happens when a function is called over and over again with the same arguments? It is
executed over and over again, which is quite easy to understand. PostgreSQL allows a
function to declare a level of immutability so that the query executor can make some
assumptions to improve the speed of the execution.

To better understand this concept, consider the `f_human_file_size()` function shown in *Listing 46*. The function accepts a numeric argument and produces a text representation of that argument:

```
testdb=> SELECT f_human_file_size( 1234567890 );
 f_human_file_size
-------------------
 1.15MB
```

Reading the function implementation, it is clear that such a function will provide the same result for the same input every time and it would produce a huge speed boost if the query executor understood that. It could cache the result for a specified input and then avoid the execution of the function for that input. Although, for a function like `f_human_file_size()` the performance improvement is small, for other much more complex functions it might be an important gain.

How can the executor decide whether to avoid a function execution under the same input-value circumstances? It does so by considering a property of the function itself. A function can be declared to be either VOLATILE, STABLE, or IMMUTABLE. The default immutability property, when none is specified, is VOLATILE. This means the function must be executed every time, even if the input values are always the same. Since no immutability property has been specified in the definition of *Listing 46*, the function is treated as a VOLATILE one. On the contrary, if the function never changes its output value when the same input is provided and does not interact with the underlying database (to select or update existing tuples), the function can be declared IMMUTABLE. This is the case for `f_human_file_size()`.

Between VOLATILE and IMMUTABLE, there is an intermediate level named STABLE. A STABLE function is not supposed to modify the underlying database, but nor does it provide the same output for the same input within the same SQL statement every time. In other words, the output of a STABLE function can change between different SQL statements or transactions, even if the same input is provided.

We can choose the right level by following the following rules:

- If the function either modifies the underlying database or returns different output values for the same input values, it must be marked as VOLATILE.
- If the function does not change its output value for the same input values, it can be either a STABLE or IMMUTABLE one:
  - If the output depends only on the input arguments and therefore the function does not interact at all with the underlying database, it can be marked as IMMUTABLE.

- If the output depends on the database status (such as a lookup table) and does not change within a single SQL statement, the function can be marked as STABLE.

Be aware that marking a function with the wrong level can lead to incorrect execution and unexpected results, so be careful when dealing with the previously mentioned levels.

In the IMMUTABLE family of functions, we have mathematical functions such as sin() that provide a result depending on the input value only. The STABLE family of functions include the timestamp set of functions (such as now() and current_timestamp); their output does not depend on any input value but does not change within a transaction boundary, meaning it can change across SQL statements outside of a transaction boundary. The VOLATILE family of functions include random() and timeofday(), the output of which does not depend on the underlying database status or any input argument, but changes each time the function is invoked.

We can improve the f_human_file_size() function by specifying that it can be considered IMMUTABLE, as shown in *Listing 57*.

```
testdb=> CREATE OR REPLACE FUNCTION
f_human_file_size( f_size numeric )
RETURNS text AS $code$
   DECLARE
        size_kb CONSTANT int    := 1024 * 1024;
        size_mb CONSTANT bigint := size_kb * 1024;
        size_gb CONSTANT bigint := size_mb * 1024;
        unit text := 'bytes';
   BEGIN
     IF f_size > size_gb THEN
        f_size := f_size / size_gb;
        unit   := 'MB';
     ELSEIF f_size > size_mb THEN
        f_size := f_size / size_mb;
        unit   := 'MB';
     ELSEIF f_size > size_kb THEN
        f_size := f_size / size_kb;
        unit   := 'KB';
     ELSE
        unit := 'bytes';
     END IF;
     RETURN round( f_size, 2 ) || unit;
END $code$ LANGUAGE plpgsql IMMUTABLE;
```

Listing 18: Defining the f_human_file_size function as IMMUTABLE

On the other hand, the `f_files_from_directory()` function defined in *Listing 54* cannot be declared either `STABLE` or `IMMUTABLE` even if it seems that it does not depend on or interact with the underlying database and that its output only depends on the input value. On a closer look, it is possible to see that the output of the function depends on another function, `nextval()`, which returns a different value each time and is marked as `VOLATILE`. This therefore means that the `f_files_from_directory()` function cannot be anything but `VOLATILE`, because it depends on another `VOLATILE` function (which, in turn, depends on the underlying database status). Consider what would happen if the function were marked as non-volatile: its results can't remain the same since the function depends on an external resource (in this case the filesystem), which can change by itself.

PostgreSQL allows functions to be used as index expressions, but only `IMMUTABLE` functions can be used for this purpose. It is clear that the index must be built depending on the return values of the function, and these must be the same for the same input values or the index will not be able to cover the underlying table values.

Costs

It is possible to provide hints to the executor about the cost of a function. PostgreSQL query optimizer is a cost-based optimizer, which means it will carefully evaluate the cost of each operation and choose the execution path with the lowest cost. Explaining the cost system and the optimizer is out of the scope of this book, but it is important to know that functions can have a cost estimation.

There are two properties that provide this cost estimation:

- `COST` is a positive number indicating how many CPU operations the function will use
- `ROWS` is an estimation of the rows returned from a `RETURNS SETOF` (or `RETURNS TABLE`) function

The `COST` property is the more straightforward one: it expresses how many CPU operations the whole execution of the function will use. CPU operations have a cost of `cpu_operator_cost` each, which is, by default, 1/40 the cost of performing a sequential read from disk. If not specified, the `COST` for a PL/pgSQL or any non-C language is set to 100.

If the function returns a result set, `COST` is intended to be the cost of a single tuple from the function result set. Moreover, it is possible to provide the optimizer with a hint about how many tuples a function will return by specifying a positive `ROWS` number.

As a simple example, a function that performs a simple limited tag query can be declared to have a ROWS property set to the limit itself:

```
testdb=> CREATE FUNCTION get_ten_tags()
RETURNS SETOF tag AS   $code$
  BEGIN
    RETURN QUERY SELECT *
                 FROM tags
                 LIMIT 10;
  END $code$ LANGUAGE plpgsql
ROWS 10; -- it is clear this function cannot return more rows
```

Tuning cost properties can quickly become a complicated task, so it is recommended to add these properties only when they are really needed and to check the impact on query execution carefully.

Moving functions to other schemas

As with many other database objects, it is possible to place a function into a schema that is different from the default one, which is public. All we need to do is either fully qualify the name of the function at the time it is created or issue an ALTER FUNCTION command.

Listing 19 shows the two ways to add the function f_greetings() to the schema my_library:

1. By declaring the function with the schema qualifier before its name, such as my_library.f_greetings
2. By issuing an ALTER FUNCTION SET SCHEMA command to move the function from one schema to another

```
    -- first ensure there is the schema
testdb=> CREATE SCHEMA my_library;
    -- and then add the function to the schema
testdb=> CREATE OR REPLACE FUNCTION
    my_library.f_greetings( who text )
    RETURNS text AS $code$
      BEGIN
        RETURN 'Hello dear ' || who;
      END $code$ LANGUAGE plpgsql IMMUTABLE;

    -- or to move an already existing function
testdb=> ALTER FUNCTION f_greetings( text ) SET SCHEMA my_library;
```

Listing 19: Declaring a function in a specific schema

For security reasons, it is not possible to change the schema of an existing function into the `pg_temp` one, since this would transform the function into a temporary one. Similarly, a function that has been already defined as temporary cannot be moved to a non-temporary schema.

Temporary functions

Like other temporary objects (such as tables), a temporary function is a function that exists only for the current session and is destroyed once the session ends. There is no explicit way to declare a function as temporary; rather, we have to place the function into the special `pg_temp` namespace. This tells the database engine that the function must be destroyed at the end of the session.

For security reasons, it is not possible to invoke a temporary function with its relative name. Instead, we have to use the fully qualified name including the `pg_temp` namespace. *Listing 20* shows a very simple example of a temporary function, which is declared as such by prepending the `pg_temp` namespace of the function name. As you can see, once the session is closed, the function is thrown away:

```
testdb=> CREATE FUNCTION pg_temp.f_greetings( who text )
RETURNS text AS $code$
  BEGIN
    RETURN 'Hello dear ' || who;
  END $code$ LANGUAGE plpgsql;

testdb=> SELECT pg_temp.f_greetings( 'Luca' );
   f_greetings
----------------
 Hello dear Luca

-- close the session and start it again
testdb=> \q
...
testdb=> SELECT pg_temp.f_greetings( 'Luca' );
ERROR:  schema "pg_temp" does not exist
LINE 1: SELECT pg_temp.f_greetings( 'Luca' );
```

Listing 20: A temporary function example

Where is my function?

The pg_proc special catalog table stores information about every routine (including functions and procedures) defined in the system. It also includes an entry for each overloaded version. There are some fields that can be used to introspect the function definitions:

- proname is the name of the function
- prosrc is the implementation of the function, which is anything specified as the block code after the AS clause
- prokind is set to f for a function and to p for a procedure
- proargnames and proargtypes represent an internal representation of the argument list
- prorettype and proretset indicate the return type and whether the function returns a scalar or a result set
- provolatile assumes a value of v for VOLATILE, s for STABLE, or i for IMMUTABLE
- prosecdef is set to true to indicate a SECURITY DEFINER property
- prolang is an internal representation of the language in which the function is implemented

With this knowledge, it is possible to query the system catalog to get information about a function. For example, to get back the code block of the function created in *Listing 15* and *Listing 21* queries the pg_proc table and returns the plpgsql string that is used as the function implementation. It is interesting to note that the output string (the content of pg_proc.prosrc) is the string that is contained in the dollar quoting, with spaces, indentations, and comments:

```
testdb=> SELECT prosrc FROM pg_proc
WHERE proname = 'f_files_from_directory' AND    prokind = 'f';
                                      prosrc
---------------------------------------------------------------------------------
------
+
   DECLARE
+
     current_tuple files%rowtype;
+
     current_file   text;
+
     name_parts     text[];
+
```

```
    BEGIN
+
+
    RAISE DEBUG 'Reading files into %', dir;
+
+
    FOR current_file IN SELECT pg_ls_dir( dir ) LOOP
+
+
        RAISE DEBUG 'Building tuple for file [%]', current_file;
+
...
```

Listing 21: Getting back the code block for a function

There are a couple of utility functions that help to get text representations of arguments and return types:

- The pg_get_function_result() provides information about a function return type
- The pg_get_function_arguments() provides information about a function argument list

These functions operate on the information contained in pg_proc and other system catalog tables. They decode the information and provide a way to get back all the information about how the function has been defined. By adding the pg_language special catalog table, which stores information about the procedural languages, it is possible to get full details about a function, which is shown in *Listing 22*:

```
testdb=> SELECT pro.proname AS function_name
    , pg_get_function_arguments( pro.oid ) AS arguments
    , pg_get_function_result( pro.oid )  AS returns
    , pro.prosrc AS code_block
    , lan.lanname AS language
FROM pg_proc pro JOIN pg_language lan ON lan.oid = pro.prolang
WHERE pro.proname = 'f_files_from_directory' AND pro.prokind = 'f';
-[ RECORD 1 ]-+-----------------------------------------------------------
-------------------
function_name | f_files_from_directory
arguments     | dir text DEFAULT '.'::text
returns       | SETOF files
code_block    |
+
              |     DECLARE
+
```

```
            |    current_tuple files%rowtype;
 +
            |    current_file   text;
 +
            |    name_parts     text[];
 +
            |  BEGIN
 +
            |
 +
            |    RAISE DEBUG 'Reading files into %', dir;
 +
            |
 +
               . . . .
            |
 language   |  plpgsql
```

Listing 22: Getting back more information about a function

Putting it all together, it is also possible to build a stored procedure to get the source code of another stored procedure, which is shown in *Listing 23*.

The `f_dump_function()` function accepts a function name to search for in the system catalog and, with a query similar to the one in *Listing 61*, extracts a textual representation of the function body, argument list, and return type. This information is then structured into a giant text string called `function_declaration`, via a `format()` call. It is interesting to note that the `format()` template string is built up on a dollar-quoted string to provide better code formatting with new-line characters and indentation. Since each overloaded function has an entry in `pg_proc`, the function produces a textual representation of the function source code for each row by means of a `FOR` loop. It also returns the source code of the declaration of each function as a results set:

```
testdb=> CREATE OR REPLACE FUNCTION f_dump_function( function_name text )
RETURNS SETOF text AS $code$
  DECLARE
    function_count int := 0;
    current_body text;
    current_args text;
    current_returns text;
    current_language text;
    current_volatile text;
    current_security text;
    function_declaration text;
    function_template text;
  BEGIN
    -- search for a function with the given name
```

```
SELECT COUNT( prosrc ) INTO  function_count
FROM  pg_proc WHERE proname = function_name AND   prokind = 'f';
IF NOT FOUND THEN
    RAISE EXCEPTION 'No function with the given name found!';
END IF;

-- how is supposed the function to look like?
-- use the format() %I for identifiers and %s for strings
function_template := $ft$CREATE OR REPLACE FUNCTION
                       %I(%s)
                       RETURNS %s
                       AS $$
                       %s
                       $$
                       LANGUAGE %I
                       SECURITY %s
                       %s;
                    $ft$;


RAISE DEBUG 'Found % functions with name [%]', function_count,
function_name;
    -- iterate on each found entry
    FOR i IN 1 .. function_count LOOP
          SELECT pg_get_function_arguments( pro.oid )
             , pg_get_function_result( pro.oid ), pro.prosrc ,
lan.lanname
             , CASE pro.prosecdef WHEN true THEN   'DEFINER'
                                         ELSE 'INVOKER'
                END
             , CASE pro.provolatile WHEN 'i' THEN 'IMMUTABLE'
                                    WHEN 's' THEN 'STABLE'
                                    ELSE 'VOLATILE'
                END
          INTO current_args,  current_returns, current_body,
current_language, current_security, current_volatile
          FROM pg_proc pro JOIN pg_language lan ON lan.oid = pro.prolang
          WHERE pro.proname = function_name AND prokind = 'f';

          -- build the function declaration
          function_declaration := format( function_template,
                                          function_name,
                                          current_args,
                                          current_returns,
                                          current_body,
                                          current_language,
                                          current_security,
                                          current_volatile );

          -- this entry is complete
```

```
            RETURN NEXT function_declaration;
    END LOOP;
    RETURN;
END $code$ LANGUAGE plpgsql;
```

Listing 23: A function that inspects the system catalog to provide source code of other functions

The result of *Listing 62* is really close to the result of the `psql` special command, `\sf` (**source of function**), which can be used to get the function declaration and implementation.

Permissions

It is possible to limit the execution of some functions to specified users. The GRANT and REVOKE SQL statements include an EXECUTE permission that is used for the execution of functions. As an example, the following snippet of code allows only the database user `luca` to execute the `f_fake_small_files` function:

```
-- avoid anyone to execute the function
testdb=> REVOKE EXECUTE ON FUNCTION f_fake_small_files FROM public;
-- allow only luca to execute the function
testdb=> GRANT EXECUTE ON FUNCTION f_fake_small_files TO luca;
```

A tag insertion function

As an example, let's build a function that accepts a single string to represent a tag hierarchy, which is a list of tags separated by a predefined character or string. The function needs to disassemble the string, extract each tag, and insert them with references to their parents. So, for instance, the string `'holidays > 2018 > sicily > family'` must be split up into tag pieces (`holidays`, `2018`, `sicily`, and `family`) and each tag must be placed into the right place of the hierarchy. In this case, 2018 is the child of holidays and the parent of Sicily).

The function shown in *Listing 24* shows a possible implementation of this behavior. The `f_insert_tags()` function accepts two arguments: the tag string (`'holidays > 2018 > sicily > family'`) and an optional string that is the separator between the tags. Since the function works on the tags table, it declares a `current_tuple`, a row-type of tags, which will be used both to insert a tuple into the tags table and to return the tuple inserted as a result set to the caller. The tag string is split into single tags by means of the `string_to_array()` function, which provides an array as its output, in which each piece is a single tag. Then, a FOREACH loop is performed against the array.

This means that every tag is assigned to the t_name field of current_tuple on each iteration. Within the loop, the name of the tag is trimmed (extra spaces are removed) and the t_child_of field is set to the last seen pk (on the first iteration both are set to NULL). This ensures that every time a new tuple is inserted, it points to the previous one (to the parent tuple). The tuple is then stored by means of a regular INSERT where no pk is specified, so that the sequence attached to the table will generate a new value. Please note that the INSERT has a RETURNING * clause that will insert every value of the fresh tuple into the current_tuple variable. Lastly, if INSERT succeeded, the FOUND Boolean variable is set and so the function issues RETURN NEXT to insert the tuple into the result set for the caller. Otherwise, an exception is thrown. Once the FOREACH loops end and no more tags need to be processed, the function ends too:

```
testdb=> CREATE OR REPLACE FUNCTION
f_insert_tags( tag_string text, separator text DEFAULT '>' )
RETURNS SETOF tags         -- returns the inserted tuples
AS $code$
  DECLARE
    tag_array text[];
    current_tuple tags%rowtype;
  BEGIN
    -- firs of all get all the tags
    tag_array := string_to_array( tag_string, separator );
    FOREACH current_tuple.t_name IN ARRAY tag_array LOOP
       current_tuple.t_child_of := current_tuple.pk;
       current_tuple.t_name      := trim( current_tuple.t_name );
       RAISE DEBUG 'Inserting tag [%] child of [%]', current_tuple.t_name,
current_tuple.t_child_of;
       -- execute an insert and get back the table data
       INSERT INTO tags( t_name, t_child_of )
       VALUES ( current_tuple.t_name, current_tuple.pk )
       RETURNING * INTO current_tuple;
       IF FOUND THEN
          RETURN NEXT current_tuple;
       ELSE
          RAISE EXCEPTION 'Cannot insert tag [%] as child of [%]',
current_tuple.t_name, current_tuple.t_child_of;
       END IF;
    END LOOP;
    RETURN;
  END $code$ LANGUAGE plpgsql STRICT VOLATILE;

testdb=> SET client_min_messages TO debug;
testdb=> SELECT * FROM f_insert_tags( 'holidays > 2018 > sicily > family'
);
DEBUG:  Inserting tag [holidays] child of [<NULL>]
DEBUG:  Inserting tag [2018] child of [21]
```

```
DEBUG:  Inserting tag [sicily] child of [22]
DEBUG:  Inserting tag [family] child of [23]
 pk |  t_name  | t_child_of
----+----------+------------
 21 | holidays |
 22 | 2018     |         21
 23 | sicily   |         22
 24 | family   |         23
```

Listing 24: Inserting the tag hierarchy through a function

Compile and runtime problem detection

When a function is defined, PostgreSQL compiles the PL/pgSQL code to check for errors. The fact that the function compiles, however, does not mean it does not contain errors or common mistakes. In order to help the developer identify common problems, PostgreSQL allows the configuration of two particular variables:

- The `plpgsql.extra_warning` emits warning messages at compile time to inform the developer that the function contains potentially common mistakes.
- The `plpgsql.extra_errors` emits error messages at compile time and stops the function definition. This means that errors must be fixed before the function can be used.

Both variables accept the same values, so choosing to define one or the other is only a matter of how strict the search for errors should be. In PostgreSQL 11, the allowed values are only `shadowed_variables` and the two `none` (check disabled) and `all` (checks enabled) special values. In the upcoming PostgreSQL 12, the range of values will extend to the following:

- `none` disables all the checks.
- `all` enables all the checks.
- `shadowed_variables` detects each time a variable masks another one. For example, this might be nested blocks that define the same variable name.
- `too_many_rows` detects when a statement with an `INTO` clause returns more than one row, therefore throwing away part of the result set in the variable assignment.
- `strict_multi_assignment` detects when a multi-variable assignment, like a `SELECT INTO`, differs with regard to the number of values and variables.

While `shadowed_variables` is a compile-time check, `too_many_rows` and `strict_multi_assignment` are runtime checks.

In order to demonstrate the utility of the `shadowed_variables` value, consider *Listing 25*. The main code block redefines the variable p1, which masks the function argument. The inner code block redefines the p3 variable, which masks the outer block variable:

```
testdb=> CREATE OR REPLACE FUNCTION
f_test_shadow( p1 int DEFAULT 1, p2 text DEFAULT 'Hello' )
RETURNS void AS $code$
  DECLARE
    p1 char(2) := 'P1'; -- masks function argument!
    p3 int     := 10;
  BEGIN
    RAISE DEBUG 'p1 is %', p1;
    DECLARE
      p3 text := 'Gosh!'; -- masks outer block variable!
    BEGIN
     RAISE DEBUG 'p3 is %', p3;
    END;
    RAISE DEBUG 'p2 is %', p2;
END $code$ LANGUAGE plpgsql;
```

Listing 25: An example of function to test shadowed_variables

If `plpgsql.extra_warning` is enabled, the function can be compiled but a warning message is emitted. Still, the function can be used, as shown in *Listing 26*:

```
-- catch masked variables at compile time
testdb=> SET plpgsql.extra_warnings TO 'shadowed_variables';
-- create the function
testdb=> CREATE OR REPLACE FUNCTION
f_test_shadow( p1 int DEFAULT 1, p2 text DEFAULT 'Hello' )
RETURNS text AS $code$  ... $cpde$ LANGUAGE plpgsql;

WARNING:  variable "p1" shadows a previously defined variable
LINE 7:     p1 char := 'P1'; -- masks function argument!
            ^
WARNING:  variable "p3" shadows a previously defined variable
LINE 13:      p3 text := 'Gosh!'; -- masks outer block variable!

-- the function is usable!
testdb=> SELECT f_test_shadow( 2, 'Luca' );
DEBUG:  p1 is P1
```

```
DEBUG:  p3 is Gosh!
DEBUG:  p2 is Luca
```

Listing 26: Compile time warnings

However, if `plpgsql.extra_warning` is enabled, it takes precedence and prevents the creation of the function. This means it is not possible to invoke the function because it will not be created, as shown in *Listing 27*:

```
-- catch masked variables at compile time
testdb=> SET plpgsql.extra_errors TO 'shadowed_variables';
-- create the function
testdb=> CREATE OR REPLACE FUNCTION
f_test_shadow( p1 int DEFAULT 1, p2 text DEFAULT 'Hello' )
RETURNS text AS $code$   ... $cpde$ LANGUAGE plpgsql;

ERROR:  variable "p1" shadows a previously defined variable
LINE 7:      p1 char(2) := 'P1'; -- masks function argument!
             ^

-- and the function has not been created!
testdb=> SELECT f_test_shadow( 2, 'Luca' );
ERROR:  function f_test_shadow(integer, unknown) does not exist
LINE 1: SELECT f_test_shadow( 2, 'Luca' );
```

Listing 27: Compile time errors

One obvious difference between using `plpgsql.extra_errors` and `plgpsql.extra_warnings` is that the former aborts the compilation upon the first error and therefore does not catch all the masked out variables in a single pass.

Procedures

A procedure is a an executable unit of code that can interact with transaction boundaries. It can commit a piece of work, roll back another piece of work, and so on. Procedures were introduced with PostgreSQL 11, and are first-class entities. A procedure is declared in a way that is similar to functions and can be implemented in any supported language. However, a procedure has fewer properties than a function and has no concept of stability, cost, or estimated return values.

Procedures are created with the CREATE PROCEDURE statement, which also supports the OR REPLACE clause. A procedure has a name, an argument list, and an implementation body. A typical procedure template looks as follows:

```
CREATE OR REPLACE PROCEDURE <procedure_name>( <arguments> )
AS <block-of-code>
LANGUAGE <implementation-language>;
```

A procedure is uniquely identified by the following:

- A mnemonic name
- An argument list

A procedure is invoked by means of the CALL statement and therefore procedures cannot be used in regular SQL statements such as SELECT or INSERT, UPDATE, DELETE. In fact, if a procedure is invoked via one of the former statements, PostgreSQL will abort the execution and report an error that specifies that we need to use the CALL statement:

```
testdb=> SELECT p_my_procedure();
ERROR:   p_my_procedure() is a procedure at character 8
HINT:   To call a procedure, use CALL.
```

On the other hand, calling a function via CALL will result in the opposite error:

```
testdb=> CALL f_insert_tags( 't1 > t2 > t3' );
ERROR:   f_insert_tags() is not a procedure at character 6
HINT:   To call a function, use SELECT.
```

The main difference between using a procedure or a function is that a function operates within transaction boundaries, which means that it cannot control the current transaction in any way. On the other hand, a procedure has the ability to commit or roll back single units of work from within the procedure itself, which means it can interact with the containing transaction. A procedure does this by means of sub-transactions, which can be rolled back without aborting the main (top-level) transaction.

Procedure argument list

A procedure, like a function, can accept arguments. The same rules for function parameters apply to procedure parameters, including their naming, type, default values, and the variadic property. It is worth noting that procedure parameters have only two directions: IN (the default) and INOUT (when a procedure provides an output to the caller). There is no explicit OUT direction.

Returning values to the caller

A procedure does not have any return values, so using a RETURN statement with a value other than NULL results in an execution error. If the code needs to exit, then RETURN NULL is the correct statement to use. Otherwise, the code can reach the end without any such statements.

The only way to return values to the caller is by mean of INOUT parameters. In this case, a single tuple will be returned with the final value of the specified values.

Security

Like functions, procedures can be defined with a security property that indicates which set of permissions are applied when the procedure is invoked:

- SECURITY INVOKER is the default setting. This means that the procedure will execute with the same permissions as the user that invoked it.
- SECURITY DEFINER specifies that the procedure will execute with the permissions of the user that defined it, even if the current user has fewer privileges.

Permissions

Similar to what happens for FUNCTIONS, GRANT and REVOKE support the EXECUTE permission on a PROCEDURE, so that it is possible to restrict the execution of a procedure to specified users only. As an example, the following snippet of code restricts the execution of a procedure to just the database user luca:

```
-- avoid anyone executing the procedure
testdb=> REVOKE EXECUTE ON PROCEDURE p_my_procedure FROM public;

-- allow only luca to execute the procedure
testdb=> GRANT EXECUTE ON PROCEDURE p_my_procedure TO luca;
```

It is worth noting that both GRANT and REVOKE support the ROUTINE keyword to reference to either a procedure or a function, so that the previous snippet of code could also have been written as follows:

```
-- avoid anyone executing the procedure
testdb=> REVOKE EXECUTE ON ROUTINE p_my_procedure FROM public;

-- allow only luca to execute the procedure
testdb=> GRANT EXECUTE ON ROUTINE p_my_procedure TO luca;
```

Moving procedures to other schemas

Similar to functions, procedures can be placed in specific schemas other than the default public one. In order to move an existing procedure to another schema, we have to issue an ALTER PROCEDURE SET SCHEMA command, for instance:

```
testdb=> ALTER PROCEDURE p_insert_tags SET SCHEMA my_library;
```

It is also possible to specify the schema for a procedure at creation time, qualifying the name of the procedure with the schema, such as my_library.p_insert_tags.

Temporary procedures

Like functions, procedures can be defined as temporary, meaning they will be destroyed at the end of the current session. The workflow for defining a temporary procedure is the same as for a temporary function: the name of the procedure must be qualified with the special pg_temp schema and the procedure must be called with the fully qualified name.

As for functions, it is not possible to move an already existing procedure into or out of the pg_temp schema.

Where is my procedure?

The pg_proc system catalog stores the same information for procedures and functions. The only difference is the value of the prokind character flag, which, in the case of procedures, is set to p. Therefore, the same considerations made for functions apply to procedures too, as well as the \df special commands in the psql terminal.

Interacting with transactions

Let's take as an example the `f_insert_tags()` function of *Listing 24*. This splits a string into an array of tags and inserts each tag into the `tags` table. It is possible to convert the function into a procedure in order to ensure each tuple is committed and does not get lost if the function unexpectedly aborts. The procedure shown in *Listing 28* performs the exact same operations as the function in *Listing 24*, so it will not be re-detailed here. However, as you can see, after every `INSERT`, an explicit `COMMIT` is issued so that each single tuple is stored even if the very next loop iteration aborts:

```
testdb=> CREATE OR REPLACE PROCEDURE
p_insert_tags( tag_string text, separator text DEFAULT '>' )
AS $code$
  DECLARE
    tag_array text[];
    current_tuple tags%rowtype;
  BEGIN
    -- first of all get all the tags
    tag_array := string_to_array( tag_string, separator );
    FOREACH current_tuple.t_name IN ARRAY tag_array LOOP
        current_tuple.t_child_of := current_tuple.pk;
        current_tuple.t_name      := trim( current_tuple.t_name );
        RAISE DEBUG 'Inserting tag [%] child of [%]',
                                current_tuple.t_name,
                                current_tuple.t_child_of;
        -- execute an insert and get back the table data
        INSERT INTO tags( t_name, t_child_of )
        VALUES ( current_tuple.t_name, current_tuple.pk )
        RETURNING * INTO current_tuple;

        RAISE DEBUG 'Committing [%]', current_tuple.t_name;
        COMMIT;
      END LOOP;
  END $code$ LANGUAGE plpgsql;

testdb=> SET client_min_messages TO debug;
testdb=> CALL p_insert_tags( 'Pets > Cats > Sofia' );
DEBUG: Inserting tag [Pets] child of [<NULL>]
DEBUG: Committing [Pets]
DEBUG: Inserting tag [Cats] child of [98]
DEBUG: Committing [Cats]
DEBUG: Inserting tag [Sofia] child of [99]
DEBUG: Committing [Sofia]
```

Listing 28: A procedure to insert a tag hierarchy from a string into the files table

In order to see how a procedure can interact with transaction boundaries, consider the same procedure as *Listing 28* but add the following constraints:

- Specify the maximum number of tags to insert. If the tag string produces too many tags, the procedure should not continue.
- Specify a list of tags to skip, which means to remove them from the hierarchy.

This is shown in *Listing 29*. The procedure accepts two more arguments, which are max_tag_count, an integer value that limits the number of tags that will be inserted, and a variadic argument, tags_to_skip, which represents a list of tags that must be removed from the hierarchy. As an example, when invoked as in *Listing 68*, the procedure will remove the tag BAD from the hierarchy connecting the tags Pets and Cats. Moreover, once it has inserted three tags, it will stop its execution.

The implementation of the new constraints requires an inner FOREACH loop that scans the tags_to_skip variadic array and compares the just-inserted current_tuple.t_name tag with any of the tags on the list to skip. If a match is found, the procedure issues a ROLLBACK that aborts the last performed INSERT statement and therefore erases the just-inserted record. On the other hand, if the tag is not a bad value, and the tag count (held by the insert_count variable) has not reached the max_tag_count limit, COMMIT is issued in order to confirm the last performed INSERT and make it persistent. Otherwise, another ROLLBACK is issued to remove the effects of the last INSERT. Finally, an empty RETURN exits from the procedures without evaluating other tags. Since, in this version, a tag can be removed from the hierarchy on the fly, we need to separate the last successful inserted tuple (represented by current_tuple) and the parent tuple (which, in the case of a ROLLBACK, is not handled by current_tuple but by parent_tuple). The debug messages shown in the output of the procedure call should make the execution flow clear:

```
testdb=> CREATE OR REPLACE PROCEDURE
p_insert_tags( tag_string text, separator text,
               max_tag_count INOUT int, VARIADIC tags_to_skip text[])
AS $code$
  DECLARE
    tag_array text[];
    current_tuple tags%rowtype;
    parent_tuple tags%rowtype;
    insert_count int := 1;
    current_skip text;
  BEGIN
    -- firs of all get all the tags
    tag_array := string_to_array( tag_string, separator );
<<TAG_LOOP>>
    FOREACH current_tuple.t_name IN ARRAY tag_array LOOP
        current_tuple.t_child_of := parent_tuple.pk;
```

```
        current_tuple.t_name       := trim( current_tuple.t_name );
        RAISE DEBUG 'Inserting tag [%] child of [%]', current_tuple.t_name,
current_tuple.t_child_of;
        -- execute an insert and get back the table data
        INSERT INTO tags( t_name, t_child_of )
        VALUES ( current_tuple.t_name, current_tuple.pk )
        RETURNING * INTO current_tuple;

        FOREACH current_skip IN ARRAY tags_to_skip LOOP
          IF current_tuple.t_name = current_skip THEN
            -- need to skip this particular tag
            RAISE WARNING 'Aborting for tag [%]', current_tuple.t_name;
            ROLLBACK;
            -- adjust values for the next INSERT
            current_tuple := parent_tuple;
            CONTINUE TAG_LOOP;
          END IF;
        END LOOP;

        -- if here the tag should not be skipped, so commit and keep parent
tuple
        IF insert_count <= max_tag_count THEN
          RAISE DEBUG 'Committing tag [%] with pk %', current_tuple.t_name,
current_tuple.pk;
          COMMIT;
          parent_tuple := current_tuple;
          insert_count := insert_count + 1;
        ELSE
          RAISE WARNING 'Aborting [%], too much tags!',
current_tuple.t_name;
          ROLLBACK;
          RETURN;
        END IF;
      END LOOP;
      -- feedback about committed tuples
      max_tag_count := insert_count;
  END $code$ LANGUAGE plpgsql;

testdb=> CALL p_insert_tags( 'Pets > BAD > Cats > Sofia > Winter', '>', 3,
'BAD' );
DEBUG:  Inserting tag [Pets] child of [<NULL>]
DEBUG:  Committing tag [Pets] with pk 93
DEBUG:  Inserting tag [BAD] child of [93]
2018-07-20 19:38:27.642 CEST [806] WARNING:  Aborting for tag [BAD]
2018-07-20 19:38:27.642 CEST [806] CONTEXT:  PL/pgSQL function
p_insert_tags(text,text,integer,text[]) line 31 at RAISE
WARNING:  Aborting for tag [BAD]
DEBUG:  Inserting tag [Cats] child of [93]
```

```
DEBUG:   Committing tag [Cats] with pk 95
DEBUG:   Inserting tag [Sofia] child of [95]
DEBUG:   Committing tag [Sofia] with pk 96
DEBUG:   Inserting tag [Winter] child of [96]
2018-07-20 19:38:27.644 CEST [806] WARNING:   Aborting [Winter], too much
tags!
2018-07-20 19:38:27.644 CEST [806] CONTEXT:   PL/pgSQL function
p_insert_tags(text,text,integer,text[]) line 51 at RAISE
WARNING:   Aborting [Winter], too much tags!
 max_tag_count
---------------
        3
```

Listing 29: A more complex procedure that performs Commits and Rollbacks

It is interesting to note that the `max_tuple_count` parameter is `INOUT`, so it is accepted as an argument and returned as a value from the function execution. This parameter is used to get feedback about the inserted (and committed) tags and, in particular, when the tag string is shorter than the limit itself, as in the second procedure call.

It is clear that the same process could have been implemented in a different way by anticipating checks that would result in a `ROLLBACK`. However, even a simple example shows how powerful handling transaction boundaries from within a procedure can be.

Nesting transactions and procedures

A `CALL` statement cannot be wrapped into an explicit transaction, or the procedure will not be able to execute transaction control statements (such as `COMMIT`). Here is what happens if the `p_insert_tags()` is executed within an explicit transaction:

```
testdb=> BEGIN;
testdb=> CALL p_insert_tags( 't1 > t2', '>', 10, NULL );
ERROR:   invalid transaction termination
CONTEXT:   PL/pgSQL function p_insert_tags(text,text,integer,text[]) line 47
at COMMIT
```

In order to better understand the transaction interaction, consider the procedure of *Listing 30*, which accepts a numeric value and, if set to `1`, performs a `COMMIT`. If set to `0`, it does nothing. Otherwise, it performs `ROLLBACK`.

As you can see, the procedure cannot interfere with the top-level transaction by issuing an explicit commit or rollback. Therefore, procedures must operate on their own sub-transactions:

```
testdb=> CREATE OR REPLACE PROCEDURE
p_tx_action( what int DEFAULT 0 )
AS $code$
  BEGIN
    IF what = 0 THEN
      RAISE DEBUG 'doing nothing!';
    ELSIF what = 1 THEN
      RAISE DEBUG 'Issuing a commit!';
      COMMIT;
    ELSE
      RAISE DEBUG 'Issuing a rollback';
      ROLLBACK;
    END IF;
  END $code$ LANGUAGE plpgsql;

-- the procedure does not operate on the top level transaction
testdb=> BEGIN;
testdb=> CALL p_tx_action();
testdb=> COMMIT;


-- the procedure forces a commit
testdb=> BEGIN;
testdb=> CALL p_tx_action( 1 );
ERROR:  invalid transaction termination
CONTEXT:  PL/pgSQL function p_tx_action(integer) line 7 at COMMIT
STATEMENT:  CALL p_tx_action(1);

-- the procedure forces a rollback
testdb=> BEGIN;
testdb=> CALL p_tx_action( 2 );
ERROR: invalid transaction termination
CONTEXT: PL/pgSQL function p_tx_action(integer) line 10 at ROLLBACK
STATEMENT: CALL p_tx_action(2);References
```

Listing 30: A procedure that performs a rollback or a commit

Summary

Functions and procedures are powerful building blocks that allow the implementation of reusable server side code. Thanks to their properties, it is possible to write programs that can interact with the underlying database and the current transaction.

In the next chapter, we will learn how functions and procedures can be developed using "external" programming languages such as Perl and Java.

References

- PostgreSQL Functions, official PostgreSQL 11 documentation available at: `https://www.postgresql.org/docs/11/static/sql-createfunction.html`
- PostgreSQL Procedures, official PostgreSQL 11 documentation available at: `https://www.postgresql.org/docs/11/static/xproc.html`

5
PL/Perl and PL/Java

In Chapter 4, *Stored Procedures*, we saw how to implement functions and procedures using the PL/pgSQL language. PostgreSQL allows developers to implement their executable code in pretty much any language they want. In order to demonstrate this, this chapter will show you how to implement code using Perl 5 and Java.

In particular, this chapter will focus on:

- PL/Perl and PL/Java as possible implementation languages
- The re-implementation of some of the code discussed in Chapter 4, *Stored Procedures*, using both of the above languages
- The differences between using a scripting language and a compiled language in server-side programming and deployment

PL/Perl

PL/Perl is one of the foreign languages available for PostgreSQL. It implements a Perl 5 environment in order to allow executable code to be interpreted as a Perl 5 program. This makes it possible to write functions, procedures, and other related executable units (such as triggers) in Perl.

There are two variants of PL/Perl, which are:

- A trusted version, named `plperl`
- An untrusted version, named `plperlu`

The trusted version cannot interact with Operating System resources (such as opening files and sockets), nor can it load external modules (by means of `require` or `use`). This makes it suitable for every non-administrator role. On the other hand, the untrusted version can exploit full Perl features, including loading external modules and interacting with Operating System resources. However, by default, its usage is limited to database administrators, because a malicious `plperlu` piece of code can ruin an entire database.

Usually, there is no need to install anything on the PostgreSQL side, since the database ships with PL/Perl on board. Nevertheless, in order to run Perl 5, we need to have a Perl 5 interpreter installed on the server that PostgreSQL runs on. Even if this is already installed, PL/Perl is, by default, not enabled, so in order to use it within a database, the language must be installed into the database itself. This can be done by means of a CREATE EXTENSION command that specifies which version of PL/Perl to use. In order to install plperlu, as shown in the following snippet, the user must be a database administrator:

```
-- as normal user
testdb=> CREATE EXTENSION plperl;
-- as database administrator
testdb=# CREATE EXTENSION plperlu;
```

Both versions of PL/Perl can coexist on the same database at the same time.

It is worth noting that the DO statement does support PL/Perl (both versions) as a language. This must be specified with the LANGUAGE keyword and can be used to run a Perl 5 snippet of code.

Database interaction

Unlike PL/pgSQL, where each unknown statement is sent to the backend as a regular SQL statement, PL/Perl interprets every statement as a Perl 5 one. For this reason, in order to send SQL statements to the backend, a set of built-in functions must be used.

In fact, PL/Perl comes with a set of so-called **Service Provider Interface (SPI)** functions that act as a PostgreSQL-specific database driver, allowing the code to access and interact with the underlying database.

The main SPI functions are the following:

- spi_exec_query(): This accepts a textual SQL statement and an optional number of rows to limit the returning result set. This function returns a hash with the following keys:
    - processed: The number of rows affected by the query (the number of inserted rows)
    - status: The value that indicates whether the query succeeded or not
    - rows: This is an array of hashes (starting from zero), each one representing a single tuple

- spi_query(): This is similar to spi_exec_query() but does not accept a result set limit; instead, it returns an object that must be evaluated after a call to spi_fetch_row(), which in turn returns a hash with the tuple structure
- spi_prepare(), spi_query_prepared(), spi_exec_prepared(), and spi_freeplan(): These handle prepared statements
- spi_commit() and its counterpart spi_rollback(): These control the current transaction

spi_exec_query() and spi_exec_prepared() return the same hash structure, with the result set contained under the rows key. The spi_query() and spi_query_prepared() functions return an object that must be passed to spi_fetchrow() in order to get a hash representing the current tuple. The status of an SPI function is coded in a set of global variables, in particular a set of the following SPI_OK variables:

- SPI_OK_SELECT and SPI_OK_SELINTO for SELECT and SELECT INTO respectively
- SPI_OK_INSERT and SPI_OK_INSERT_RETURNING for an INSERT with and without a RETURNING clause
- SPI_OK_DELETE and SPI_OK_DELETE_RETURNING for a DELETE with and without a RETURNING clause
- SPI_OK_UPDATE and SPI_OK_UPDATE_RETURNING for an UPDATE with and without a RETURNING clause

Testing the status of an executed statement is, of course, a good habit when creating a robust Perl function.

The elog() function works in the same way as the RAISE statement: it accepts a level and a message to display or to propagate as an exception. The available levels are the same as in the RAISE statement.

It is possible to put all of this together with a DO block that performs a query against the files table, as shown in the following listing. The block of code defines a lexically scoped variable, $query, which holds the text of the SQL statement to execute. This SQL statement is then executed via the spi_query() function. The result is then popped one tuple at a time via spi_fetchrow(), which returns a hash reference that is held in the $tuple variable. For each tuple found, the elog() function is used to display the content of the tuple:

```
testdb=> SET client_min_messages TO debug;
testdb=> DO LANGUAGE plperl $code$
  my $query = sprintf "SELECT f_name, f_hash FROM files";
```

```
    my $statement = spi_query( $query );
    while ( my $tuple = spi_fetchrow( $statement ) ) {
        elog( DEBUG, "Found file name $tuple->{ f_name } and hash $tuple->{
f_hash }" );
    }
$code$;

DEBUG:  Found file name picture1.png and hash
22347625d4e6462022657daa85bb77a1
DEBUG:  Found file name picture2.png and hash
323412345666462022657daa85bb77a2
DEBUG:  Found file name picture3.png and hash
823412345666462022657daa85bb77a3
DEBUG:  Found file name audio1.mp3 and hash
fdeab2345666462022657daa85bb77bb
```

Listing 1: PL/Perl DO block example

Since the preceding listing handles a quite small result set, it is possible to rewrite it as shown in the following snippet, using the `spi_exec_query()` function. The `spi_exec_query()` function returns a reference to a hash from which every single row is extracted, looping from zero to the number of rows found. Every row is represented by a hash reference that is assigned to the `$tuple` variable and then every field value is extracted into the separated variables `$file_name` and `$file_hash` respectively. It would have been possible to write the following piece of code in a more compact way, but for the sake of readability, intermediate variables have been used.

```
testdb=> DO LANGUAGE plperl $code$
   my $query = sprintf "SELECT f_name, f_hash FROM files";
   my $result_set = spi_exec_query( $query );
   # did the query run ok?
   elog( EXCEPTION, "Query failed!" ) if ( $result_set->{ status } !=
SPI_OK_SELECT );
   for my $i ( 0 .. $result_set->{ processed } - 1 ){
      my $tuple = $result_set->{ rows }[ $i ];
      my $file_name = $tuple->{ f_name };
      my $file_hash = $tuple->{ f_has };
      elog( DEBUG, "Row $i holds file $file_name with hash $file_hash" );
   } $code$;
```

Listing 2: PL/Perl DO block example with a larger result set

Function arguments and return types

Arguments are passed as they are in a regular Perl 5 subroutine—within the @_ array. Values are returned either with an explicit `return` statement or by the implicit value of the last evaluated expression, as in regular Perl 5 subroutines. Database NULL values are handled as `undef` values in Perl. An `undef` parameter means a function has been invoked with a NULL argument. Similarly, returning `undef` means that the function returns a NULL SQL value.

Functions in PL/Perl can only return scalar values, meaning they are always executed in a scalar context. It is possible to return complex values (such as an array) using references to these structures. PostgreSQL arrays are managed as references to Perl arrays, while composite types (such as the row type) are managed by means of Perl hashes, where each key represents a field name.

Returning tuples is performed by either returning a single hash (by returning a single tuple) or by issuing a `return_next()` function call and specifying which hash to return as an argument. Similar to PL/pgSQL, once the result set has been completed, an explicit `return undef` must be issued too.

Re-implementing functions in PL/Perl

In order to see these concepts in action, take a look at the following listing, which uses PL/Perl to implement the same function that we saw in Chapter 4, *Stored Procedures*, when generating fake tuples. As you can see, the declaration of the function (the CREATE FUNCTION part) is the same as the PL/pgSQL counterpart, while the function implementation (the AS part) is pure Perl 5 code. Since the function needs to compute a hash using an external module (Digest), the function is declared as `plperlu`.

The function first assigns a context variable, $max, to the first and only argument passed to the function itself, which is the limit of the result set to be generated. After that, a scalar variable, $current_tuple, is used as a hash reference for the tuple to generate on each iteration. The `for` loop iterates from one to the $max value, and the hash is initialized with the required values. Please note that each hash field has the same name as the tuple to be returned. It is also interesting to note that a few Perl functions are called from within the function: `rand()`, `localtime()`, and `md5_base64` (from the Digest module), which clearly shows that pretty much all of Perl's power is exploitable.

However, as you can see, extracting the next value from a sequence is a little more complicated than the PL/pgSQL implementation. This is because Perl needs to issue a regular SQL query to the database, extract the result set, get the first row (which is row number 0), and then get the exact column. This is what the `spi_exec_query()` call is used for. Database interaction is a little more complex than in the PL/pgSQL case; this is not a drawback, however, but a natural consequence of using a programming language within PostgreSQL.

The following listing illustrates how to generate a fake tuple with PL/pgSQL:

```
testdb=> CREATE OR REPLACE FUNCTION
f_fake_files( int DEFAULT 10 )
RETURNS SETOF files AS $code$
    use Digest::MD5 qw(md5_base64);
    my ( $max ) = @_;
    my $current_tuple;   # hash to store a single tuple

    for my $i ( 1 .. $max ){
                    # issue a query to invoke the 'nextval' function
        my $pk = spi_exec_query( 'SELECT nextval( \'files_pk_seq\' )', 1 )
                    ->{ rows }[ 0 ]    # get the first row
                    ->{ nextval };     # get the only 'nextval' column
        $current_tuple->{ pk } = $pk;
        $current_tuple->{ f_name } = "File_$i";
        $current_tuple->{ f_size } = rand() * 1024 * 1024 / rand();
        $current_tuple->{ f_type } = 'txt' if ( $i % 3 == 0 );
        $current_tuple->{ f_type } = 'png' if ( $i % 3 == 1 );
        $current_tuple->{ f_type } = 'mp3' if ( $i % 3 == 2 );
        $current_tuple->{ f_hash } = md5_base64( $current_tuple->{ f_name }
);
        $current_tuple->{ ts }      = localtime();
        elog( 'DEBUG', "Generated $i = $current_tuple->{ f_name }" );
        return_next( $current_tuple );
    }
    # all done
    return undef;
$code$ LANGUAGE plperlu;
```

Listing 3: Generating fake tuples via a PL/Perl function

When you re-implement a function in another language, you need to drop the existing function first, or PostgreSQL will not be able to understand which function you are referring to. In other words, it is not possible to overload a function using a different language.

Thanks to the untrusted version of PL/Perl, it is also possible to re-implement the function of listing 16 in the previous chapter, which scans a directory in order to build real tuples to insert into the files table. The following *Listing 4*, shows a possible implementation in pure Perl. Since the function needs to both interact with the file system and load external modules (to compute the hash of the file content), the function must be implemented with the plperlu untrusted language.

The function gets a named argument, $dir, which is the directory from which we get content by calling opendir(). On each iteration of readdir(), a new hash reference is initialized with appropriate values and appended to the result set via return_next(). It is interesting to note how much simpler it is to get the file size, the modification time, and type compared to the PL/pgSQL counterpart implementation. On the other hand, as we have already seen, getting the next value of the sequence is a little harder in PL/Perl that it is in PL/pgSQL, as follows:

```
testdb=> CREATE OR REPLACE FUNCTION
f_files_from_directory( text DEFAULT '.' )
RETURNS SETOF files AS $code$
 use Digest::MD5 qw(md5_base64);
 my ( $dir ) = @_;
 my $current_tuple;
 elog( DEBUG, "Reading files into $dir" );
 opendir( my $dir_handle, $dir ) || elog( EXCEPTION, "Cannot open $dir
directory" );
   while ( my $current_file = readdir( $dir_handle ) ) {
         elog( DEBUG, "Building tuple for entry $current_file" );
         # transform the name to absolute
         my $absolute_file  = $dir . '/' . $current_file;
         # skip directories
         next if not -f $absolute_file;
         my $pk = spi_exec_query( 'SELECT nextval( \'files_pk_seq\' )', 1 )
                             ->{ rows }[ 0 ]    # get the first row
                             ->{ nextval };     # get the only 'nextval'
column
         $current_tuple->{ pk } = $pk;
         $current_tuple->{ f_name } = $current_file;
         $current_tuple->{ f_size } = ( stat( $absolute_file ) )[ 7 ];
         $current_tuple->{ ts }     = localtime( ( stat( $absolute_file ) )[
9 ] );
         $current_tuple->{ f_hash } = md5_base64( $absolute_file );
         $current_tuple->{ f_type } = ( split /\./, $current_file )[ -1 ] ||
'txt';
         return_next( $current_tuple );
```

```
    }
    return undef;
    $code$ LANGUAGE plperlu;
```

Listing 4: Reading a directory to implement file tuples

As a final example, consider the f_insert_tags() function of the following *Listing 5*, which is the Perl translation of the PL/pgSQL function of *Listing 24* in the previous chapter. The function accepts a single hierarchical tag string and an optional separator and splits the string into its single pieces (tags). Each tag is then inserted with the appropriate parent (the previous pk) and appended to the result set. The interesting part of the implementation is that we are using a prepared statement, by means of the spi_prepare() function. This holds a query with two arguments marked by $ positional placeholders, the type of which is specified by its name (for example, 'text' refers to a text value type). The $prepared_statement variable holds the prepared statement and, at each iteration, it is passed to the spi_exec_prepared() function along with the argument values for $1 ($current_tuple->{ t_name]) and $2 ($current_tuple->{ t_child_of }). The result set extracted from the execution of the INSERT prepared statement is then appended (in the case of success) to the output result set by means of return_next(), as shown in the following snippet:

```
testdb=>  CREATE OR REPLACE FUNCTION
  f_insert_tags( text, text DEFAULT '>' )
  RETURNS SETOF tags AS $code$
    my ( $tag_string, $separator ) = @_;
    my $current_tuple;
    my $prepared_statement = spi_prepare( 'INSERT INTO tags( t_name,
t_child_of )VALUES( $1, $2 ) RETURNING *',
                                          'text',
                                          'int' );
    for my $tag  ( split $separator, $tag_string ) {
      ( $current_tuple->{ t_name }  = $tag ) =~ s/^\s+|\s+$//g;
      $current_tuple->{ t_child_of } = $current_tuple->{ pk };
      elog( DEBUG, "Inserting tag $current_tuple->{ t_name } child of
$current_tuple->{ t_child_of } " );
      my $result_set = spi_exec_prepared( $prepared_statement,
                                   $current_tuple->{ t_name },
                                   $current_tuple->{ t_child_of } );
      if ( $result_set->{ status } == SPI_OK_INSERT_RETURNING ) {
        $current_tuple = $result_set->{ rows }[ 0 ];
        return_next( $current_tuple );
      }
      else {
        elog( EXCEPTION, "Cannot insert tag $current_tuple->{ t_name } " );
      }
```

```
}
  return undef;
$code$ LANGUAGE plperl STRICT VOLATILE;
```

Listing 5: Inserting tag tuples from a single hierarchical string

Implementing routines in PL/Perl

When we need to control a transaction from within a unit of code, a procedure must be used. PL/Perl can be used as a language to implement procedures. As an example, the following listing shows a PL/Perl implementation of the `p_insert_tags` procedure seen in *Listing 29* in `Chapter 4`, *Stored Procedures*. This implementation follows its PL/pgSQL counterpart pretty much step-by-step.

The main differences are that the `spi_exec_query()` function is used to issue `COMMIT` and `ROLLBACK` when required and that a prepared statement is used (held in the `$prepared_statement` variable) to repeat the `INSERT` statements within the main loop. It is interesting to note that in this implementation, due to the nature of Perl, it is a lot easier to search for tags to skip. Similarly, when `FOREACH` loops were required previously (see *Listing 63* in `Chapter 4`, *Stored Procedures*), here, only a single `grep()` function call is needed. However, since the procedure has an `INOUT` argument named `max_tag_count`, the PL/Perl code must return a tuple-like structure with a single row made of a single column named `max_tag_count`, which means returning a hash structure with a single `max_tag_count` key.

This is what the lines with `return { max_tag_count => $insert_count }` do: they return to the caller a value named `max_tag_count` with `$insert_count value`. Without such an explicit `return`, PostgreSQL will be confused about which values are returned from the procedure. Remember that a procedure does not have a formal return type:

```
testdb=> CREATE OR REPLACE PROCEDURE
p_insert_tags( text, text, max_tag_count INOUT int, VARIADIC  text[])
AS $code$
  my ( $tag_string, $separator, $max_tag_count, $tags_to_skip ) = @_;
  my ( $current_tuple, $parent_tuple, $insert_count ) = ( undef, undef, 1
);
  $insert_count    = 1;
  my $prepared_statement = spi_prepare( 'INSERT INTO tags( t_name,
t_child_of )VALUES( $1, $2 ) RETURNING *', 'text', 'int' );
TAG_LOOP:
  for my $current_tag_name ( split /$separator/, $tag_string ){
 # trim the tag name
      ( $current_tuple->{ t_name }   = $current_tag_name ) =~
```

```perl
s/^\s+|\s+$//g;
    $current_tuple->{ t_child_of } = $parent_tuple->{ pk } if ( defined
$parent_tuple );
    elog( DEBUG, "Building tuple for [$current_tuple->{ t_name }] child
of [$current_tuple->{ t_child_of }]" );
  # build up the query
  my $result_set = spi_exec_prepared( $prepared_statement,
                                      $current_tuple->{ t_name },
                                      $current_tuple->{ t_child_of } );
  if ( $result_set->{ status } == SPI_OK_INSERT_RETURNING ) {
    $current_tuple = $result_set->{ rows }[ 0 ];
  }

  # skip bad tags
  if ( grep( /$current_tuple->{ t_name }/, @$tags_to_skip ) ){
    elog( WARNING, "Aborting for tag $current_tuple->{ t_name }" );
    spi_exec_query( "ROLLBACK" );
    $current_tuple = $parent_tuple;
    next TAG_LOOP;
  }

  if ( $insert_count <= $max_tag_count ){
    elog( DEBUG, "Committing tag [$current_tuple->{ t_name }] with pk
$current_tuple->{ pk }" );
    spi_exec_query( "COMMIT" );
    $parent_tuple = $current_tuple;
    $insert_count++;
  }
  else {
      elog( WARNING, "Aborting [$current_tuple->{ t_name }], too much
tags!" );
      spi_exec_query( "ROLLBACK" );
      return { max_tag_count => $insert_count };
  }
}
return { max_tag_count => $insert_count };
$code$ LANGUAGE plperl;
```

Listing 6: Implementing the p_insert_tags procedure in PL/Perl

A possible output of the preceding procedure would be as follows:

```
testdb=> call p_insert_tags( 'conferences > linuxday > italy > 2018', '>',
3, 'b' );
DEBUG:  Building tuple for [conferences] child of []
```

```
DEBUG:   Committing tag [conferences] with pk 239
DEBUG:   Building tuple for [linuxday] child of [239]
DEBUG:   Committing tag [linuxday] with pk 240
DEBUG:   Building tuple for [italy] child of [240]
DEBUG:   Committing tag [italy] with pk 241
DEBUG:   Building tuple for [2018] child of [241]
WARNING:  Aborting [2018], too much tags!
CONTEXT:  PL/Perl function "p_insert_tags"
WARNING:  Aborting [2018], too much tags!
 max_tag_count
--------------
         4
```

PL/Java

PL/Java is a binding for the Java language that allows you to run Java code directly within the PostgreSQL server. The language does not come included with the official PostgreSQL release, so we have to install it.

Installing PL/Java

Installing PL/Java requires several steps. Luckily, it uses Apache Maven as a project management, dependency, and build system, so many of these steps are performed automatically. Here, the PL/Java version 1.5.1 Beta 1 will be installed, since it is the latest one available. This is not recommended for production use, so read the project release notes and installation instructions carefully before installing it in production environments.

To get a bleeding-edge version of PL/Java, it is possible to clone the Git repository and compile the sources. The result will be the production of an auto-installing Jar archive that will be placed into the PostgreSQL shared libraries directory; the exact location of such directory will be determined automatically during the Jar build process. A typical installation workflow is as follows:

```
% git clone https://github.com/tada/pljava.git
% cd pljava
% git checkout refs/tags/1_5_1b1
% mvn clean install
...
% sudo java -jar pljava-packaging/target/pljava-pg11.99-amd64-FreeBSD-gpp.jar
```

As you an see, the very last step installs the PL/Java engine on the PostgreSQL server and must therefore be done with high privileges (using `sudo`).

Once PL/Java has been installed on the PostgreSQL server without requiring a database restart, it needs to be properly configured by a database administrator. In particular, PL/Java needs to know where the Java libraries are for the current system. The configuration is kept in the PostgreSQL variable `pljava.libjvm_location` (which is created by installing PL/Java). For example, the following code snippet configures PL/Java to use OpenJDK version 8:

```
-- where are Java libraries?
testdb=# SET pljava.libjvm_location TO
'/usr/local/openjdk8/jre/lib/amd64/server/libjvm.so';
-- now create the language in this database
testdb=# CREATE EXTENSION pljava;
-- make library changes permanent
testdb=# ALTER DATABASE testdb SET pljava.libjvm_location FROM CURRENT;
```

After PL/Java has been configured, it can be used on the specific database as an available language. PL/Java makes the following two languages available (please note that there is no pl prefix):

- `java`: The trusted Java language
- `javau`: The untrusted Java language

PL/Java main concepts

Before illustrating a couple of PL/Java examples, let's think about some important terminology, workflows, and concepts. First of all, all code must be packaged as a Jar and deployed to the PostgreSQL server. This, of course, make things a little more complex than in other scripting languages, such as PL/Perl or PL/pgSQL, since further compilation and packaging steps are required. An easy way to deal with these extra steps is to configure Apache Maven for the PL/Java project that is going to be deployed. Explaining the Apache Maven `pom.xml` configuration file is out of our scope here, but a working example can be found within the source code of the book and can be used as a starting template for other PL/Java projects.

Once the Jar archive has been produced, it can be deployed to the PostgreSQL server manually or with a few utility functions that PL/Java installs into the `sqlj` schema. These include the following:

- `install_jar()`: This takes the URL of the Jar and installs it with a name that can be used to refer to it later on; this is the deploy action
- `remove_jar()`: This removes the Jar from the server and is the un-deploy action
- `replace_jar()`: This substitutes an already installed Jar with another version and is the re-deploy action

Each Jar is associated with a mnemonic name that is used to reference the Jar within the database. Classes within the Jar must be reachable, which means that a classpath must be set, as it is in normal Java applications. PL/Java forces a classpath setting for each schema, so we have to add a Jar to each classpath from which PL/Java code will be executed. The function `set_classpath()` accepts a mnemonic Jar name and a schema name and then binds the two so that the schema can access the Jar content.

The typical workflow for the deployment of a PL/Java project is as follows:

1. Deploy with `install_jar()`
2. Set the classpath for each required schema using `set_classpath()`
3. Create PostgreSQL objects (such as `FUNCTION`, which invokes Java methods)
4. Re-deploy updated versions of the Jar archive using `replace_jar()`

Step 4 is, of course, optional. Even step 3 can be skipped, if desired. In fact, PL/Java allows for a declarative mapping of Java objects into PostgreSQL objects (such as a Java method into a PostgreSQL function) by means of annotations.

Annotations are converted into objects named deployment descriptors, which are a set of PostgreSQL statements that act as `'glue-code'`. When a deployment is performed by either `install_jar()` or `replace_jar()`, the deployment descriptor is read and the statements are executed, leaving Java objects automatically exposed on the PostgreSQL side.

The Java implementation must have an entry-point method, which must be declared as `static`. This is similar to Java's main method for normal applications. Each static method can be used as an entry point for PostgreSQL to enter the Java world. From there, we can invoke other methods, create instances, and carry out a regular Java workflow.

Each method can have arguments and return types, which are appropriately converted from and into PostgreSQL types. The main Java types work as expected, therefore a Java `String` can be mapped from and into PostgreSQL `text` or `varchar`, a Java `Integer` can be mapped into a PostgreSQL `integer`, and so on. It is also possible to map a Java custom type into an SQL one, but the conversion logic must be written within the Java type.

If a Java method returns a result set of some kind, it must either return a Java `Iterator` or implement a specific PL/Java interface that will help populate the result set one tuple at a time. In the following sections, we will look at a few examples of how to return a result set.

Implementing a PL/Java function without a deployment descriptor

In order to demonstrate PL/Java in action, imagine that we need to write a function named `splitTagString`, which accepts a string that represents a hierarchy of tags and a separator. The function must return a result set with the separated tags, one for each tuple. In order to implement this feature, we have to set up a Java class with a static method that will be invoked from the PostgreSQL server. This method will receive the same argument list as its SQL counterpart as input, and must return an iterable collection, which in this case is a collection of text strings. Since PL/Java maps the PostgreSQL type `text` to the Java type `String`, the method will accept `String` arguments and return an `Iterable<String>` Java type.

The Java code that implements this desired behavior is shown in the following listing. The `splitTagString()` method accepts two `String` values, uses a `Logger` to emit log messages (like `RAISE` in PL/pgSQL or `elog()` in PL/Perl), and builds a `List` of `Strings` that are individual tags. This list is then returned in the form of an `Iterator`.

Note that in the following code we have used Java features, such as `String.split()`, to emphasize that PL/Java provides not only a way to express code in Java syntax, but also to use Java libraries:

```
package pg11ssp;
import org.postgresql.pljava.*;
import java.util.logging.Logger;
import java.util.*;

public class Functions {
    public static Iterator<String> splitTagString ( String tagString,
String delimiter ){
        Logger logger = Logger.getAnonymousLogger();
        // set a default value for the delimiter
        if ( delimiter == null || delimiter.isEmpty() )
            delimiter = ">";
        logger.info( "Splitting tag string [" + tagString + "] with [" +
delimiter + "]" );
        List<String> tags = new ArrayList<String>();
    for ( String currentTag : tagString.split( delimiter ) )
```

```
                tags.add( currentTag.trim() );
                return tags.iterator();
        }
    }
```

Listing 7: A PL/Java implementation of splitting the tag string (Java code only)

Once the Java code has been written, it needs to be compiled and packaged, which can easily be done via Maven, as shown in the following example:

```
% mvn clean package
...
[INFO] ---------------------< pg11ssp:pg11ssp-pljava >--------------------
----
[INFO] Building PostgreSQL 11 Server Side Programming - PL/Java 0.0.1
[INFO] ------------------------------[ jar ]------------------------------
----
...
[INFO] Building jar: /usr/home/luca/pljava-examples/target/pg11ssp-
pljava-0.0.1.jar
[INFO] -------------------------------------------------------------------
----
[INFO] BUILD SUCCESS
```

If there are no compilation errors, a .jar file named pg11ssp-pljava-0.0.1.jar will be placed into the subdirectory of the target project. It is now time to deploy the .jar file into the PostgreSQL server. This can be done with the install_jar() function, followed by the set_classpath() call, which will make the Jar content available within the current database schema. In the following example, this is public:

```
testdb=# SELECT sqlj.install_jar( 'file:///usr/home/luca/pljava-
examples/target/pg11ssp-pljava-0.0.1.jar',
        'PG11SSP', false );
testdb=# SELECT sqlj.set_classpath( 'public', 'PG11SSP' );
```

The package will be available with the mnemonic name PG11SSP.

It is now possible to create a function that invokes the Java code, as shown in the following listing. As you can see, from a database perspective, the function is really simple and contains only the qualified name for the static method to invoke, which is the package (pgsqp11), the class (Functions), and the method name (splitTagString). As already stated, please note that the function language is Java and not pljava, as one might expect:

```
testdb=# CREATE OR REPLACE FUNCTION f_j_split_tag_to_string( text, text )
RETURNS SETOF text
AS 'pg11ssp.Functions.splitTagString' LANGUAGE java;
```

```
testdb=# SELECT f_j_split_tag_to_string( 'holidays > 2018 > sicily', '>' );
INFO: pg11ssp.Functions Splitting tag string [holidays > 2018 > sicily]
with [>]
 f_j_split_tag_to_string
--------------------------
 holidays
 2018
 sicily
```

Listing 8: A PL/Java implementation of splitting the tag string

Implementing a PL/Java function with a deployment descriptor

In this section, we will implement a method to scan a directory and get the metadata of all files, which would then be exposed to the database server. The implementation of this method is similar to the previous *Listing 4* (PL/Perl) in this chapter, as well as *Listing 16* in Chapter 4, *Stored Procedures* (PL/pgSQL).

The PL/Java implementation is a little more complex because it means we have to deal with the `ResultSetProvider` interface. This is how PL/Java allows a function to return a result of a complex data type, which in this case is the `files` tuples.

`ResultSetProvider` requires the implementation of the following two methods:

- `assignRowValues(..)`, which is invoked once for every tuple to be added to a result set. The function must return `true` if a new tuple has been successfully added to the result set, or `false` to indicate that no more tuples are going to be added.
- `close()`, which is invoked when the result set is either completed (when `assignRowValues(..)` returns `false`) or if the query has been terminated from the executor using a `LIMIT` clause.

Other than these two methods, the class must implement the entry point for the stored procedure, which is a static method. For this particular example, the method will be called `scanDirAndBuildTuples(..)`. It will accept a directory name as a text path and must return the `ResultSetProvider`, which will, in turn, return the tuples. This method is shown in the following listing.

First of all, the method is annotated with the @Function annotation, which describes how to automatically connect the Java method to a PostgreSQL function named f_j_files_from_directory. The annotation exploits the onNullInput property to declare the function with the STRICT property. This means that it is not invoked on the NULL input and immediately returns a NULL value. Similarly, the effects property in the annotation means that the function is declared with the VOLATILE property.

Finally, the trusted property makes the system declare the function as being executable by an untrusted PL/Java implementation (javau). Thanks to this descriptive annotation, there will be no need for an explicit CREATE FUNCTION once the Jar archive has been installed in the PostgreSQL server. The implementation of the scanDirAndBuildTuples(..) method is pretty straightforward: a new FileTupleBuilder object is created, the specified directory is read, and all files found are then added to the private instance list files. Once the object has been properly initialized, it is returned to the caller so that the PL/Java engine can start building the tuples, shown as follows:

```
public class FileTupleBuilder implements ResultSetProvider {
  private List<File> files = new ArrayList<File>();
  private static Logger logger = Logger.getAnonymousLogger();

  @Function( type = "files",
      name = "f_j_files_from_directory",
      trust = Function.Trust.UNSANDBOXED, // untrusted
      effects = Function.Effects.VOLATILE,
      onNullInput = Function.OnNullInput.RETURNS_NULL // strict
      )
  public static ResultSetProvider scanDirAndBuildTuples( String dir )
throws SQLException {
    FileTupleBuilder tupleBuilder = new FileTupleBuilder();
    try {
      File dirHandle = new File( dir );
      if ( ! dirHandle.isDirectory() )
        throw new SQLException( "Not a directory" );

      for ( File currentEntry : dirHandle.listFiles() ){
        if ( ! currentEntry.isFile() )
          continue;

        logger.info( "Building tuple for file " + currentEntry.getPath() );
        tupleBuilder.files.add( currentEntry );
      }
      return tupleBuilder;
    } catch ( Exception e ){
      logger.warning( "Cannot scan directory " + dir );
```

```
        throw new SQLException ( e );
    }
  }
}
```

Listing 9: The entry point method

Tuples are effectively built by the `assignRowValues(..)` method shown in the following listing. The method accepts the current result set that is already positioned on the next tuple to be produced (which is why the result set is named `currentTuple`), as well as the tuple number within this result set (the `currentRow` argument). Since each tuple must correspond to a file, and files are stored in the in-memory list files, the `currentRow` index is used to get the `currentFile` object out from the list. Then, the `currentTuple` result set is appropriately initialized with values computed from the current file object, such as the name or the size.

As we saw with the PL/Perl case, even PL/Java cannot interact directly with the underlying database, and instead does this in the **Java DataBase Connectivity** (**JDBC**) way. This means that in order to get the next sequence value for the `pk` field, a regular query must be issued. Luckily, PL/Java provides a default connection named `jdbc:default:connection`, which returns the current connection to the database and can therefore be used as a normal JDBC connection to issue queries. This is how we properly initialize the `currentTuple` pk column. The computation of the file hash is a little more complex, since it involves the `MessageDigest` Java class and being able to read the file content while printing out the hex string one piece at a time. Again, different languages can do the same thing in different ways, but this example emphasizes that the Java library can be used when required, shown as follows:

```
public boolean assignRowValues ( ResultSet currentTuple, int currentRow )
throws SQLException {
  if ( files.isEmpty () || currentRow >= files.size () )
    return false;

  File currentFile = files.get ( currentRow );
  logger.info ( "File " + currentFile.getPath () + " at tuple number " +
currentRow );

  /* update some fields on this tuple */
  currentTuple.updateString ( "f_name", currentFile.getName () );
  currentTuple.updateLong ( "f_size", currentFile.length () );
  currentTuple.updateTimestamp ( "ts", new Timestamp (
System.currentTimeMillis () ) );
  /* get the sequence next value */
  ResultSet resultSet = DriverManager
      .getConnection ("jdbc:default:connection")
```

```
    .createStatement()
    .executeQuery( "SELECT nextval( 'files_pk_seq' )" );
  if ( resultSet.next() )
    currentTuple.updateInt( "pk", resultSet.getInt( 1 ) );
  else
    throw new SQLException( "Cannot get primary key value from sequence" );
  /* compute the type of the file from its extension */
  int extensionIndex = currentFile.getName().lastIndexOf( "." );
  if ( extensionIndex > 0 )
    currentTuple.updateString( "f_type", currentFile.getName().substring(
extensionIndex + 1 ) );
  else
    currentTuple.updateString( "f_type", "txt" );
  /* compute the hash of the file */
  try{
    MessageDigest digestEngine = MessageDigest.getInstance("SHA-1");
    StringBuffer sha1String = new StringBuffer();
    if (digestEngine != null) {
      byte[] sha1 = digestEngine.digest( Files.readAllBytes( Paths.get(
currentFile.getAbsolutePath() ) ) );
      for (byte b : sha1)
        sha1String.append( String.format("%02x", b) );
    }
    currentTuple.updateString( "f_hash", sha1String.toString() );
  } catch ( Exception e ){
    logger.warning( "Cannot compute the hash" );
    currentTuple.updateString( "f_hash", "n/a" );
  }
  return true;  // adds the tuple to the result set
}
```

Listing 10: The tuple builder method

The `ResultSetProvider.close()` method has an empty implementation, since there is no particular task to perform. In other cases, it might be required to release external resources, clean up memory, and so on. The code is therefore complete, but in order to get the @Function annotation to work transparently, we need to set the SQLJDeploymentDescriptor property in the pom.xml Maven file to true, shown as follows:

```
<SQLJDeploymentDescriptor>
   true
</SQLJDeploymentDescriptor>
```

With all of this in place, it is possible to recompile and package the `.jar`, as already seen, and instruct the PostgreSQL server to re-deploy the current `.jar` using the `replace_jar()` function. We can then immediately test the function, as shown in the following listing:

```
testdb=# SELECT sqlj.replace_jar( 'file:///usr/home/luca/pljava-
examples/target/pg11ssp-pljava-0.0.1.jar',
 'PG11SSP', true );
testdb=# SELECT * FROM f_j_files_from_directory( '/home/luca/pljava-
examples/src/main/java/pg11ssp' );

INFO:  Building tuple for file /home/luca/pljava-
examples/src/main/java/pg11ssp/Functions.java
INFO:  Building tuple for file /home/luca/pljava-
examples/src/main/java/pg11ssp/FileTupleBuilder.java
INFO:  File /home/luca/pljava-examples/src/main/java/pg11ssp/Functions.java
at tuple number 0
INFO:  File /home/luca/pljava-
examples/src/main/java/pg11ssp/FileTupleBuilder.java at tuple number 1
 pk  |         f_name         | f_size |                 f_hash
| f_type |           ts
-----+------------------------+--------+------------------------------------
------+--------+------------------------
 246 | Functions.java         |    689 |
d97d6cf18455b0e67f99c5e6bd0182ae29cdcdd9 | java    | 2018-07-24 14:07:56.168
 247 | FileTupleBuilder.java  |   3235 |
002b9daf0d4b4f8bbe2fac0ff1608fbcc3532690 | java    | 2018-07-24 14:07:56.184
```

Listing 11: Re-deploying and testing the PL/Java function

Please note that the function has been installed automatically without any need for an explicit CREATE FUNCTION on the PostgreSQL side.

Summary

One powerful feature of PostgreSQL is its ability to host pretty much any programming language on the server-side, meaning that code can be deployed to the server and run locally on the data.

This chapter has shown you how to use Perl 5 and Java as hosted—or foreign—languages. The choice of which language to use as an alternative to SQL or PL/pgSQL depends on several factors, including the knowledge of the language and the specific task to be accomplished. This decision might also be driven by the deployment phase; for example, it is much simpler to deploy a Perl 5 function or procedure than a Java one. Another influencing factor might be the ecosystem of the language, including the libraries and the existing code.

In the next chapter, we will use functions to implement triggers, a way to react to data changes from within the database itself. The aim is to implement business logic to enforce *local* constraints over data in a way that is totally independent from any external application.

References

- The PL/Perl Language, official PostgreSQL 11 documentation available at `https://www.postgresql.org/docs/11/static/plperl.html`
- The PL/Java Language, project web-site available at `https://github.com/tada/pljava/wiki`
- The PL/Java API Documentation, available at `https://tada.github.io/pljava/pljava-api/apidocs/index.html`
- Apache Maven Project Management software, official web-site available at `http://maven.apache.org/`

6
Triggers

Triggers are a powerful way to react to database events. Each time a new tuple is added to a table, a trigger can fire in order to perform some kind of data validation or propagation, or, in general, apply business rules. Triggers are nowadays a fundamental part of any DBMS system, and provide an infrastructure that helps the administrator to enforce data validation and constraints.

The main idea behind a trigger is that when a specific event happens (such as some data changing), a trigger is fired and a specific piece of executable code runs. PostgreSQL implements triggers by means of functions, so the executable code of a trigger must be implemented as a FUNCTION. As we will see, this function must have a particular prototype and it must be able to access a set of pre-defined variables that keep information about what fired the trigger.

PostgreSQL provides two main type of triggers, which are fired in reaction to either data manipulation or data definition. This chapter focuses on the powerful trigger infrastructure that PostgreSQL provides.

This chapter will go through the following concepts:

- Data manipulation triggers, the most common implementation of triggers, used to validate and propagate data
- Data definition triggers, a database-wide set of triggers that can intercept DDL statements, allowing you to audit and monitor database DDL activity
- Implementing trigger behavior in foreign languages, such as Perl and Java

Data manipulation triggers

A data manipulation trigger (DML trigger), is a trigger that fires in response to a DML statement (such as INSERT, UPDATE, DELETE, or TRUNCATE) that is executed against a particular table. DML triggers are defined by means of the following:

- A *name*
- A *timing* for when the trigger should react
- An *event* that fires the trigger
- The *table* over which the trigger is fired
- The *level*, which is the set of data handled by the trigger

The *event* is any of the supported DML statements: INSERT, UPDATE, DELETE, or TRUNCATE.

The *timing* indicates whether the trigger should react before or after the event (the DML statement) completes. It can therefore be one of the following choices:

- BEFORE: This means that the trigger is executed before the event consolidates the data
- AFTER: This means that the trigger executes after the event has consolidated data
- INSTEAD OF: This is a particular case and means the trigger will be executed instead of the event

The *level* defines which data the trigger handles when it is fired. A **row-level** trigger is a trigger that fires once for each tuple modified, while a **statement-level** trigger fires once for every SQL statement. The options to define the trigger level are the following:

- FOR EACH ROW: This defines a row-level trigger
- FOR EACH STATEMENT: This defines a statement-level trigger

Each trigger must be attached to a single table, or, in some cases, to a view. It therefore reacts to particular statements (events) on that table. However, since a trigger executes a PostgreSQL FUNCTION, the same function can be reused to create different triggers on different tables.

To make it a little clearer, let's assume an INSERT statement creates two new tuples in a table. The event is INSERT and a BEFORE timing means the trigger will execute before the INSERT statement completes: the two new tuples are not yet committed to the underlying table. On the other hand, an AFTER timing means the trigger will execute once the two new tuples have been consolidated to the underlying table.

If the trigger has been defined with a FOR EACH ROW level, the trigger will execute twice, once per tuple. If the trigger has been defined as FOR EACH STATEMENT, however, the trigger executes once with an input made by two tuples.

Not all the combinations of event, level, and timing are possible or useful. The following table indicates which combinations are currently supported:

Event	Timing	Level	Target
INSERT or UPDATE or DELETE	BEFORE or AFTER	FOR EACH ROW or FOR EACH STATEMENT	tables or views
TRUNCATE	BEFORE or AFTER	FOR EACH STATEMENT	tables
INSERT or UPDATE or DELETE	INSTEAD OF	FOR EACH ROW	views

Triggers fired with a FOR EACH ROW level can be customized with a WHEN predicate that restricts the trigger to fire only for particular values (we will discuss this in more detail later on).

Trigger names matter! You can define as many triggers as you want on the same table and even on the same timing and event. However, triggers fired under the same circumstances will be executed in alphabetical order.

Since each trigger is attached to a table or a view, it is defined in the same namespace as the table or view it is attached to. In other words, it is not possible to manually specify a schema for a trigger, which means the trigger name is always a simple name without the schema qualifier.

A trigger is created by means of the CREATE TRIGGER statement, which accepts all the trigger properties, including the trigger function name. The basic syntax for creating a trigger is as follows:

```
CREATE TRIGGER <name>
<timing> <event>
ON <table>
<level>
EXECUTE PROCEDURE <trigger_function_name>;
```

Please note that the PROCEDURE keyword in the CREATE TRIGGER command does not refer to a PROCEDURE as defined in the previous chapter. A trigger only ever executes a FUNCTION. It is important to note that the FUNCTION used as trigger function must be marked as VOLATILE (the default behavior), because if not it will not see any of the table changes that fire it. Remember that non-volatile functions cannot depend on the underlying database status.

A trigger can be removed via the DROP TRIGGER command. There is also an ALTER TRIGGER command that mainly serves as a way to rename a trigger.

The trigger function

The trigger function is a regular PostgreSQL FUNCTION written in any of the supported languages. It must have a specific prototype: it does not accept any argument and does return the special TRIGGER type.

The return value of a trigger function must be either a NULL value or a record value, with the record having the same structure as the table the trigger is attached to. The return value is evaluated differently depending on the trigger type. In particular, the return value of a statement-level trigger is always ignored. A row-level trigger that returns a not-null record makes the current operation continue with the values contained in the tuple (either another trigger fires or the statement succeeds). If a NULL value is returned, the operation is terminated and the tuple is skipped.

Inside the trigger function, PostgreSQL has a few special variables that can be really useful to understand what fired the trigger and how to react. These represent the *trigger context*. In particular, there are two record type variables (generic tuples) called OLD and NEW, which are available in row-level triggers. The OLD record holds the tuple *before* the statement execute, while NEW holds the tuple *after* the statement manipulated it. As you can imagine, OLD and NEW records can co-exist only when an UPDATE statement is executed. INSERT does not have any OLD tuple, while DELETE cannot have any NEW tuple. This is represented in the following table:

Statement	OLD	NEW
INSERT	-	the incoming tuple
UPDATE	the not updated tuple	the updated tuple
DELETE	the deleted tuple	-

Statement-level triggers cannot access either OLD nor NEW. Once a trigger function is invoked, the NEW and OLD records have default values, which are column defaults that are applied before any trigger.

There are other variables that can be used to perform introspection and to understand what instances, how, and when the trigger is fired. These variables are exported in different ways depending on the language used to implement the function; however, they have the same meaning. In PL/pgSQL these variables are as follows:

- `TG_NAME` is the name of the trigger
- `TG_TABLE_NAME` and `TG_TABLE_SCHEMA` are the name and schema of the table the trigger is attached to
- `TG_OP` is a string that can have a value of `'INSERT'`, `'UPDATE'`, `'DELETE'`, or `'TRUNCATE'` indicating the event that fired the trigger
- `TG_LEVEL` is a string that assumes either a value of `'ROW'` or `'STATEMENT'` indicating the trigger level
- `TG_WHEN` is a string indicating the timing, and can be `'BEFORE'`, `'AFTER'`, or `'INSTEAD OF'`

As we will see, thanks to the previous variables, a trigger function can inspect its running context and behave accordingly.

Creating a simple trigger

It is now time to see all the preceding concepts in action. The first trigger function to examine is the one shown in *Listing 1*, which acts as a notifier that the statement has executed, simply writing out information. The trigger function, implemented in PL/pgSQL, analyzes the trigger's variables and prints out information about what fired the trigger. Since this function is going to be executed for each tuple, this means it is for a row-level trigger. It will raise an exception if it is used for a statement-level trigger (`TG_LEVEL` is different from `'ROW'`). Depending on the statement that fired the trigger, which is contained in `TG_OP`, the trigger function knows if OLD, NEW, or both record variables are available and simply displays the primary key (the `pk` column) of both. The trigger returns NULL at the end, meaning that the whole operation will gracefully fail:

```
testdb=> CREATE OR REPLACE FUNCTION f_tr_notifier()
RETURNS TRIGGER AS $code$
  BEGIN
    -- display some information about what fired me up
    RAISE DEBUG 'Trigger [%] fired [%] [%] [%] against %.%',
              TG_NAME,        -- trigger name
              TG_WHEN,        -- BEFORE, AFTER, INSTEAD OF
              TG_OP,          -- INSERT, UPDATE, DELETE, TRUNCATE
              TG_LEVEL,       -- ROW, STATEMENT
              TG_TABLE_SCHEMA, TG_TABLE_NAME;

    -- this can executed only for low level triggers
    IF TG_LEVEL <> 'ROW' THEN
        RAISE EXCEPTION 'This trigger function can be invoked only for row-
level triggers!';
    END IF;
```

```
    IF TG_OP = 'INSERT' THEN
        -- here only NEW is defined
        RAISE DEBUG 'NEW tuple: pk = %', NEW.pk;
    ELSIF TG_OP = 'UPDATE' THEN
        -- here both NEW and OLD are defined
        RAISE DEBUG 'NEW tuple pk = %, OLD tuple pk = %', NEW.pk, OLD.pk;
    ELSIF TG_OP = 'DELETE' THEN
        -- here only OLD is defined
        RAISE DEBUG 'OLD tuple pk = %', OLD.pk;
    END IF;

    -- abort the current operation
    RETURN NULL;
END $code$ LANGUAGE plpgsql;
```

Listing 1: A simple trigger function that displays information about what fired the trigger

Listing 2 shows the definition of the trigger with the previous function. The CREATE TRIGGER command is used to attach the trigger to the files table, to make it execute the function on every tuple, and before every data manipulation statement:

```
testdb => CREATE TRIGGER tr_notifier
            BEFORE                              -- timing
            INSERT OR UPDATE OR DELETE          -- event
            ON files                            -- table
            FOR EACH ROW                        -- level
            EXECUTE PROCEDURE f_tr_notifier(); -- trigger function
```

Listing 2: A row-level trigger that fires before every statement

If we define this trigger and execute the statements, we will see some debugging information from the trigger and nothing will happen. This is because the trigger function always returns NULL, meaning the executor skips the manipulation of the current tuple. This is shown in *Listing 3*, where a set of statements are executed with the RETURNING clause to emphasize that nothing hits the underlying table:

```
testdb=> SET client_min_messages TO DEBUG;
testdb=> UPDATE files SET ts = current_timestamp
            WHERE f_type = 'txt' RETURNING *;

DEBUG:  Trigger [tr_notifier] fired [BEFORE] [UPDATE] [ROW] against
public.files
DEBUG:  NEW tuple pk = 27, OLD tuple pk = 27

 pk | f_name | f_size | f_hash | f_type | ts
----+--------+--------+--------+--------+----
(0 rows)
```

```
testdb=> INSERT INTO files( f_name, f_size, f_hash, f_type )
          VALUES( 'chapter4.pdf', 1778965,
'f029d04a81c322f158c608596951c1aa', 'pdf' )
          RETURNING *;

DEBUG:  Trigger [tr_notifier] fired [BEFORE] [INSERT] [ROW] against
public.files
DEBUG:   NEW tuple: pk = 255

 pk | f_name | f_size | f_hash | f_type | ts
----+--------+--------+--------+--------+----
(0 rows)

testdb=> DELETE FROM files WHERE f_type = 'txt' RETURNING *;

DEBUG:  Trigger [tr_notifier] fired [BEFORE] [DELETE] [ROW] against
public.files
DEBUG:   OLD tuple pk = 27

 pk | f_name | f_size | f_hash | f_type | ts
----+--------+--------+--------+--------+----
(0 rows)
```

Listing 3: Executing the row-level trigger

Since the trigger function is not tied to the `files` table, it is possible to define another trigger against the `tags` table that exploits the same function, as shown in *Listing 4*. If we then try some statements against the `tags` table, we will receive a similar output without modifying the data:

```
testdb=> CREATE TRIGGER tr_notifier
          BEFORE INSERT OR UPDATE OR DELETE ON tags
          FOR EACH ROW EXECUTE PROCEDURE f_tr_notifier();
```

Listing 4: Reusing the same trigger function in another table

As you can imagine, having the capability to reuse the same trigger function in different triggers is a good approach because it improves maintainability. The drawback is that the function must be written generically and must make an effort in order to understand which event fired it, in which context it is running, and therefore to understand what to do on the target table.

Discovering if a table has triggers

How can we tell if a table has associated triggers? One common approach is to use the \d (**describe**) command from the psql command-line interface. This will report an entry for each attached trigger with the same definition as that passed to the CREATE TRIGGER statement. The following is the output of \d against the files table:

```
testdb=> \d files
                                 Table "public.files"
...
Triggers:
    tr_notifier BEFORE INSERT OR DELETE OR UPDATE
                ON files FOR EACH ROW
                EXECUTE PROCEDURE f_tr_notifier()
```

Trigger information is stored in the special pg_trigger catalog table, so it is also possible to query that table to get information about a trigger. For instance, as shown in *Listing 5*, it is possible to see all the trigger's names and functions for the files table. A trigger is said to be internal if it is automatically constructed by PostgreSQL to enforce table constraint, such as foreign keys. Since user-defined triggers are not internal, the tgisinternal condition excludes all constraint triggers from the output:

```
testdb=> SELECT tgname, tgrelid::regclass, proname
         FROM pg_trigger JOIN pg_proc ON tgfoid = pg_proc.oid
         WHERE tgrelid = 'files'::regclass AND tgisinternal = false;

  tgname     | tgrelid |    proname
-------------+---------+---------------
 tr_notifier | files   | f_tr_notifier
```

Listing 5: Getting basic information about triggers

If all you need to know is whether a table has attached triggers, you can also simply check the pg_class.relhastrigger value, as shown in *Listing 6*:

```
testdb=> SELECT relname,
                CASE relhastriggers
                WHEN true THEN 'with triggers!'
                ELSE 'without triggers'
                END
         FROM pg_class
         WHERE relname IN ('files', 'tags' );
```

```
relname |       case
---------+---------------
tags     | with triggers!
files    | with triggers!
```

Listing 6: Discovering if a table has a trigger

Disabling Triggers

Sometimes, we want to be able to execute statements without the interference of a trigger. It is possible to disable one or all of the triggers that are attached to a table. Be aware that this could lead to data corruption, especially if your triggers are there to check and keep data consistent. In any case, issuing an ALTER TABLE command can disable, and later re-enable, a trigger. For instance, if you want to disable the tr_notifier trigger on the files table, you can issue the following command:

```
testdb=> ALTER TABLE files DISABLE TRIGGER tr_notifier;
```

When you are ready to re-enable the trigger, you can issue the opposite command:

```
testdb=> ALTER TABLE files ENABLE TRIGGER tr_notifier;
```

It is possible to use the special ALL trigger name as an alias to execute the command against all triggers attached to the table. For example, the following statement will disable all the triggers on the files table:

```
testdb=> ALTER TABLE files ENABLE TRIGGER ALL;
```

The system catalog pg_trigger has the tgisenabled column, which assumes the D value for a disabled trigger.

Using triggers to modify data on the fly

In this section, we will look at how a trigger can be used to modify manipulated data according to specific rules. For example, what happens if the type of the file (f_type) is not specified when a tuple is inserted or updated? It might be possible to infer the file type from its name extension. In order to do this, a row-level trigger must be implemented; the trigger will fire before any INSERT or UPDATE completes, and this will allow you to modify each tuple on the fly, inspect the current value of the incoming or updating f_name value, and extract the file type from its extension.

The trigger function is shown in *Listing 7*. First, it checks its running context to ensure the function has not been executed for a wrong statement, and raises an exception if the trigger is not invoked at row level for an INSERT or UPDATE. Then, both the INSERT and UPDATE triggers see the NEW special record variable, and, in this particular case, NEW will hold the tuple that is going to be inserted or has been updated respectively. This means the trigger function can focus just on NEW and its f_name and f_type values. A statement can either insert a new file without specifying the extension, in which case the trigger has to infer it, or it can also provide a file type that should not be overridden with the file extension. This is a rule that depends on the situation. In this example, we assume that when a user explicitly provides a file type, this type must be kept. This is why the function checks the NEW.f_type value for NULL (which is related to an INSERT operation). If the value is NULL, the user does not explicitly specify a file type, so the function must do its job; otherwise, the user has specified an explicit value of NEW.f_type and such a value must be kept, therefore the function does nothing to the incoming data. If a file type must be computed, the function splits the file name into '.' separated pieces. If there are at least two pieces, the last one will be used as the file type and placed into NEW.f_type, otherwise the default 'txt' type is used.

It does not matter whether the function modifies the NEW tuple or not. This record is returned to the caller to mean OK, continue with this data:

```
testdb=> CREATE OR REPLACE FUNCTION
f_tr_infer_file_type_from_extension()
RETURNS TRIGGER AS $code$
  DECLARE
    name_parts text[];
  BEGIN
    -- check that this is fired for ROW level, BEFORE, INSERT or UPDATE
    IF TG_LEVEL <> 'ROW'
       OR TG_WHEN <> 'BEFORE'
       OR TG_OP NOT IN ( 'INSERT', 'UPDATE' ) THEN
          RAISE EXCEPTION 'This trigger cannot help you!';
    END IF;

    -- if the user has specified a f_type, do not override it
    IF NEW.f_type IS NOT NULL AND TG_OP = 'INSERT' THEN
          RAISE DEBUG 'Preserving file type %', NEW.f_type;
    ELSE
       -- here we need to compute the file type
          name_parts := string_to_array( NEW.f_name, '.' );
          IF array_length( name_parts, 1 ) > 1 THEN
             NEW.f_type := name_parts[ array_length( name_parts, 1 ) ];
             RAISE DEBUG 'Automatically selected file type %', NEW.f_type;
          ELSE
             NEW.f_type := 'txt';
```

```
        RAISE DEBUG 'No name extension, using default file type txt';
      END IF;
    END IF;
    -- proceed
    RETURN NEW;
  END $code$ LANGUAGE plpgsql;
```

Listing 7:The trigger function that infers the file type

The definition of the trigger is as follows:

```
testdb=> CREATE TRIGGER tr_infer_file_type
         BEFORE INSERT OR UPDATE ON files
         FOR EACH ROW EXECUTE PROCEDURE
f_tr_infer_file_type_from_extension();
```

Listing 8: Trigger definition

It is now time to see the trigger in action, so let's try to insert a new tuple without explicitly specifying the file type:

```
testdb=> INSERT INTO files( f_name, f_hash )
         VALUES( 'chapter4.pdf', '14b87625d4e6462022657daa85bb77bb' );

DEBUG:  Preserving file type txt
INSERT 0 1
```

Before executing any writing statements (such as INSERT) against the files table, you need to disable the trigger of *Listing 1* with the following line: ALTER TABLE files DISABLE TRIGGER tr_notifier;.

After running the previous command, we can see that something went wrong: the trigger is *preserving* a file type that was not specified. This demonstrates the concept that once a trigger is fired, it receives the tuples with their default values already set. In this case, the f_type column has been defined with a default value of 'txt', so when the trigger fires and the trigger function runs, the value of NEW.f_type is not NULL, therefore the trigger cannot discriminate whether the value was explicitly set by the user or by something else. In this case, let's drop the DEFAULT column value on f_type and do all the work through the trigger (which, as you can see, already handles the default 'txt' file type. Set the default value for f_type to NULL and execute a couple of statements against the files table, as shown in *Listing 9*:

```
testdb=> ALTER TABLE files ALTER COLUMN f_type SET DEFAULT NULL;
testdb=> INSERT INTO files( f_name, f_hash )
         VALUES( 'chapter5.pdf', '14b87625d4e6462cc2657daa85bb77bb' );
```

```
DEBUG:  Automatically selected file type pdf

testdb=> UPDATE files SET f_name = 'chapter5.odt' WHERE f_name =
'chapter5.pdf';

DEBUG:  Automatically selected file type odt
```

Listing 9: Dropping the column default value to make the trigger do the check

This time, the trigger function works in both cases and automatically infers the file type from its name. Even a simple trigger like the previous one hides potential problems. Consider an explicit UPDATE where the f_type column value is specified:

```
testdb=> UPDATE files SET f_name = 'chapter5.pdf', f_type = 'mp3'
         WHERE f_name = 'chapter5.odt';

DEBUG:  Automatically selected file type pdf
```

The preceding statement makes the trigger select the 'pdf' type from the file name, even if the user has specified a f_type value. Assuming the user always wins, in order to deal with such cases, the trigger function must be re-factored to include some more conditionals.

Don't panic! It is possible to replace the function implementation without having to touch the trigger definition. *Listing 10* shows the new, improved trigger function. When executed, the function tries to extract the file name extension and, therefore, the file type, without any regard to the specific operation. The file type is then kept in the computed_file_type variable. There are two main branches, discriminated by the executed statement. In the case of INSERT, the file type is inferred only if the user does not specify any value. The UPDATE case is a little more complicated. First, the function checks if the f_type column has a NULL value (which is either specified by the user explicitly or comes from a wrong tuple already in the table). If the previous tuple does not have a file type set to NULL, the last known file type can be used. Otherwise, even if the OLD tuple does not have a good file type (the tuple has a NULL value in the table), computed_file_type is used as a good one. Then, if the file type value does not change across the update, but the file name does, the function uses computed_file_type as a hint for a file type change. If the NEW.f_type value does not match the computed_file_type one, the file name change forces a file type change too:

```
testdb=> CREATE OR REPLACE FUNCTION f_tr_infer_file_type_from_extension()
RETURNS TRIGGER AS $code$
  DECLARE
    name_parts text[];
    computed_file_type text;
  BEGIN
```

```
    IF TG_LEVEL <> 'ROW'
        OR TG_WHEN <> 'BEFORE'
        OR TG_OP NOT IN ( 'INSERT', 'UPDATE' ) THEN
            RAISE EXCEPTION 'This trigger cannot help you!';
    END IF;

    name_parts := string_to_array( NEW.f_name, '.' );
    IF array_length( name_parts, 1 ) > 1 THEN
        -- got the extension
        computed_file_type := name_parts[ array_length( name_parts, 1 ) ];
    ELSE
        computed_file_type := NULL;
    END IF;

    IF TG_OP = 'INSERT' THEN
        IF NEW.f_type IS NULL THEN
            -- here infer the type from the name
            NEW.f_type := computed_file_type;
        ELSE
            RAISE DEBUG 'Explicitly specified file type % on INSERT',
NEW.f_type;
        END IF;
    ELSE
        -- update case
        IF NEW.f_type IS NULL THEN
            IF OLD.f_type IS NOT NULL THEN
                RAISE DEBUG 'Preserve old file type %', OLD.f_type;
                NEW.f_type := OLD.f_type;
            ELSE
                RAISE DEBUG 'Switch NULL type to %', computed_file_type;
                NEW.f_type := computed_file_type;
            END IF;
        END IF;

        IF NEW.f_type = OLD.f_type
            AND NEW.f_name <> OLD.f_name THEN

            RAISE DEBUG 'Name updated from % to % but no type changed',
NEW.f_name, OLD.f_name;

            IF computed_file_type <> NEW.f_type THEN
                RAISE DEBUG 'Name update lead to file type %',
computed_file_type;
                NEW.f_type := computed_file_type;
            END IF;

        END IF;
    END IF;
```

```
    -- proceed
    RETURN NEW;
END $code$ LANGUAGE plpgsql;
```

Listing 10: Improved trigger function to catch more cases

There are further situations in which the function might not lead to expected results, but you get the point: in order to use a trigger to modify data on the fly, we must be aware of all the possible rules to apply and think about all possible statement and value combinations.

It is possible to limit the action of the trigger to particular conditions using the WHEN predicate. As an example, the trigger can be redefined, as shown in *Listing 11*, where a WHEN condition is applied to NEW.t_type. Here, the trigger will only fire when f_type is NULL. It is worth noting that the WHEN condition does not apply to the executed statement. This means the trigger will only fire when an explicit value of f_type is set to NULL. This does not solve the UPDATE problem seen before, since UPDATE without an explicit f_type does not means the latter is NULL, rather that NEW.f_type will be set to OLD.f_type, which cannot be null:

```
testdb=> DROP TRIGGER IF EXISTS tr_infer_file_type ON files;
testdb=> CREATE TRIGGER tr_infer_file_type
         BEFORE INSERT OR UPDATE ON files
         FOR EACH ROW
         WHEN ( NEW.f_type IS NULL )
         EXECUTE PROCEDURE f_tr_infer_file_type_from_extension ();
```

Listing 11. Trigger with an explicit check on the NEW tuple

Again, this demonstrates how important it is to evaluate whether the input and output from each statement were as expected when using triggers to modify data on the fly.

Parametric triggers

The trigger function can accept implicit arguments, which are imposed at the time the trigger is created and are accessible via the following special variables:

- TG_ARGV: An array of arguments
- TG_NARG: An integer that holds the number of arguments, if there are any

In order to demonstrate how to use trigger arguments, let's consider a simplified version of the function that infers the file type. This time, instead of analyzing the file name, the function will apply an argument as the default type every time the incoming tuple has f_type set to NULL.

First of all, let's consider how the trigger is defined. As shown in *Listing 12*, the only difference is that the trigger function is now specified with an explicit parameter, which, in this case, is 'md', to represent the default file type of Markdown:

```
testdb=> DROP TRIGGER IF EXISTS tr_infer_file_type ON files;
testdb=> CREATE TRIGGER tr_infer_file_type
 BEFORE INSERT OR UPDATE ON files
 FOR EACH ROW EXECUTE PROCEDURE f_tr_infer_file_type_from_extension( 'md'
);
```

Listing 12: A trigger that passes an argument to the trigger function

The trigger will therefore invoke the trigger function with the first argument set to 'md'. This argument is exposed via TG_ARGV[0], and, as shown in *Listing 13*, the function will use this value when the NEW.f_type column is set to NULL:

```
testdb=> CREATE OR REPLACE FUNCTION f_tr_infer_file_type_from_extension()
RETURNS TRIGGER AS $code$
  DECLARE
    name_parts text[];
    computed_file_type text;
  BEGIN
    IF TG_LEVEL <> 'ROW'
       OR TG_WHEN <> 'BEFORE'
       OR TG_OP NOT IN ( 'INSERT', 'UPDATE' ) THEN
          RAISE EXCEPTION 'This trigger cannot help you!';
    END IF;

    IF NEW.f_type IS NULL THEN
       RAISE DEBUG 'Setting default file type to %', TG_ARGV[ 0 ];
       NEW.f_type := TG_ARGV[ 0 ];
    END IF;

    -- proceed
    RETURN NEW;
END $code$ LANGUAGE plpgsql;
```

Listing 13: Trigger function that access an argument via TG_ARGV

Listing 14 shows the trigger in action. As you can see, this time, the default md value is set to f_type:

```
testdb=> SET client_min_messages TO debug;
testdb=> INSERT INTO files( f_name, f_hash )
         VALUES ( 'chapter6.pdf', '14b87625d4e6462cc2657daa85bb77cf' );
DEBUG:  Setting default file type to md
```

Listing 14: The parametric trigger in action

Thanks to trigger arguments, it is easier to reuse the same trigger function with different triggers and scenarios.

Aborting the current statement

A trigger that fires before the statement consolidates its data can abort the statement, throwing away one or more tuples. As a simple example, consider a trigger that must validate a file hash. The only check to perform is that the hash string contains only allowed characters in the range a–f and numbers in the range 0–9.

Let's start from the trigger function, which is shown in *Listing 15*. The function, after checking its running context, ensures the f_hash field of the incoming NEW tuple is set. Otherwise, the trigger can immediately skip the tuple by issuing RETURN NULL;. As already stated, in a before trigger, returning a null value means skipping the current operation. To check for the formal correctness of the hash field, the function exploits the regexp_matches() PostgreSQL function. This function accepts text to search for and a regular expression to apply. It returns an array of text strings that represent each single match. The regular expression '[a-f0-9]{32}' means "each character in the range from 'a' to 'f' and each number from '0' to '9', for exactly 32 characters in length". The idea of the function is therefore to match the hash against the regular expression. If the hash is correctly written, exactly one string will match the whole hash value. If the result of regexp_matches() is more than one, or if what it matches is not the exact string passed into the operation (such as NEW.f_hash), the SQL statement must stop. This is done by issuing RETURN NULL:

```
testdb=> CREATE OR REPLACE FUNCTION f_tr_check_hash()
RETURNS TRIGGER AS $code$
  DECLARE
    matches text[];
  BEGIN
    IF TG_LEVEL <> 'ROW'
       OR TG_WHEN <> 'BEFORE'
```

```
        OR TG_OP NOT IN ( 'INSERT', 'UPDATE' ) THEN
          RAISE EXCEPTION 'This trigger cannot help you!';
    END IF;

    IF NEW.f_hash IS NULL
       OR length( NEW.f_hash ) = 0 THEN
       RAISE WARNING 'The hash must be specified!';
       -- abort
       RETURN NULL;
    END IF;

    -- hash always in lowercase
    NEW.f_hash := lower( NEW.f_hash );
    matches := regexp_matches( NEW.f_hash, '[abcdef0-9]{32}' );
    IF array_length( matches, 1 ) = 1
      AND matches[ 1 ] = NEW.f_hash THEN
      -- ok
      RETURN NEW;
    ELSE
     -- abort
     RAISE WARNING 'Illegal hash [%]', NEW.f_hash;
     RETURN NULL;
    END IF;
END $code$ LANGUAGE plpgsql;
```

Listing 15: A trigger function that checks for a file hash format

Listing 16 shows the trigger definition, which, as you can imagine, is for a before trigger that executed on each tuple:

```
testdb=> CREATE TRIGGER tr_check_hash
         BEFORE INSERT OR UPDATE ON files
         FOR EACH ROW EXECUTE PROCEDURE f_tr_check_hash();
```

Listing 16: Trigger definition

It is now possible to test the trigger. As shown in *Listing 17,* each time a multiple tuple transaction is executed, each single tuple that passes the trigger function will hit the underlying table. Each tuple that does not will be skipped:

```
testdb=> INSERT INTO files( f_name, f_hash )
         VALUES ( 'Conclusions.pdf', 'aabbccddeeff00ZZaabbccddeeff00ZZ' )
         , ('Introduction.txt', '1234567890abcdef1234567890abcdef' );

WARNING: Illegal hash [aabbccddeeff00zzaabbccddeeff00zz]
INSERT 0 1 -- only one tuple out of two has been inserted!
```

Listing 17: The trigger refusing the insertion of a tuple with a wrong hash

The WHEN condition

In the example of *Listing 13*, we saw how a trigger can have a WHEN additional filter on the tuples that indicates whether to fire the trigger or not. The WHEN clause accepts any SQL Boolean condition, and can therefore be used to tune the trigger accurately.

For instance, we can specify a condition as follows:

```
WHEN ( NEW.f_type IS DISTINCT FROM OLD.f_type )
```

This makes the trigger fire every time the f_type column changes its value. This simplifies the trigger function, since it no longer has to check for a changed condition on that column. A more general condition is as follows:

```
WHEN ( NEW.* IS DISTINCT FROM OLD.* )
```

This makes the trigger fire when at least one column changes across the SQL statement.

The REFERENCING clause

A statement trigger can see the whole result set of the affected tuples. We can think of it as two result sets made of NEW and OLD tuples. This is particularly useful because it allows the trigger function to have a look at the so called *transitional* table, which is a pseudo-table made by the result set of incoming changes.

Transitional tables are made aliases via the REFERENCING clause, followed by NEW TABLE AS and OLD TABLE AS for the incoming and old tuples respectively. Inside the trigger function, these result sets are managed as regular tables. As in the case of NEW and OLD record aliases, NEW TABLE and OLD TABLE are not always available. For INSERT, only NEW TABLE can be aliased, while for UPDATE, both can be aliased and for DELETE, only OLD TABLE can be aliased.

In order to see the transitional tables in action, consider the need to implement a logic that transforms any DELETE operation against the files table into an archive operation. Each deleted tuple must be copied into an archive table, which is named archive_files. In order to achieve this, it is possible to build a statement trigger that fires after a DELETE statement and copies each deleted tuple into the target table. Let's start from the trigger, which is shown in *Listing 18*. The trigger is defined as an AFTER trigger against a DELETE statement and fires once per statement (FOR EACH STATEMENT). The deleted tuples will be available via a pseudo-table named deleting. The trigger function accepts an argument, which is the archive table name. This is not mandatory, but shows how to make the trigger a little more reusable:

```
testdb=> CREATE TRIGGER tr_archiver
         AFTER DELETE ON files
         REFERENCING OLD TABLE AS erasing
         FOR EACH STATEMENT EXECUTE PROCEDURE f_tr_archive_files(
'archive_files' );
```

Listing 18: A delete trigger referencing deleted tuples

The `f_tr_archive_files()` trigger function is shown in *Listing 19* and is straightforward. It defines a `rowtype` variable `current_tuple` and iterates on the `deleting` pseudo-table, assigning each row of the table to the former variable. At each iteration, a dynamic `INSERT` statement is built in order to transfer tuple values from the original table into the target table, the name of which is contained in the first `TG_ARGV[ 0 ]` argument. As you can see, once the loop has ended, the function returns a `NULL` value, since the value returned in an after trigger does not matter:

```
testdb=> CREATE OR REPLACE FUNCTION f_tr_archive_files()
RETURNS TRIGGER AS $code$
  DECLARE
    current_tuple files%rowtype;
  BEGIN

    FOR current_tuple IN SELECT * FROM erasing LOOP
        RAISE DEBUG 'Moving tuple [%] with name [%] to %',
current_tuple.pk, current_tuple.f_name, TG_ARGV[ 0 ];

        EXECUTE 'INSERT INTO ' || TG_ARGV[ 0 ]
               || ' SELECT $1.*'
               USING current_tuple;
    END LOOP;
    RETURN NULL;
  END $code$ LANGUAGE plpgsql;
```

Listing 19: The trigger function that references the old table

With this trigger in place, each `DELETE` performed against the files table will result in the copying of files from one table to another, as shown in *Listing 20*:

```
testdb=> SET client_min_messages TO DEBUG;
testdb=> DELETE FROM files WHERE f_type = 'org';
DEBUG:  Moving tuple [26] with name [Introduction.txt] to archive_files
DEBUG:  Moving tuple [28] with name [File2] to archive_files
DEBUG:  Moving tuple [30] with name [File4] to archive_files
DEBUG:  Moving tuple [32] with name [File6] to archive_files
DEBUG:  Moving tuple [34] with name [File8] to archive_files
DEBUG:  Moving tuple [36] with name [File10] to archive_files
```

```
DEBUG:   Moving tuple [27] with name [File1] to archive_files
DEBUG:   Moving tuple [29] with name [File3] to archive_files
DEBUG:   Moving tuple [31] with name [File5] to archive_files
DEBUG:   Moving tuple [33] with name [File7] to archive_files
DEBUG:   Moving tuple [35] with name [File9] to archive_files
DELETE 11

testdb=> SELECT * FROM files WHERE f_type = 'org';

 pk | f_name | f_size | f_hash | f_type
----+--------+--------+--------+--------
(0 rows)

testdb=> SELECT * FROM archive_files WHERE f_type = 'org';

 pk | f_name           | f_size | f_hash                           | f_type
----+------------------+--------+----------------------------------+-------
-
 26 | Introduction.txt | 0.0000 | 1234567890abcdef1234567890abcdef | org
 28 | File2            | 0.0000 | c81e728d9d4c2f636f067f89cc14862c | org
 30 | File4            | 0.0000 | a87ff679a2f3e71d9181a67b7542122c | org
 32 | File6            | 0.0000 | 1679091c5a880faf6fb5e6087eb1b2dc | org
 34 | File8            | 0.0000 | c9f0f895fb98ab9159f51fd0297e236d | org
 36 | File10           | 0.0000 | d3d9446802a44259755d38e6d163e820 | org
 27 | File1            | 0.0000 | c4ca4238a0b923820dcc509a6f75849b | org
 29 | File3            | 0.0000 | eccbc87e4b5ce2fe28308fd9f2a7baf3 | org
 31 | File5            | 0.0000 | e4da3b7fbbce2345d7772b0674a318d5 | org
 33 | File7            | 0.0000 | 8f14e45fceea167a5a36dedd4bea2543 | org
 35 | File9            | 0.0000 | 45c48cce2e2d7fbdea1afc51c7c6ad26 | org
```

Listing 20: The trigger reacting to deletions

Using a trigger to perform multiple statements

A trigger function can be used to perform other SQL statements when it fires. In order to demonstrate this feature, imagine that each time a new music file (a file with the type mp3) is added to the files table, it must be automatically tagged with the tag music. To perform this action, once the INSERT of a new mp3 files happens, another INSERT must be performed in the j_files_tags join table to associate the file to the appropriate tag.

Let's implement this behavior with a trigger, starting with the trigger function. *Listing 21* shows the simplest implementation of the cascading insert to the join table. As you can see, the function simply performs INSERT into the j_files_tags table, exploiting the NEW.pk value and extracting the tag's primary key from the tags table. Searching for tags is specified via the TG_ARGV[0] trigger parameter:

```
testdb=> CREATE OR REPLACE FUNCTION f_tr_add_music_tag()
RETURNS TRIGGER AS $code$
  BEGIN
    INSERT INTO j_files_tags( f_pk, t_pk )
    SELECT NEW.pk, t.pk
    FROM    tags t
    WHERE   t.t_name = TG_ARGV[ 0 ];

    RETURN NEW;
  END $code$ LANGUAGE plpgsql;
```

Listing 21: The trigger function to cascade an INSERT

Therefore, the trigger definition will look like that in *Listing 22*, where the trigger fires after the tuple has been inserted in the files table and only if the incoming tuple has an mp3 type. In this case, the trigger function is called with the music argument:

```
testdb=> CREATE TRIGGER tr_add_music_tag
          AFTER INSERT ON files
          FOR EACH ROW
          WHEN ( NEW.f_type = 'mp3' )
          EXECUTE PROCEDURE f_tr_add_music_tag( 'music' );
```

Listing 22: Trigger definition to cascade INSERTs

The whole system works because the trigger has been defined as AFTER. This is the tuple that has already been inserted into the files table and so the foreign key from j_files_tags to files can be validated.

Trigger examples in foreign languages

As already emphasized, since triggers are associated to a function, it is possible to use any supported language to write the trigger function. In this section, we will see a few examples of rewriting previous trigger functions into PL/Perl and PL/Java, just to demonstrate the basic concepts behind the use of these languages to implement trigger behaviors.

PL/Perl Triggers

The PL/Perl trigger functions have access to a hash reference named `$_TD`, which has the following keys:

- `old` and `new` hold a hash reference to the OLD and NEW tuples in row-level triggers respectively
- `name`, `event`, `level`, and `when` hold a text string indicating the name of the trigger, the SQL statement that generated it, the moment the trigger fired, and the level (such as `STATEMENT` or `ROW`) respectively
- `table_name` and `table_schema` are the name of the table on which the trigger has been attached, and the name of the schema the trigger belongs to, respectively
- `argc` is the number (if any) of the trigger arguments
- `argv` is an array with the list of the trigger arguments

A row-level trigger function must return either a `MODIFY` text string, to indicate the NEW tuple has been modified and that it must be used within the current operation, or `SKIP`, to indicate that the current operation should be aborted.

In order to see how the preceding variables and concepts fit together, let's implement again the trigger in *Listing 15*, which validates a hash value. The PL/Perl re-implementation is shown in *Listing 23*. First of all, the function checks the `$_TD` event, `level`, and `when` to ensure that the trigger has been invoked at a row level, before any `INSERT` or `UPDATE`. Then, the function compares the `f_hash` column of the new tuple with a regular expression, and, if the column value does not match, the trigger function returns the special value `SKIP`, to indicate the operation must be aborted. Otherwise, the trigger function returns the `MODIFY` special value to indicate that we should continue with the new tuple values (the trigger function has modified the `f_hash` column value by putting the hash code in lowercase letters):

```
testdb=> CREATE OR REPLACE FUNCTION f_tr_check_hash_plperl()
RETURNS TRIGGER AS $code$
    return "SKIP" if ( $_TD->{level} ne 'ROW'
                       || $_TD->{when} ne 'BEFORE'
                       || ! grep { $_TD->{event} == $_ } ( 'INSERT', 'UPDATE'
) );

    if ( ! $_TD->{new}->{ f_hash } ) {
        elog( WARNING, 'The hash must be specified' );
        return "SKIP";
    }
```

```
# hash always in lower case
$_TD->{new}->{ f_hash } = lc $_TD->{new}->{ f_hash };

return "SKIP" if ( $_TD->{new}->{ f_hash } !~ /[abcdef0-9]{32}/ );

return "MODIFY";
$code$ LANGUAGE plperl;
```

Listing 23: A PL/Perl trigger function implementation to check the file hash format

The trigger definition is straightforward and pretty much the same as the analogous PL/pgSQL implementation, as shown in *Listing 24*:

```
testdb=> DROP TRIGGER IF EXISTS tr_check_hash ON files;
testdb=> CREATE TRIGGER tr_check_hash
         BEFORE INSERT OR UPDATE ON files
         FOR EACH ROW EXECUTE PROCEDURE f_tr_check_hash_plperl();
```

Listing 24: Trigger that exploits a PL/Perl function

PL/Java Triggers

The PL/Java trigger function must be a `static` method returning `void` and must accept a single argument of the `TriggerData` type. The `TriggerData` interface provides the following main methods to inspect the trigger execution context:

- `isFiredForStatement()` and its counterpart `isFiredForEachStatement()`, which return `true` if the trigger is a statement or row level one respectively
- `isFiredBefore()` and its counterpart `isFiredAfter()`, which return `true` if the trigger has been fired before or after an event respectively
- `isFiredByInsert()`, `isFiredByUpdate()`, and `isFiredByDelete()`, which return `true` if the trigger has been fired by an `INSERT`, an `UPDATE`, or a `DELETE` statement respectively
- `getNew()` and `getOld()` provide the `ResultSet` instance for the new and old row-level tuples

The trigger function can throw `SQLException`, or its specialized subclass, `TriggerException`, to abort the current transaction. This will abort the whole transaction, not just the current operation.

The trigger to check the hash file shown in *Listing 15* can therefore be re-implemented in PL/Java by the `TriggerCheckHash.triggerCheckHash()` method shown in *Listing 25*:

```
package pg11ssp;
import org.postgresql.pljava.*;
import java.util.*;
import java.sql.*;

public class TriggerCheckHash {

    public static void triggerCheckHash( TriggerData triggerData )
        throws SQLException {
        if ( ! triggerData.isFiredForEachRow()
            || ! triggerData.isFiredBefore()
            || ! ( triggerData.isFiredByInsert() ||
triggerData.isFiredByUpdate() ) )
            throw new TriggerException( triggerData,
                                        "This function cannot be invoked by
the trigger!" );

        // get the new tuple
        ResultSet newTuple = triggerData.getNew();
        String hash = newTuple.getString( "f_hash" );

        if ( hash == null
            || hash.isEmpty() )
            throw new TriggerException( triggerData,
                                        "The hash must have a value" );

        // convert to lower case
        newTuple.updateString( "f_hash", hash.toLowerCase() );

        if ( ! hash.matches( "[abcdef0-9]{32}" ) )
            throw new TriggerException( triggerData,
                                        "Not a valid hash" );


    }

}
```

Listing 25: Check Hash trigger in PL/Java

A little more glue code is required here. The PL/Java function must be visible from the PostgreSQL side and then the trigger can be defined against the function. The following code snippet shows the declaration of the trigger function and of the trigger itself. Remember that it is possible to use PL/Java annotation and the deployment descriptor to automatically create the function on the PostgreSQL side:

```
testdb=> CREATE OR REPLACE FUNCTION f_tr_check_hash_pljava()
RETURNS TRIGGER AS
  'pg11ssp.TriggerCheckHash.triggerCheckHash'
LANGUAGE java;

testdb=> CREATE TRIGGER tr_check_hash
        BEFORE INSERT OR UPDATE ON files
        FOR EACH ROW EXECUTE PROCEDURE f_tr_check_hash_pljava();
```

As explained in the previous chapter, the Jar archive must be deployed to the server. This can be achieved using the `pom.xml` Maven. The schema classpath must be appropriately set, so implementing a single trigger in PL/Java usually requires more effort than other languages such as PL/Perl. However, as already emphasized, the trigger function will have access to the whole Java ecosystem, including your own specific libraries and utilities, which is the advantage of implementing triggers in PL/Java.

Data definition triggers

Data definition language triggers (**DDL triggers**), also known as event triggers, are special triggers that, instead of being associated with a table, are associated with a whole database. An event trigger fires when a particular event happens within the database. Instead of being attached to regular SQL statements, an event trigger is attached to commands, which are statements that manage database objects (hence the name *DDL triggers*).

For DML triggers, an event trigger is defined by the event and the timing and executes a stored procedure (a `FUNCTION`). Events that fire DDL triggers are DDL statements, such as `CREATE`, `ALTER`, `DROP`, `GRANT`, `REVOKE`, and some other utility commands such as `SECURITY LABEL` and `COMMENT`.

The event is specified by the execution of one of the preceding commands, grouped in any of the following categories:

- `ddl_command_start` happens at the very beginning of the command execution
- `ddl_command_end` happens just after the command execution
- `sql_drop` happens immediately before the end of a command that drops database objects (such as `DROP`)
- `table_rewrite` happens just before a table is totally rewritten

In future releases, it will be possible to gain more event choices. It is also interesting to note that the `table_rewrite` timing is fired only by ALTER TABLE or ALTER TYPE commands, and not by other utility commands such as VACUUM or CLUSTER (even if these do an effective table rewrite).

The statement that fired the event is exposed by means of a *command tag*, which is a textual representation of the command itself. For instance, an `ALTER TABLE files ADD COLUMN foo int;` command has a tag of `ALTER TABLE`.

Since DDL commands are transactional, the function executed when an event trigger fires is also executed within the transaction of the command itself. As a consequence, if a `ddl_command_start` trigger function fails with an error, the command itself will not be executed because the transaction is aborted. On the other hand, if the command itself fails, no `ddl_command_end` trigger will fire.

Similar to DML triggers, event triggers are created by a particular CREATE EVENT TRIGGER command that cannot be subjected to the triggering mechanism itself (to avoid infinite recursion). It is possible to define multiple triggers on the same timing and event. In this case, the triggers will fire in alphabetical order.

Event triggers can only be defined by superusers. Since they can intercept almost any command, they could be maliciously used to spy on database activity. Event triggers are used for logical replication and other internal mechanics. They should not be used for regular database activity since they are still under heavy development and improvement.

The trigger function

The trigger function of an event trigger is a regular FUNCTION that does not accept any implicit arguments and that returns the EVENT_TRIGGER special type.

Within the trigger function, it is possible to invoke another set of utility functions to get some information about what fired the trigger. The following are the main functions:

- `pg_event_trigger_ddl_commands()` returns a result set of commands that fired the triggers and their related information. It can be used only with `ddl_command_end` timing and returns a row for every command executed.
- `pg_event_trigger_dropped_objects()` returns a result set of objects that have been dropped by a DROP (or similar) command
- `pg_event_trigger_table_rewrite_oid()` and `pg_event_trigger_table_rewrite_reason()` return the object identifier and a reason (coded as an integer value) for the rewriting of a table

A first event trigger

In order to demonstrate event triggers in action, consider the trigger definition of *Listing 26*. This intercepts the `sql_drop` event, which is the removal of a database object:

```
testdb=> CREATE EVENT TRIGGER
            etr_notifier ON sql_drop
            EXECUTE PROCEDURE f_etr_notifier();
```

Listing 26: A trigger that handles drop events

The `f_etr_notifier()` trigger function is shown in *Listing 27*. As you can see, the function iterates over the results of `pg_event_trigger_ddl_commands()` to display a message with the name and command executed against an object. The result set of `pg_event_trigger_ddl_commands()` has a field named `command_tag`, which identifies the SQL command (such as `ALTER TABLE`), and a field named `object_identity`, which identifies the fully qualified name of the object to which the command applies.

The function then performs another iteration over the results set of the `pg_event_trigger_dropped_objects()` function. This contains a column named `object_identity` with the fully qualified name of the object dropped, and a column named `object_type`, which contains a textual representation of the object type:

```
testdb=# CREATE OR REPLACE FUNCTION f_etr_notifier()
RETURNS EVENT_TRIGGER AS $code$
  DECLARE
    event_tuple record;
  BEGIN
    FOR event_tuple IN SELECT *
                        FROM pg_event_trigger_ddl_commands()  LOOP
        RAISE DEBUG 'Event fired by command [%] on [%]',
                event_tuple.command_tag,    -- statement
                event_tuple.object_identity;
    END LOOP;

    FOR event_tuple IN SELECT *
                        FROM pg_event_trigger_dropped_objects()  LOOP
      RAISE DEBUG 'Dropped object [%] of type [%]',
                    event_tuple.object_identity,
                    event_tuple.object_type;
    END LOOP;
  END $code$ LANGUAGE plpgsql;
```

Listing 27: A trigger function that handles drop events

With the trigger in place, let's see what happens if the `f_size` column of the `files` table is dropped. *Listing 28* shows a transaction that is rolled back (to avoid the effective deletion of the column) and an `ALTER TABLE DROP COLUMN` statement. From the trigger function output, we can see that the trigger finds that an `ALTER TABLE` statement has been issued, thanks to `pg_event_trigger_ddl_commands()`. Then, in order to drop the `f_size` column, three objects have to be dropped. The first one is the column itself (of the `table column` type), the second is the column default value (of the `default value` type) and the last is the `CHECK` constraint (of the `table constraint` type). All of these dropped objects have been reported by `pg_event_trigger_dropped_objects()`:

```
testdb=# SET client_min_messages TO DEBUG;
testdb=# BEGIN;
testdb=# ALTER TABLE files DROP COLUMN f_size;

DEBUG:   Event fired by command [ALTER TABLE] on [public.files]
DEBUG:   Dropped object [public.files.f_size] of type [table column]
DEBUG:   Dropped object [for public.files.f_size] of type [default value]
DEBUG:   Dropped object [files_f_size_check on public.files] of type [table
constraint]
ALTER TABLE

testdb=# ROLLBACK;
```

Listing 28: Event trigger fired

Using event triggers to avoid specific commands

We can use event triggers to abort commands. If the trigger function raises an exception, the wrapping transaction will not commit and neither will the executed command. As an example, let's say that we want to deny the removal of a function. We need to avoid any `DROP FUNCTION` commands being executed within the database. This can be implemented by an event trigger that analyzes each dropped object (via `pg_event_trigger_dropped_objects()`) and if any of these is a *function*, it raises an exception. The implementation therefore is as straightforward as shown in *Listing 29*:

```
testdb=# CREATE OR REPLACE FUNCTION f_etr_avoid_drop_function()
RETURNS EVENT_TRIGGER AS $code$
  DECLARE
    event_tuple record;
  BEGIN
    FOR event_tuple IN SELECT *
                   FROM pg_event_trigger_dropped_objects()   LOOP
        IF event_tuple.object_type = 'function' THEN
```

```
          RAISE EXCEPTION 'Cannot drop a function!';
        END IF;
  END LOOP;
    END $code$ LANGUAGE plpgsql;
```

In order to make `pg_event_trigger_dropped_objects()` work, the trigger must be attached to the `sql_drop` event category, as shown in *Listing 30*:

```
testdb=# CREATE EVENT TRIGGER
         etr_avoid_drop_function ON sql_drop
         EXECUTE PROCEDURE f_etr_avoid_drop_function();
```

Having defined the previous trigger, a function deletion aborts, as shown in *Listing 31*:

```
testdb=# DROP FUNCTION f_tr_check_hash CASCADE;
ERROR: Cannot drop a function!
CONTEXT: PL/pgSQL function f_etr_avoid_drop_function() line 8 at RAISE
```

Filtering specific commands

One problem related to the event trigger in *Listing 29* is that it is executed any time a DROP (or related) command is executed, even if it is not a specific DROP FUNCTION command. Event triggers provide a mechanism to filter the event (the command) on which they fire a little more accurately by means of a WHEN predicate. This accepts a list of variables that must match a list of choices. At the time of writing, the only supported variable is TAG, which assumes the values of the *command tag* (such as DROP FUNCTION).

Thanks to the WHEN predicate, it is possible to re-define the trigger of *Listing 30* to that in *Listing 32*. The trigger will only fire when a DROP FUNCTION command is issued.

```
testdb=# DROP EVENT TRIGGER IF EXISTS etr_avoid_drop_function;
testdb=# CREATE EVENT TRIGGER
etr_avoid_drop_function
ON sql_drop WHEN  TAG IN ( 'DROP FUNCTION' )
EXECUTE PROCEDURE f_etr_avoid_drop_function();
```

Managing event triggers

Event triggers can be modified by means of an ALTER EVENT TRIGGER command. They can also be removed by means of a DROP EVENT TRIGGER command.

It is possible to disable an event trigger without removing it from the system. This is done via ALTER EVENT TRIGGER, as follows:

```
testdb=# ALTER EVENT TRIGGER etr_avoid_drop_function DISABLE;
```

We can use DISABLE or ENABLE to disable or re-enable the trigger.

Event triggers can be listed with the psql special command \dy:

```
testdb=# \dy
                                   List of event triggers
          Name             |  Event   |  Owner   | Enabled |
Procedure        |     Tags
-------------------------+----------+----------+---------+-----------------
----------+---------------
 etr_avoid_drop_function | sql_drop | postgres | enabled |
f_etr_avoid_drop_function | DROP FUNCTION
```

Event trigger definitions are stored in the pg_event_trigger special catalog, where the columns evtname and evtevent contain the trigger name and event category respectively. The evtenabled column contains a letter indicating whether or not the trigger is enabled (D means disabled, A means *always enabled*, O means *enabled* and R has the special meaning of *replica*, which is outside the scope of this book). The evtfoid column contains the function identifier and the evttags column contains an array of WHEN filters. Therefore, the following simple queries provide basic information about the event triggers installed in the database:

```
testdb=# SELECT evtname AS trigger_name
             , evtevent AS event_category
             , CASE evtenabled
                     WHEN 'D' THEN 'disabled'
                     ELSE 'enabdled' END AS trigger_status
             , evtfoid::regproc AS trigger_function
             , array_to_string( evttags, ',') AS trigger_when
FROM pg_event_trigger;

     trigger_name        | event_category | trigger_status |
trigger_function        | trigger_when
-------------------------+----------------+----------------+---------------
-----------+---------------
```

```
etr_avoid_drop_function | sql_drop        | enabdled       |
f_etr_avoid_drop_function | DROP FUNCTION
```

Event trigger examples in foreign languages

Like DML triggers, event triggers can also have a trigger function written in any supported language. However, built-in support for event triggers is still pretty limited in foreign languages. In this section, a few examples will be shown to give you an idea about how to exploit language facilities to write event trigger functions.

PL/Perl

The idea behind a PL/Perl event trigger function is similar to that in a DML trigger scenario. The special $_TD hash reference holds information about the trigger context. $_TD has the following keys:

- tag: The command tag (the textual representation of the command) of the command that fired the trigger
- event: The event on which the trigger is fired

The return value of the event trigger function is ignored.

As an example, consider listing 33. This re-implements the trigger of *Listing 29*, which avoids the execution of a DROP FUNCTION command. As you can see, the knowledge of the value of $_TD->{tag} is not sufficient to implement the function behavior, since it is also required to know the name of the dropped object. This can be achieved by querying the pg_event_trigger_dropped_objects() function . Since the return value of the function does not have any effect, the only way to abort the operation is to throw an exception, hence the die() invocation to abort the function and the transaction:

```
testdb=# CREATE OR REPLACE FUNCTION f_etr_avoid_drop_function_plperl()
RETURNS EVENT_TRIGGER AS $code$
  elog( DEBUG, "Trigger fired on $_TD->{event} for command $_TD->{tag}" );

  for my $event_tuple ( @{ spi_exec_query( 'SELECT * FROM
pg_event_trigger_dropped_objects()' )
                          ->{ rows } } ) {
     die( "Cannot drop a function!" ) if ( $event_tuple->{ object_type } ==
'function' );
```

```
}
    $code$ LANGUAGE plperl;
```

Listing 33: A PL/Perl function for an event trigger that prevents DROP FUNCTION commands

The trigger definition is straightforward, and is shown in *Listing 34*:

```
testdb=# DROP EVENT TRIGGER IF EXISTS etr_avoid_drop_function;
testdb=# CREATE EVENT TRIGGER
 etr_avoid_drop_function ON sql_drop
 EXECUTE PROCEDURE f_etr_avoid_drop_function_plperl();
```

Listing 34: The event trigger that executes a PL/Perl function

PL/Java

PL/Java does not yet offer any specific support for event triggers, so a trigger function must be written only using regular PL/Java facilities.

In order to see what this means, consider the re-implementation of the trigger function in *Listing 29*, which avoids the execution of a DROP FUNCTION. The function implementation is shown in *Listing 35*. The method must be static, return a String type (the value does not matter), and not accept any argument. As you can see, the method implements normal PL/Java behavior and throws an exception if a command with the specified object type of *function* is dropped:

```
package pg11ssp;
import org.postgresql.pljava.*;
import org.postgresql.pljava.annotation.*;
import java.sql.*;
import java.util.logging.Logger;

public class DDLTrigger {

    @Function( name = "f_etr_avoid_drop_function_pljava",
               type = "event_trigger" )
    public static String avoidDropFunction()
        throws SQLException {
        ResultSet eventTuples = DriverManager
            .getConnection("jdbc:default:connection")
            .createStatement()
            .executeQuery( "SELECT * FROM
pg_event_trigger_dropped_objects()" );

        if ( eventTuples.next() )
            if ( eventTuples.getString( "object_type" ).equals( "function"
) )
                throw new SQLException( "Cannot drop a function!" );
```

```
        return "";
    }
}
```

Listing 35: A Java implementation of an event trigger function to avoid DROP FUNCTION commands

Since the code in *Listing 35* uses the PL/Java deployment annotation, the function will be immediately available on the server side with the name `f_etr_avoid_drop_function_pljava`, so the trigger can be immediately defined. This is shown in *Listing 36*:

```
testdb=# DROP EVENT TRIGGER IF EXISTS etr_avoid_drop_function;
testdb=# CREATE EVENT TRIGGER
 etr_avoid_drop_function ON sql_drop
 EXECUTE PROCEDURE f_etr_avoid_drop_function_pljava();
```

Listing 36: An event trigger that invokes a Java function

Since the function must return an `EVENT_TRIGGER` type, the annotation in *Listing 35* explicitly sets the return type.

Summary

Triggers are powerful tools that allow a database developer to better restrict data. Thanks to triggers, it is possible to perform on-the-fly validation, modification, and propagation of incoming data. PostgreSQL provides a very powerful trigger infrastructure that, being based on functions, allows you to write a trigger in any supported language. While other database systems allow you to manage DML triggers only, PostgreSQL also provides an infrastructure for database-wide DDL triggers that open new scenarios in database management and auditing.

In `Chapter 7`, *Rules and the Query Rewriting System*, we will introduce the Query Rewriting System (also known as the *rule system*). With this knowledge, we will be able to intercept and change an SQL statement on the fly.

References

- The PostgreSQL official documentation on Triggers is available at: `https://www.postgresql.org/docs/11/static/triggers.html`
- The PostgreSQL official documentation on Event Triggers is available at: `https://www.postgresql.org/docs/11/static/event-triggers.html`

7
Rules and the Query Rewriting System

The query rewriting system is a PostgreSQL component that intercepts statements and optionally rewrites them into other forms. Thanks to this component, statements can be bounced from one target to another or they can be modified into a totally different statement, therefore providing a very dynamic mechanism to handle users' queries.

The query rewriting system can be exploited by developers by mean of *rules*, which are definitions of how the statement transformations must happen. As you will see, this allows PostgreSQL to implement dynamic views and much more.

This chapter will focus on the following topics:

- The query rewriting system and how it works
- The rule system, the interface to the query rewriting system
- How dynamic views are created by means of rules
- How to exploit rules to bounce statements from one table to another, or to transform a statement into another statement or even multiple statements

Introducing the query rewriting system

In this section, we will look at what the query rewriting system is and when and where are the rules used by PostgreSQL.

What is the query rewriting system?

The query rewriting system is an internal component that is responsible for disassembling and rewriting a statement, transforming it into another. There are particular cases in which a statement cannot be executed, but must be transformed into another statement in order for the system to be able to perform the job.

The query rewriting system is responsible for understanding and carrying out transformation on the fly. Thanks to this feature, we can bounce a query against table A to a query against another table, B, transparently. Your clients and applications will not see this transformation and will think they are interacting with table A, while the real data is actually stored in table B. This example is one of many, however, thanks to the query rewriting system, it is possible to transform a statement into a completely different statement, such as transforming DELETE into UPDATE, or combining several statements into one.

If this reminds you of triggers, you'd be right! The query rewriting system does a job that is really close to that of triggers. However, the query rewriting system acts before any trigger fires and is done at a syntactic level, not at a semantic level. In other words, the query rewriting system fires depending only on the type of statement, while a trigger fires depending on the type of statement, the underlying table, the timing, and other data-dependent conditions.

When and where are rules used by PostgreSQL?

The first place where PostgreSQL uses the query rewriting system is in the dynamic view definition. A dynamic view, or a *view* for short, can be thought of as an alias for a complex query—each time the view is queried, the complex query runs and actual data is used.

Let's make this clearer with an example. The following listing shows the definition of a dynamic view named vw_text_files, which executes the query against the underlying files table to get out all files with a txt type. The view can be thought of as a phantom table named vw_text_files. When asked for data, it goes to the files table and extracts the files of type txt, as shown in the following snippet:

```
testdb=> CREATE OR REPLACE VIEW vw_text_files AS
         SELECT * FROM files
         WHERE f_type = 'txt';
```

Listing 1: An example of a dynamic view

In other words, when you perform `SELECT` against the phantom table, `vw_text_files`, PostgreSQL intercepts the statement and rewrites it as `SELECT` against the files table. This is the job of the query rewriting system: it detects that the statement in the following listing has something wrong (in this case, a phantom table) and rewrites it to make it work as expected:

```
testdb=> SELECT * FROM vw_text_files;
 pk  |   f_name    | f_size |        f_hash        | f_type |
ts
-----+-------------+--------+----------------------+--------+------------
----------------
 274 | chapter5.txt |  22.10 | aabb4455667788aacb3e | txt    | 2018-08-02
22:56:51.645603
```

Listing 2: Using a view

Rules

Rules are the user-interface of the query rewriting system. They allow the user to define how the rewriting will happen, and therefore define how to transform a statement into another.

Before executing the examples of this chapter, it is better to remove all triggers defined in `Chapter 6`, *Triggers*, or at least disable them, with the following code:

```
testdb=# DROP EVENT TRIGGER IF EXISTS etr_avoid_drop_function;
testdb=> ALTER TABLE files DISABLE TRIGGER all;
```

The syntax of rules

The syntax for creating a rule is similar to the syntax of defining a trigger, but there is no function to execute. A rule is identified by the following criteria:

- A name
- An event (an SQL statement)
- A target table on which the statement applies
- The actual rewriting rule

Rules are created by the CREATE RULE command, which supports the optional OR REPLACE predicate for re-defining an existing rule. We can remove a rule using the DROP RULE command. The template for creating a rule, therefore, is as follows:

```
CREATE OR REPLACE RULE <name>
AS ON <INSERT, UPDATE, DELETE, SELECT>
TO <table>
DO <rule>
```

 Rules are executed in alphabetical order. You can have as many rules you want on the same event and target table, but they will always be executed in alphabetical order.

The actual rule is identified by the query to be executed. This can be a standard SQL statement or the special keyword, NOTHING, which means that the original statement must be removed. The rule can be preceded by one of the two following keywords:

- ALSO: This is the default behavior; it means that the original statement (the event) must be executed and that the rule statement must be performed.
- INSTEAD: This means that the original statement (the event) must not be executed; instead, the rule must be performed.

Within the rule definition, it is possible to refer to the special table aliases, NEW and OLD. These work similarly to the record aliases in row level triggers, as follows:

- NEW is available for INSERT and UPDATE events and refers to the tuples that are going to be stored.
- OLD is available for UPDATE and DELETE events and refers to original tuples.

Let's make this clearer by looking at an example. In order to prevent any DELETE statements being used on the file table, it is possible to write a rule as follows:

```
testdb=> CREATE OR REPLACE RULE r_avoid_delete_files
        AS ON DELETE TO files
        DO INSTEAD NOTHING;
```

The preceding code states that each time DELETE is issued against the files table, the system must actually do NOTHING. This means that the event statement (DELETE) should be thrown away.

As another example, we can enforce that each time `DELETE` is issued against the files table, the archive table `archive_files` must also be truncated. This is an example of the `DO ALSO` rule, shown as follows:

```
testdb=> CREATE OR REPLACE RULE r_cascade_delete_files
         AS ON DELETE TO files
         DO ALSO DELETE FROM archive_files;
```

When the preceding rule is in place, it is like issuing the following query each time:

```
testdb=> DELETE FROM files;
```

The previous statement can be transformed into a two-statement transactions as follows:

```
testdb=> BEGIN;
testdb=> DELETE FROM files;
testdb=> DELETE FROM archive_files;
testdb=> COMMIT;
```

This is just the surface level of the rule system. As already explained, a rule is used to implement a dynamic view. Consider again the view defined in *Listing 1*. We are now going to re-implement it with rules.

First of all, we must create a table with the same structure as the resulting view, but with no data in it. This can be achieved easily by cloning the files table with the `CREATE TABLE ( LIKE )` command as follows:

```
testdb=> CREATE TABLE vw_rule_text_files( LIKE files );
```

It is now time to implement a rule to intercept `SELECT` against `vw_rule_text_files`, the newly created—and empty—table, and bounce it to the files table. This rule must have the special name `"_RETURN"` (with quotes), shown as follows:

```
testdb=> CREATE RULE "_RETURN"
         AS ON SELECT TO vw_rule_text_files
         DO INSTEAD SELECT * FROM files;
```

Each time `SELECT` is issued against the empty table `vw_rule_text_files`, the code declares that the query should be redirected to the files table instead. The special name `"_RETURN"` makes PostgreSQL aware that the previously created table, `vw_rule_text_files`, is a placeholder for a view instead, as shown in the following snippet:

```
testdb=> \d vw_rule_text_files
                    View "public.vw_rule_text_files"
   Column |         Type         | Collation | Nullable | Default
```

```
---------+-----------------------------+-----------+-----------+--------
pk       | integer                     |           | not null  |
f_name   | text                        |           | not null  |
f_size   | numeric(18,2)               |           |           |
f_hash   | text                        |           | not null  |
f_type   | text                        |           |           |
ts       | timestamp without time zone |           |           |
```

 Since a SELECT rule must be named "_RETURN", you can have only one SELECT rule per table.

A rule example – archiving tuples on deletion

In Chapter 6, *Triggers*, we looked at triggers that fired after a DELETE statement and that moved deleted tuples from the files table to the archive_files table. Let's now look at how to implement the same behavior with a rule.

First of all, the rule will be attached to the files table on the DELETE event. The rule must do the following:

- Permit the event to do its job, such as delete the tuples
- Perform a tuple moving

Since this is a DELETE event, the deleted tuples will be available via the OLD table alias. The rule definition is shown in the following listing. It doesn't make sense to keep both the rule and the trigger active on the same table, since they serve the same purpose. However, remember that rules works before the trigger has a chance to be fired:

```
testdb=> CREATE OR REPLACE RULE r_archive_tuples_on_deletion
 AS ON DELETE TO files
 DO ALSO
 INSERT INTO archive_files
 SELECT OLD.*;
```

Listing 3: A rule to archive files

Where is my rule?

Rules can be seen in the output of the *describe* `psql` special command, `\d`, as shown in the following snippet:

```
testdb=> \d files
                                          Table "public.files"
...
Rules:
    r_archive_tuples_on_deletion AS
    ON DELETE TO files DO  INSERT INTO archive_files (pk, f_name, f_size,
f_hash, f_type, ts)   SELECT old.pk,
               old.f_name,
               old.f_size,
               old.f_hash,
               old.f_type,
               old.ts
```

Please note that the rule has been rewritten with all of the column names explicitly specified.

Rule definitions are kept in `pg_rewrite`, the system catalog, with the following main columns:

- `rulename`, which is the name of the rule
- `ev_class`, which is the identifier of the table the rule is attached to
- `ev_type`, which is a value representing the event (the statement) that the rule refers to (`'1'` = SELECT, `'2'` = UPDATE, `'3'` = INSERT, and `'4'` = DELETE)
- `ev_enabled` means that the rule is disabled if set to `'D'`
- `ev_action`, which is the action to execute for this rule in an internal PostgreSQL form

Thanks to the utility function, `pg_get_ruledef()`, it is possible to convert the internal PostgreSQL rule form into a human readable (SQL-like) form. Therefore, the following query provides information about which rules are active on the files table:

```
testdb=> SELECT rulename
            , ev_class::name AS table_name
            , CASE ev_type WHEN '1'  THEN 'SELECT'
                           WHEN '2'  THEN 'UPDATE'
                           WHEN '3'  THEN 'INSERT'
                           WHEN '4'  THEN 'DELETE'
              END AS event
            , pg_get_ruledef( oid, true ) AS rule_definition
            FROM pg_rewrite
```

```
                    WHERE ev_class = 'files'::regclass;

          rulename            | table_name | event  |
rule_definition
------------------------------+------------+--------+----------------------
------------------------------------------------------------------------
---------------
  r_archive_tuples_on_deletion | 16663     | DELETE | CREATE RULE
r_archive_tuples_on_deletion AS
+
                              |            |        |        ON DELETE TO
files DO  INSERT INTO archive_files (pk, f_name, f_size, f_hash, f_type,
ts)   SELECT old.pk,+
                              |            |        |
old.f_name,
+
                              |            |        |
old.f_size,
+
                              |            |        |
old.f_hash,
+
                              |            |        |
old.f_type,
+
                              |            |        |              old.ts;
(1 row)
```

It is not possible to modify a rule definition once it has been created. The only command supported by ALTER RULE is the RENAME command, which is used to change the rule's name. If you need to change a rule, you have to either drop it via DROP RULE and re-create it, or use the CREATE OR REPLACE RULE command to re-define it.

Conditional rules

The application of a rule can be filtered by means of a WHERE predicate. The rule will only apply if the WHERE Boolean condition is true for the applied tuples. Within the WHERE predicate, it is possible to refer to the OLD and NEW table aliases.

To make it clearer, consider the rule of *Listing 3*. This rule will archive any file that is going to be deleted from the files table. If you simply want to delete files without archiving them, you can write a rule like the one shown in the following listing. This applies to all files with an f_type, other than bak (which is backup, in this example). Files for which the WHERE predicate results are true will be deleted and archived, while all other files will simply be deleted because the rule will not be applied:

```
testdb=> CREATE OR REPLACE RULE r_archive_tuples_on_deletion
         AS ON DELETE TO files
         WHERE ( OLD.f_type <> 'bak' )
         DO ALSO
         INSERT INTO archive_files
         SELECT OLD.*;
```

Listing 4: A rule to archive files excluding backup ones

Using a rule to execute multiple statements– the playlist example

As already stated, a rule can be used to execute multiple statements at once thanks to the DO ALSO predicate. In order to demonstrate this feature, let's consider an automatic playlist population. Every time a new mp3 file is added to the files table, the same file name must be queued in the playlist table. In other words, INSERT must be split into two operations: the real insertion and a cascading insertion to another table. This is simple to achieve using rules.

As shown in the following listing, it is possible to create a DO ALSO rule on every INSERT against the files so that, if the file has a type of mp3, INSERT against the playlist table is also performed:

```
testdb=> CREATE OR REPLACE RULE r_append_to_playlist
         AS ON INSERT TO files
         WHERE ( NEW.f_type = 'mp3' )
         DO ALSO
            INSERT INTO playlist( p_name )
            VALUES ( NEW.f_name );
```

Listing 5: A rule to queue new music files to a playlist

As you can see in the output of the following *Listing 6*, the playlist starts to become immediately populated by new files:

```
testdb=> INSERT INTO files( f_name, f_hash, f_type )
         VALUES( 'ballbreaker.mp3', '234567ba12789ab', 'mp3' );

testdb=> SELECT * FROM playlist;
 pk |       p_name
----+-----------------
  1 | ballbreaker.mp3
```

Listing 6: The effects of the previously defined rule

As you can imagine, in order to complete this simple example, we need to create a DELETE rule. Each time an mp3 file is deleted, it must also be removed from the playlist, as demonstrated in the following listing:

```
testdb=> CREATE OR REPLACE RULE r_delete_mp3
         AS ON DELETE TO files
         WHERE ( OLD.f_type = 'mp3' )
         DO ALSO
             DELETE FROM playlist
             WHERE p_name = OLD.f_name;
```

Listing 7: A rule to remove mp3 files from the playlist

The resulting output is shown in the following *Listing 8*:

```
testdb=> DELETE FROM files WHERE f_name = 'ballbreaker.mp3';
testdb=> SELECT * FROM playlist;
 pk | p_name
----+--------
```

Listing 8: The effects of deleting an mp3 file

Using a rule to route tuples

One thing rules are good at is routing tuples from one table into another. This is particularly useful when doing inheritance-based partitioning. Describing partitioning is out of the scope of this book, but for the sake of simplicity, let's assume we want to split our files table depending on the type of files. Let's say that mp3 files must go to a different table, named files_mp3. The end result is that all of our music will be contained in a separate table with the same structure of the original one, but with specific files and a reduced size.

Using rules with partitioning is, as you can imagine, really easy. Take a look at the following snippet:

```
testdb=> CREATE TABLE files_mp3() INHERITS( files );
testdb=> CREATE OR REPLACE RULE r_insert_mp3
         AS ON INSERT TO files
         WHERE ( NEW.f_type = 'mp3' )
         DO INSTEAD
            INSERT INTO files_mp3
            SELECT NEW.*;
```

Note that the very same behavior could have been achieved with a routing trigger fired before the insertion. The trigger function would perform the insert against the `files_mp3` tables.

When to use rules and when to use triggers

As we have seen, rules are a powerful mechanism that rewrite specific SQL statements on the fly in order to carry out different actions. To some extent, rules are a way to control and react to specific statements. This makes rules similar to triggers, so it can be difficult to decide on when to use a rule and when to use a trigger.

The first rule to keep in mind is that rules fire before triggers. Rules can route a statement to a totally different table, so that your original table triggers never fire. Another difference is that triggers can handle more statements, such as `TRUNCATE`, which is not possible with rules. Finally, triggers execute functions, which opens an infinite set of possibilities about what you can do with them. While you can invoke a function with a rule too, having the ability to modify the data within the function, as in the case of triggers, is often more powerful.

An example of when a rule cannot substitute a trigger is when you have foreign key constraints. In the previous chapter, we saw how to use an after trigger to associate a music file to the music tag. The same thing cannot be easily achieved with a rule because `j_files_tags` has a foreign key constraint on files. This means that the following rule, even if it appears correct, will not work:

```
testdb=> CREATE OR REPLACE RULE r_associate_music_tag
AS ON INSERT TO files
WHERE ( NEW.f_type = 'mp3' )
DO ALSO
  INSERT INTO j_files_tags( f_pk, t_pk )
  SELECT NEW.pk, t.pk FROM tags t
  WHERE t.t_name = 'music';
```

In fact, when `INSERT` is performed against the files table, `DO ALSO` is executed too. However, the tuple of `files` has not yet been consolidated, so there is a constraint violation:

```
testdb=> INSERT INTO files( f_name, f_hash, f_type ) VALUES(
'ballbreaker.mp3', 'ab23de45bb765432af', 'mp3' );
ERROR:  insert or update on table "j_files_tags" violates foreign key
constraint "j_files_tags_f_pk_fkey"
DETAIL:  Key (f_pk)=(286) is not present in table "files".
```

Note that situations like this cannot be solved even with a deferable transaction, a transaction that will check foreign key constraints only at the commit.

Last but not least, a rule is fired once for each statement. It rewrites the whole statement once and only once, without any regard to how many tuples the statement is manipulating. On the other hand, a trigger can be fired once per tuple, and this can give you better control on each single bit of data at the cost of more resources. In conclusion, the best approach depends on the specific scenario.

Summary

Rules provide a powerful interface for interacting with the PostgreSQL query rewriting system. Thanks to rules, it is possible to transform a statement syntactically into another one or even into multiple ones. While this can also often be achieved by means of triggers, rules work at a syntactic level and are fired before any trigger. Of course, rules are not the universal solution to any problem and there are cases in which triggers are preferable and vice-versa. Knowing however how to handle statement rewriting is a valuable skill for any PostgreSQL server side developer.

In the next chapter, we will explain the PostgreSQL extension, which is a way to package your own code, including functions, procedures, triggers, tables, and so on, as well as manage its deployment and upgrade.

References

- The PostgreSQL Rule System, official documentation available at `https://www.postgresql.org/docs/11/static/rule-system.html`
- PostgreSQL Rule Creation, official documentation available at `https://www.postgresql.org/docs/11/static/sql-createrule.html`
- Inheritance Partitioning, official PostgreSQL documentation available at `https://www.postgresql.org/docs/11/static/ddl-partitioning.html#DDL-PARTITIONING-IMPLEMENTATION-INHERITANCE`

8
Extensions

SQL is a declarative textual language that allows us to create our own scripts. It does not matter how long these scripts are, whether they are one line or 1000; the script will execute one command after another. This allows us to build a very complex command set.

However, this script approach has certain drawbacks. It does not scale and it is difficult to apply changes across different script versions, which means that it is quite hard to handle scripts and versions the right way. While there are many interesting tools for versioning, making changes, and deployment control (the most notable project being Sqitch), PostgreSQL comes with its own mechanism that is based on the concept of extensions.

Extensions are widely used within the PostgreSQL ecosystem to ease the installation, upgrading, and general maintenance of a set of database commands and data.

In this chapter, you will learn about the following topics:

- What an extension is and how it is made
- How to install, manage, update, and throw away extensions
- How to create your own extensions and updated versions
- Where to find extensions on the internet and how to automate their download and installation as much as possible

Extensions

An extension is a package, a container of related SQL objects (such as functions, procedures, tables, and indexes). The advantage of packaging these related objects into a single extension, instead of using one or more scattered scripts, is that PostgreSQL will manage the whole set of objects as a single package. To some extent, it is a way of making PostgreSQL aware that these objects are related to each other, so that it can either drop or upgrade them all at once. You can still use your scripts as the backbone for an extension; you just need to make PostgreSQL aware of which files your extensions are made of.

Moreover, PostgreSQL-related tools are aware of extensions, so, for instance, when you take a backup of your database via `pg_dump`, no individual object from an extension will be dumped. Instead, a special command to reinstall the extension will be inserted in your backup archive, so that the extension will be recreated upon restoration. This means that the system does not even consider the extension objects to be individual database objects; it always knows it can restore objects from the extension itself.

If you are not yet convinced about how great this concept of packaging is, consider the script approach again. If your script creates two almost unrelated objects (such as tables), you (the database user) will be able to drop one of the objects without dropping the other. With an extension, PostgreSQL provides a layer of *extra protection* that prevents the removal of extension objects until all of them are removed (the whole extension). Again, the extension is a single package and is managed as a single entity, even if it creates several database objects. Even permissions are managed at the extension level.

Last but not least, extensions help in managing changes, versions, and upgrades. Once an extension has been created, it is possible to provide another extension with only the changes required for the upgrade. PostgreSQL will understand which steps to perform in order to apply changes and upgrade the installed extension to the latest (or the specified) version.

There is, however, an important drawback: not all objects can be included in an extension. As a rule of thumb, any object that is cluster-wide (intra-database) cannot be included (this includes roles, databases, and tablespaces). Moreover, row-level security policies cannot be part of an extension. Not being part of an extension does not mean that the extension cannot create these objects, but it does mean that these objects will not be seen as packaged with the extension and therefore will not be managed as other extension objects.

Each extension must provide two specific files to allow PostgreSQL to manage the package as a whole: a `control` file and a `script` file. These files must be placed into a path known to PostgreSQL: `SHAREDIR/extension`. It is possible to use the utility command `pg_config` to get information about where the `SHAREDIR` is located:

```
% pg_config --sharedir
/opt/pg11/share/postgresql
```

The main file is the `control` file, which also indicates where the `script` file can be found if it is installed somewhere other than the preceding directory. Both files must be named after the extension name.

When an extension is installed, all the packaged objects are placed into a database schema. If the extension can be moved to another schema, the extension is said to be *relocatable*. This is an important feature of an extension, because it allows the users to move the extensions to custom schemas.

Usually, an extension can only be installed by a database superuser. It is, however, possible to mark an extension so that it can be installed by non-superusers as well.

The control file

The `control` file is a text configuration file whose name is made up of the name of the extension and the `.control` suffix, such as `packt.control` for an extension named `packt`. The `control` file follows the same key-value syntax of the PostgreSQL `postgresql.conf` main configuration file.

A `control` file can use several directives. The main ones are as follows:

- `directory`: Specifies the path where the script file is located. If a relative path is used, this path is considered to be relative to the `SHAREDIR/extension` extension directory.
- `default_version`: The version to install as default when no specific version is required.
- `comment`: A descriptive comment about the extension, applied only at installation time.
- `requires`: An optional list of required extensions to be installed before the current one.
- `superuser`: A Boolean flag (which defaults to true) that indicates whether only database superusers can create the extension or not.
- `relocatable`: A Boolean flag that indicates if the extension can be relocated.
- `schema`: If the extension is not relocatable, it will be installed into this specific schema.

An extension must have at least one `control` file, called the main `control` file, but it can have more than one. The additional control files, called secondary `control` files, have a slightly different naming schema and can use all the same options as the primary `control` file, with the exception of `directory` and `default_version`. Secondary control files must be placed into the script directory and must be named after the extension name and the version they refer to, such as `packt--1.1.control`.

The script file

The script file is a plain SQL file that contains any command needed to create the extension objects. It is likely that your already existing SQL scripts can be converted into an extension script file seamlessly. The script file is executed within a transaction and contains any SQL command that does not interact with the wrapping transaction (such as COMMIT) or that cannot be executed within a transaction (including utility commands, such as VACUUM).

The script file must be named after the extension name and the version number, with the extension 'sql'. Version numbers are always preceded by a double dash. For example, the packt--1.4.sql name refers to the 'packt' extension, at version 1.4.

A script file can also include a double version number. This means that it must be used to upgrade an extension from the first (leftmost) version number to the second (rightmost) one. For instance, the packt--1.4--1.5.sql script file can be used to upgrade the 'packt' extension from version 1.4 to version 1.5. This is very useful because, as you will see later, it allows us to upgrade extensions with a single command.

Relocatable extensions

As already stated, an extension is relocatable if it can be moved to another schema upon installation or even afterward. On the other hand, the extension is not relocatable at all if it cannot be moved to another schema. There is also a third level, which is partially relocatable files, that allows users to specify a custom schema only upon installation. This is done by specifying relocatable = false in the control file and using the special schema name @extschema@ in the script file. When the extension is installed, the user can specify the SCHEMA option to CREATE EXTENSION, which will be dynamically substituted with every occurrence of @extschema@.

When the extension is installed, search_path is set to the real value of @extschema@ so that the extension creates all objects within the same schema. In particular, if the control file specifies a schema value, the schema used will be set to that value. Otherwise, it will be set to the first value in the user's search_path and, if none exists, to the current schema from which CREATE SCHEMA has been launched.

Extension management

Enough theory! It's now time to see how an extension is implemented. This chapter will start by implementing an extension from scratch. We will then look at how to provide upgrades to an existing extension.

Creating and removing extensions

Extensions are installed on a per-database basis. The control and script file must be available to the cluster and the extension must be loaded into every database in which it is required. An extension is created by means of the CREATE EXTENSION command, which allows us to specify the version and the schema (if the extension is relocatable). If no version is specified, the extension will be installed with the default version specified in its control file. Similarly, if no schema is specified, the extension will be installed in the target schema. Alternatively, if no schema is specified in the control file, it will be installed in the current schema.

Let's suppose that we have a relocatable extension named pg11ssp. We could install it with the following commands:

```
-- install at default version, in default schema
testdb=# CREATE EXTENSION pg11ssp;
-- install specified version in specified schema
testdb=# CREATE EXTENSION pg11ssp
        WITH VERSION '1.2' SCHEMA 'packt';
```

An extension can be dropped with the DROP EXTENSION command, as follows:

```
testdb=# DROP EXTENSION pg11ssp;
```

This command will drop all extension objects at once.

There is also an ALTER EXTENSION command which can be used to change the schema of a relocatable extension, add an object on the fly (and remove an object), and change the version of the installed extension. More examples on the usage of these commands will be shown later.

Which extensions are installed?

In order to see which extensions are installed in the system, at which version, it is possible to use the `psql` special command `\dx` (**describe extension**), as shown in the *Listing 1* as follows:

```
testdb=> \dx
                         List of installed extensions
   Name   | Version |   Schema    |                 Description
----------+---------+-------------+------------------------------------------
----------------
 plperl   | 1.0     | pg_catalog  | PL/Perl procedural language
 plperlu  | 1.0     | pg_catalog  | PL/PerlU untrusted procedural language
 plpgsql  | 1.0     | pg_catalog  | PL/pgSQL procedural language
```

Listing 1: Inspecting installed extensions

The extension metadata is kept in the `pg_extension` special catalog, where the main columns are as follows:

- `extname`: The name of the extension
- `extnamespace`: An internal representation of the extension schema
- `extrelocatable`: A Boolean flag indicating if the extension is relocatable
- `extversion`: A textual representation of the extension version

The `comment` directive contained in the extension `control` file is managed as a PostgreSQL object comment and is therefore kept in the `pg_description` catalog table. Instead, the query of *Listing 2* can be used to get information about the installed extensions:

```
testdb=> SELECT extname
       , extnamespace::regclass AS namespace
       , extversion AS version
       , CASE extrelocatable WHEN true THEN 'RELOCATABLE'
                                        ELSE 'NOT-RELOCATABLE'
         END AS relocatable_status
       , c.description AS comment
FROM pg_extension LEFT JOIN pg_description c
     ON c.objoid = oid
ORDER BY 1, 3;

  extname | namespace | version | relocatable_status |
comment
---------+-----------+---------+--------------------+----------------------
-----------------------------------
 plperl  | 11        | 1.0     | NOT-RELOCATABLE    | PL/Perl procedural
```

```
language
 plperlu | 11         | 1.0      | NOT-RELOCATABLE     | PL/PerlU untrusted
procedural language
 plpgsql | 11         | 1.0      | NOT-RELOCATABLE     | PL/pgSQL procedural
language
```

Listing 2: A query to get information about the extensions

Creating your own extension

In this section, we will learn how to create an extension, reusing some of the code you have seen in the previous chapters. In the following subsections, we will cover how to create, update, and manage your own extension for PostgreSQL.

Starting from scratch

Let's consider the sample database used throughout this book and make an extension called `pg11ssp`. The first version of the extension, version 1.0, will define the data structure (the tables and constraints) and a few functions. Let's start with the `script` file, which is partially shown in *Listing 3*. As you can see, it is a plain SQL set of statements:

```
CREATE TABLE IF NOT EXISTS files ( ... );
CREATE TABLE IF NOT EXISTS tags( ... );
CREATE TABLE IF NOT EXISTS j_files_tags ( ... );
```

Listing 3: The script file pg11ssp–1.0.sql

Let's now consider the `control` file. This must set `default_version` to the smallest version number available, which, in this case, is 1.0. Moreover, to make things simpler, we can have the script file within the same directory as the `control` file so there is no need to have a directory directive. The extension must be installed by any user (so `superuser` is set to `false`) and cannot be `relocatable`: each object must belong to the `packt` schema. Putting all this together produces the `control` file shown in *Listing 4*:

```
comment = 'PostgreSQL 11 Server Side Programming Example Extension'
default_version = '1.0'
superuser       = false
relocatable     = false
schema          = 'packt'
```

Listing 4: The pg11ssp.control control file

Instead of manually installing the extension control and script files into the server, it is easier to use an ad hoc `Makefile`. PostgreSQL provides an infrastructure for the make files of extensions so that the only thing to do, other than include in your `Makefile` the `pgxs.mk` PostgreSQL base file, is to define the extension name and the related `control` file. The PostgreSQL `Makefile` included will allow you to install and uninstall required files. The `Makefile` for this simple extension is shown in the following code snippet: the `DATA` variable holds the name of the `control` file, while `EXTENSION` keeps the name of the extension to install. The other lines exploit the `pg_config` command to get the path to the extensions and to include the base `makefile`. In order to ease the building, installation, and removal of an extension, PostgreSQL provides an infrastructure named PGXS. Using PGXS, building the extension becomes easier and it is also easier to port to different platforms and cluster versions. In order to use the PGXS infrastructure, you must use a `Makefile` like the one shown in the following code snippet, which includes the `pgxs.mk` base `Makefile`:

```
EXTENSION = pg11ssp
DATA = pg11ssp--1.0.sql
PG_CONFIG = pg_config
PGXS := $(shell $(PG_CONFIG) --pgxs)
include $(PGXS)
```

The whole bunch of files is therefore as follows:

```
% ls
Makefile pg11ssp--1.0.sql  pg11ssp.control
```

It is of course possible to keep these under a version control system (such as `git`), archive them, and manage them as you do with all your project files. With these files in place, it is possible to install the extension using the `Makefile`:

```
% sudo make install
/bin/sh /opt/pg11/lib/postgresql/pgxs/src/makefiles/../../config/install-sh
-c -d '/opt/pg11/share/postgresql/extension'
/bin/sh /opt/pg11/lib/postgresql/pgxs/src/makefiles/../../config/install-sh
-c -d '/opt/pg11/share/postgresql/extension'
/usr/bin/install -c -m 644 .//pg11ssp.control
'/opt/pg11/share/postgresql/extension/'
/usr/bin/install -c -m 644 .//pg11ssp--1.0.sql
'/opt/pg11/share/postgresql/extension/'
```

The preceding installation simply places the `control` and `script` files in the correct place for the extension to be found by PostgreSQL. However, in order to be usable, it must be installed on each database in which it is required. Since the extension can be installed by any user, simply connecting to the database and issuing a CREATE EXTENSION will work and make the extension objects available:

```
testdb=> CREATE EXTENSION pg11ssp;
testdb=> \d packt.files
                               Table "packt.files"
 Column |              Type              | Collation | Nullable |
Default
--------+--------------------------------+-----------+----------+-------------
-----------------
 pk     | integer                        |           | not null | generated
always as identity
 f_name | text                           |           | not null |
 f_size | numeric(10,4)                  |           |          | 0
 f_hash | text                           |           | not null | 'N/A'::text
 f_type | text                           |           |          | 'txt'::text
 ts     | timestamp without time zone    |           |          | now()
Indexes:
    "files_pkey" PRIMARY KEY, btree (pk)
    "files_f_hash_key" UNIQUE CONSTRAINT, btree (f_hash)
Check constraints:
    "files_f_size_check" CHECK (f_size >= 0::numeric)
Referenced by:
    TABLE "packt.j_files_tags" CONSTRAINT "j_files_tags_f_pk_fkey" FOREIGN
KEY (f_pk) REFERENCES packt.files(pk)
```

All objects are now in their place. We can drop these in a single command, DROP EXTENSION:

```
testdb=> DROP EXTENSION pg11ssp;
```

We can then recreate the extension.

Extension objects do not clash with other example objects because the extension uses its own separated schema. As you can imagine, trying to force another existing schema to the extension fails:

```
testdb=> ALTER EXTENSION pg11ssp SET SCHEMA fluca;
ERROR:  extension "pg11ssp" does not support SET SCHEMA
```

The list of installed extensions will report information about the extensions that we just created and installed:

```
testdb=> \dx
                                List of installed extensions
    Name    | Version |   Schema   |                    Description
----------+---------+------------+---------------------------------------------
----------------
  pg11ssp | 1.0     | packt      | PostgreSQL 11 Server Side Programming
Example Extension
  ...
```

Creating an improved version

It is now time to improve the extension and release a new version. We are going to include some PL/Perl code from the previous chapters in what will be release 1.1 of the extension. The extension will also add a column to the already existing table files.

In order to make all the changes automatically, the SQL script must be named after the extension name and must include the starting version and the final version, each separated by a double dash, such as pg11ssp--1.0--1.1.sql. The PostgreSQL extension engine will consider this name to be something that will upgrade extension pg11ssp from version 1.0 to version 1.1. On the other hand, if changes have been packed into a script named pg1ssp1--1.1.sql, the extension engine will not able to upgrade it automatically, so we need to install version 1.0 and then version 1.1 manually.

Since this extension will add a dependency on PL/Perl, it is better to provide a secondary control file to automate the installation of the required dependencies. This control file is shown in the following code snippet and must be named pg11ssp--1.1.control:

```
requires = 'plperl'
```

The two files can be copied into the extension directory, so that the upgrade can be performed:

```
% sudo cp pg11ssp--1.0--1.1.sql /opt/pg11/share/postgresql/extension
% sudo cp pg11ssp--1.1.control /opt/pg11/share/postgresql/extension
```

It is now time to carry out the upgrade. This can be achieved by specifying the version to upgrade to as an argument to the ALTER EXTENSION command:

```
testdb=> ALTER EXTENSION pg11ssp UPDATE TO '1.1';
testdb=> \dx pg11ssp
```

```
                         List of installed extensions
   Name     | Version | Schema |                      Description
----------+---------+--------+------------------------------------------------
-----------
   pg11ssp | 1.1     | packt  | PostgreSQL 11 Server Side Programming Example
   Extension
```

The new extension is updated and the new objects are included.

Installing all the preceding versions

Imagine that another change is made to the simple `pg11ssp` extension, so that version 1.2 is released. This time, the changes are so minimal that only the `script` file must be provided. *Listing 5* contains a simple `ALTER TABLE`. The script is named `pg11ssp--1.1--1.2.sql`, so that PostgreSQL knows it can be used to upgrade version 1.1 to version 1.2:

```
ALTER TABLE files DROP COLUMN ts;
```

Listing 5: Another script file

Place the file into the `extension` directory, so that the `extension` directory now contains the following code:

```
% sudo ls `pg_config --sharedir`/extension/pg11ssp*
/opt/pg11/share/postgresql/extension/pg11ssp--1.0--1.1.sql
/opt/pg11/share/postgresql/extension/pg11ssp--1.0.0.sql
/opt/pg11/share/postgresql/extension/pg11ssp--1.0.sql
/opt/pg11/share/postgresql/extension/pg11ssp--1.1--1.2.sql
/opt/pg11/share/postgresql/extension/pg11ssp--1.1.control
/opt/pg11/share/postgresql/extension/pg11ssp.control
```

Now, drop away the already installed extension as follows:

```
testdb=> DROP EXTENSION pg11ssp;
```

What if you want to install the extension again, but this time at version 1.2? A simple `CREATE EXTENSION` command will install it to the default version specified in the `control` file. However, if you specify the version you want to install at the time you create the extension, PostgreSQL will start from the main `control` file, install version 1.0, then upgrade to 1.1 and go on until it reaches the required version. You cannot ask PostgreSQL to install a version you don't have the scripts for. This works as follows:

```
testdb=> CREATE EXTENSION pg11ssp WITH VERSION '1.2';
testdb=> \dx pg11ssp
   List of installed extensions Name | Version | Schema | Description -------
```

```
--+---------+--------+----------------------------------------------
---- pg11ssp | 1.2 | packt | PostgreSQL 11 Server Side Programming Example
Extension
```

As you can see, the required version has been installed in the database.

Extension data and backups

As you have already seen, an extension can include pretty much any database object, including regular tables. Such tables can be populated when the extension is installed or updated. They can also be modified by users during the life cycle of the database.

By default, backup tools such as pg_dump do not include extension objects to be dumped, since they can always be recreated from the extension scripts. However, if the user changes the data in the extension tables, this data will be lost (or, more accurately, it will not be automatically backed up).

One solution could be to back up this data manually, but this is tedious work. PostgreSQL allows us to indicate that a specific table must be included into the backup, even if it belongs to an extension. This is done by invoking the pg_extension_config_backup() special function with the following arguments:

- The name of the table or sequence to back up
- An optional WHERE clause to filter the tuples to back up

During installation, an extension manipulates search_path. It is a good idea to invoke the function with a fully qualified name, such as pg_catalog.pg_extension_config_backup().

If you need to back up the content of the files table (excluding entries where f_type is 'bak'), the script of *Listing 3* must be changed by adding an invocation to the previous function, as follows:

```
CREATE TABLE files ( ... );
SELECT pg_catalog.pg_extension_config_dump( '@extschema@.files',
                        $filter$ WHERE f_type <> 'bak' $filter$ );
...
```

Note that since we have used the @extschema@ variable to fully qualify the table name, as well as dollar quoting to correctly escape the filter string, the preceding example will configure the backup system so that files with a different type than 'bak' will be regularly dumped.

This feature should be used for every object the extension is going to create that is going to be manipulated by the user. The exclusion filter should remove every tuple the extension creates on its own, so it is a good idea to use a flag to discriminate the tuples created by the extension or manipulated by the user.

If there is no exclusion filter, the whole content of the table is going to be dumped in the backup. This only makes sense if the table has been created by the extension as an empty container, which means the extension did not insert any tuples at all.

Adding an object to an existing extension

The ALTER EXTENSION command allows for the dynamic addition of a database object to an existing extension. For instance, suppose you want the playlist table to be part of the pg11ssp extension. You can issue ALTER EXTENSION to add this table to the extension. The result will be that the table will be managed with all the other extension objects, so if you remove the extension, then the playlist table will also be removed. Similarly, the table will disappear from the regular database backup, as it is now part of the extension, unless you configure the backup for the table, as shown in the previous section. The following command ties the playlist table to the pg11ssp extension:

```
testdb=> ALTER EXTENSION pg11ssp ADD TABLE playlist;
```

On the other hand, it is possible to untie an object from an extension. For instance, if you want the packt.files table to become an independent database object, you can use the following command:

```
testdb=> ALTER EXTENSION pg11ssp DROP TABLE packt.files;
testdb=> ALTER EXTENSION pg11ssp DROP SEQUENCE packt.files_pk_seq;
```

First of all, note that the sequence on which the table depends is removed by the extension. This makes the untie work fully. Otherwise, if only the table was removed from the extension, the extension would become un-droppable because the sequence is on the extension side and the sequence consumer (the table) is on the database side. The second thing to note is that the previous commands do not drop the database objects, only the relationships between them and the extension.

The PostgreSQL Extension Network (PGXN)

The **PostgreSQL Extension Network** (**PGXN**) is a collection of extensions and tools to manage them in order to ease your experience with extensions. It is very similar to the **Comprehensive Perl Archive Network** (**CPAN**). Thanks to the PGXN, developers can share and distribute their extensions to other people, who, in turn, can download and install their extensions.

The extension ecosystem

The PGXN is made up of four main components: search, manager, API, and client.

Usually, the first entry point for a user is the PGXN Search, a website through which a user can search for an extension through categories, keywords, descriptions, and so on.

The most important part of PGXN is the manager, which is a web form to upload and distribute extensions. Developers can upload their extensions through the manager and distribute them worldwide. Extensions must be portable, which means they must be built on top of PGXS (the API). Moreover, a special JSON file must be provided for each extension. This file contains meta-information about the author, license, version, and dependencies of the extension, as well as other information needed to correctly handle and index the extension in the catalog.

Each distribution server implements a PGXN API, which provides a set of functionalities, using which the repository can be queried and extensions can be downloaded.

Finally, the PGXN client program allows for the automation of extension downloading and installation.

Getting an extension from the search website

Imagine you want to install the `pg_track_settings` extension, a utility that allows you to track changes to the server. Using this extension, we can create snapshots to inspect what has changed since the last configuration.

The first step is to browse to `http://pgxn.org` and search for the latest `pgtracksettings` extension available, which, at the time of writing, is version 1.0.1. The download link is `http://api.pgxn.org/dist/pg_track_settings/1.0.1/pg_track_settings-1.0.1.zip`. We can download this as follows:

```
% wget
http://api.pgxn.org/dist/pg_track_settings/1.0.1/pg_track_settings-1.0.1.zi
p
```

It is now time to extract it and inspect the content:

```
% unzip pg_track_settings-1.0.1.zip
...
% cd pg_track_settings-1.0.1
% ls
...
pg_track_settings--1.0.0--1.0.1.sql
pg_track_settings--1.0.0.sql
pg_track_settings.control
pg_track_settings--1.0.1.sql Makefile
META.json
```

The extension contains the `pg_track_settings.control` main `control` file, secondary control files for upgrading to the 1.0.1 version, `Makefile`, the `META.json` file required by PGXN, and a lot of other metadata that is required for the extension to compile and run.

It is possible to install the extension using the PGXS `makefile`:

```
% sudo make install
```

If everything succeeds, we can then use the extension within the database:

```
testdb=# CREATE EXTENSION pg_track_settings;
testdb=# \dx pg_track_settings
                    List of installed extensions
       Name          | Version | Schema |       Description
---------------------+---------+--------+------------------------
 pg_track_settings | 1.0.1   | public | Track settings changes
```

This is the manual approach to using PGXN for downloading and installing an extension. Of course, if you are on a different platform to Unix, the way in which you download and extract commands might change, but the main concepts remain the same. Read every extension documentation carefully, with particular regard to the installation instructions and compatibility notes.

In order to uninstall the extension, you need first to unload it from the database:

```
testdb=# DROP EXTENSION pg_track_settings;
```

Then, use the `Makefile` target `uninstall` to remove it from the cluster:

```
% sudo make uninstall
```

The PGXN Client

The PGXN Client is an external application, similar to `cpan(1)` or `cpanm(1)` for Perl. The PGXN client allows us to search for, download, and deploy an extension that is available on the PGXN repositories. It is worth noting that, while it is stable and usable, the PGXN Client application is no longer maintained.

In order to see how PGXN client works, let's install the `pgtracksettings` extension of the previous section again.

First of all, the PGXN client must be installed on the server. The program is a Python executable that can be downloaded from `https://pypi.org/project/pgxnclient/` and can be installed via `pip` (the Python installer) or with a distribution pre-built package. For instance, to install it on a Debian or Ubuntu system, carry out the following command:

```
% sudo apt install pgxnclient
```

To install on a FreeBSD server, carry out the following command:

```
% sudo pkg install pgxnclient
```

To install it via the Python installer, carry out the following command:

```
% pip install pgxnclient
```

Once the executable is installed, you should be able to run it from your favorite shell. After the installation, you should have both the `pgxnclient` and the `pgxn` executables, both working in the same way (in fact, the former is an alias for the second one which has a shorter name). In the following example, the `pgxn` and `pgxnclient` executable will be used interchangeably.

The PGXN client is a command-oriented program. The main commands that can be used are the following:

- search searches for an extension documentation containing the specified terms. It is possible to specify what to search with the extra --docs (documentation, the default), --dist (distributions), or --ext (extensions) options.
- info prints information about an extension and accepts the --details (for more details) and --readme (to see the distribution's README content) extra options.
- install deploys an extension, after downloading it, to the PostgreSQL server. Its counterpart is uninstall, which removes the extension from the server.
- load loads the extension into the database. It executes the CREATE EXTENSION in the specified database.

All options that handle extensions accept three extra arguments:

- stable (the default): This means that only extensions marked as stable must be considered
- testing: This means that also development branches must be considered for installation
- unstable: This means that any version of an extension should be accepted, even an unstable one

Let's take a look at a possible workflow with pgxnclient in order to install the pg_track_settings extension seen previously. Please note that it is better to remove this extension from your database and cluster before reinstalling it with pgxnclient.

First of all, let's gather some information about the extension. Even if we already know the extension name, perform a search in order to see which extensions are related to the terms track and settings:

```
% pgxnclient search --ext track settings

pg_track_settings 1.0.1
    A simple extension which keep *track* of postgresql *settings*
    modifications

prioritize 1.0.4
    get and *set* the priorities of backends

session_variables 0.0.4
    Functions to manipulate (get/*set*) session variables
...
```

The extension named `og_track_settings` is what we are searching for, so let's inspect it a little closer:

```
% pgxnclient info pg_track_settings
name: pg_track_settings
abstract: A simple extension which keep track of postgresql settings
modifications
...
license: postgresql
release_status: stable
version: 1.0.1
date: 2018-07-15T08:53:48Z
sha1: c19e30d6d0724bc38d61177ece35aa5fe1b7af1a
provides: pg_track_settings: 1.0.1
runtime: requires: PostgreSQL 9.1.0
```

When you are sure this is the extension you are looking for, you can install it via the `install` command. Since the default is to use a stable version, and this extension has been marked as stable, version 1.0.1 is what will be installed:

```
% pgxn install --sudo `which sudo` pg_track_settings

INFO: best version: pg_track_settings 1.0.1
INFO: saving /tmp/tmp6aq7lrjs/pg_track_settings-1.0.1.zip
INFO: unpacking: /tmp/tmp6aq7lrjs/pg_track_settings-1.0.1.zip
INFO: building extension
make: Nothing to be done for 'all'.
INFO: installing extension
Password:
/bin/sh /opt/pg11/lib/postgresql/pgxs/src/makefiles/../../config/install-sh
-c -d '/opt/pg11/share/postgresql/extension'
/bin/sh /opt/pg11/lib/postgresql/pgxs/src/makefiles/../../config/install-sh
-c -d '/opt/pg11/share/postgresql/extension'
/bin/sh /opt/pg11/lib/postgresql/pgxs/src/makefiles/../../config/install-sh
-c -d '/opt/pg11/share/doc/postgresql/extension'
/usr/bin/install -c -m 644 .//pg_track_settings.control
'/opt/pg11/share/postgresql/extension/'
/usr/bin/install -c -m 644 .//pg_track_settings--1.0.0--1.0.1.sql
.//pg_track_settings--1.0.0.sql .//pg_track_settings--1.0.1.sql
'/opt/pg11/share/postgresql/extension/'
/usr/bin/install -c -m 644 .//README.md
'/opt/pg11/share/doc/postgresql/extension/'
```

Since the deployment to the server requires superuser privileges, the `--sudo` option can be specified to make `pgxnclient` ask for the `sudo(1)` password when needed.

Now that the extension is in place, it is possible to issue `CREATE EXTENSION` in the database in which it is to be installed. Alternatively, by using `pgxnclient` again, the `load` command can be used:

```
% pgxn load -d testdb -h localhost -U luca pg_track_settings
INFO: best version: pg_track_settings 1.0.1 CREATE EXTENSION
```

The output clearly shows that the extension has been created on the target database.

As you have seen, using the PGXN client results in an easier and more customizable approach, because the program exploits the PGXN API to perform the searching for, downloading of, and installation of extensions.

Summary

Extensions are the PostgreSQL packages that allow a database to be improved by installing new types, code, and functionalities. The main advantage of these packages is that each one is managed as a whole, without any regard as to how much data and functionality it installs into the database. This makes extensions very easy to manage, maintain, and even upgrade, thanks to a well-defined standard for upgrade paths.

The PostgreSQL Extension ecosystem is continuously growing and, thanks to the PGXN, developers and administrators can find and contribute the extensions they need. Using tools such as `pgxnclient`, it is also possible to automate the extension management.

The next chapter will focus on processes, showing you how to make backend (connection) processes to share events and data and how to make them communicate with external applications. We will also look at how to plug in your own processes in the cluster life cycle.

References

- Sqitch, Sane Database Change Management, official website available at: `https://sqitch.org/`
- PostgreSQL Extension Network, official website available at: `https://pgxn.org/`
- PostgreSQL Extensions, official documentation available at: `https://www.postgresql.org/docs/11/static/extend-extensions.html`
- PGXS, official PostgreSQL documentation available at: `https://www.postgresql.org/docs/11/static/extend-pgxs.html`
- PGXN Client, GitHub official repository available at: `https://github.com/dvarrazzo/pgxnclient`

Inter Process Communication and Background Workers

9

This chapter focuses on processes. PostgreSQL uses processes to carry out all its magic. Database connections are handled by backend processes, while utility processes (such as vacuum, autovacuum, or WAL writer) run all the time to ensure that a database is in good shape.

From the user's perspective, the process-model provides strong isolation. This means that, apart from the database data being used as a communication stream, two processes cannot easily inter-communicate. For this reason, PostgreSQL provides a powerful and elegant model of event broadcasting that allows backend processes and client processes to synchronize and exchange data dynamically.

However, process communication is not the only feature shown in this chapter. PostgreSQL also allows the user to write custom processes, called background workers, that can extend the PostgreSQL set of processes and, therefore, enhance its capabilities.

In this chapter, you will learn the following:

- What IPC is and how to receive and send events from one process to another
- How to use IPC to synchronize the database with external applications and processes
- How to embed your own process within the cluster life cycle using Background Workers

Inter-Process Communication (IPC)

PostgreSQL allows for a dynamic **Inter-Process Communication** (IPC) where each backend process can communicate with other backend processes. While PostgreSQL provides a way to signal a backend process in order to terminate it—a kind of extreme IPC—the kind of communication this section focuses on is the asynchronous event model, which is known as a *channel*.

Asynchronous events

PostgreSQL provides a mechanism to publish events over a channel. Subscribers can subscribe to this channel to receive these events. The whole communication process happens asynchronously.

Each event is sent over a *channel*, which is identified by a unique name and can have an optional *payload*, in the form of a text string. If no payload is specified, the subscribers will get an empty payload string. Otherwise, they will receive the payload sent over the channel. When events are received, each subscriber receives a tuple of information including the following:

1. The *event channel name*
2. The *payload* (or an empty string), a textual string with a maximum size of 8,000 bytes
3. The **Process IDentifier (PID)** of the publisher process (the process that sent the event)

The channel name and the payload are only relevant to the application that is going to use them and do not have any particular meaning for PostgreSQL.

A session (a database connection) can use any of the following commands to interact with the asynchronous event system:

- `LISTEN` to register the session as a subscriber for a particular channel
- `UNLISTEN` to remove the subscription from a channel
- `NOTIFY` to publish an event over a channel

It is worth noting that LISTEN and UNLISTEN are applied when the transaction is committed. Therefore, if a transaction performs a rollback, the related action is not applied. Moreover, invoking any of the two commands multiple times in sequence on the same channel has no effect.

The whole event system works at transaction boundaries. Events are not sent (NOTIFY has no effect) until the publisher transaction commits. This means that an event cannot be sent if the publisher transaction aborts. On the other hand, subscribers will be notified of a pending event after the completion of the transaction in which they are currently involved (either committed or aborted). This means that this event mechanism cannot be used for real-time IPC. Therefore, in order to make this mechanism responsive, transactions should be kept as short as possible. Working at a transaction boundary, however, guarantees that events notified by the same transaction will be pushed to subscribers in the same order that they were produced. Similarly, events from different transactions will be notified to subscribers in the same order that the transactions are committed.

Another consequence of working at transaction boundaries is that the server can decide to fold multiple identical events within the same transaction. If a transaction publishes the same event with the same payload more than once, the server can decide to push only one event to the subscriber. However, outside transaction boundaries, if the same event with the same payload is sent from different transactions, the server will never group the messages into a single instance. This is an important aspect to consider when relying on the same message being delivered multiple times.

Limitations of events

A channel/event name can be any valid identifier that makes sense to the application scenario. Each event is limited in size: a maximum payload of 8,000 bytes can be sent per event. Moreover, there are no security checks on events: any user on the database (and therefore any connection) can subscribe to events and get information from channels.

Finally, bear in mind that events published before the subscriber issues a LISTEN command cannot be received. The subscription becomes active when LISTEN is executed and only for subsequent events. While these limitations are often not that important, you must take them into account when designing your IPC infrastructure.

A single process example

It is now time to see the effect of `LISTEN` and `NOTIFY` in action. We are going to look at a session that notifies itself about an event. Let's consider an event named `table_insert` and a channel with the same name, and look at how to notify an event on that channel. *Listing 1* shows a session that first accepts incoming events (`LISTEN`), then notifies an event (`NOTIFY`). Note that the default output on the `psql` terminal is to get a message with the PID of the sender process, the event type, and the payload. Finally, the session unregistered itself from the event channel (`UNLISTEN`), meaning it will no longer accept events on the channel. As you can see, the later `NOTIFY` did not have any effect on the session itself:

```
testdb=> LISTEN table_insert;
testdb=> NOTIFY table_insert, 'A new tuple has been inserted';

Asynchronous notification "table_insert" with payload "A new tuple has been
inserted" received from server process with PID 834.

testdb=> UNLISTEN table_insert;
testdb=> NOTIFY table_insert, 'Two new tuples has been inserted';
-- nothing happens ...
```

Listing 1: Self-notification

Event special functions

The `pg_notify()` special function can be used to send a notification programmatically. It accepts the same two arguments of `NOTIFY`, the channel name and the payload, and notifies the event over the channel. *Listing 2* shows how to invoke the function to perform a self-notification as in the previous section.

Another special function is `pg_listening_channels()`, which provides a result set made of the names of channels the current session is listening on. As shown in *Listing 2*, this function can be used to get back the event channels that the process is subscribed to:

```
testdb=> LISTEN insert_table;
testdb=> SELECT pg_notify( 'insert_table',                              'A
new row has been inserted!' );
 pg_notify
-----------

(1 row)
```

```
Asynchronous notification "insert_table" with payload "A new row has been
inserted!" received from server process with PID 806.

testdb=> SELECT * FROM pg_listening_channels();
 pg_listening_channels
-----------------------
 insert_table
```

Listing 2: Using special functions to notify and get back the list of subscribed channels

Channels and event queues

A channel is dynamically created each time it is referenced for the first time. All events published on a channel will be queued in an internal queue that holds the data to publish them on demand to the subscribers. The queue is generally 8 GB in size and, while this might seem like a lot, it is worth noting that unconsumed events may well fill the queue. In other words, if no subscribers are attached to receive events, the queue will begin accumulating events until it is full. This, in turn, will make it impossible to publish new events (using NOTIFY) and therefore any transaction trying to publish new events will fail.

It is therefore important to ensure that the queue is never filled. To monitor it, we have the special pg_notification_queue_usage() function which returns a number indicating the status of the queue. This number will either be between 0 (empty) and 1 (full):

```
-- on an empty queue system ...
testdb=> SELECT pg_notification_queue_usage();
pg_notification_queue_usage
-----------------------------
0
```

In order to see how the queue use increases, *Listing 3* performs a cycle to notify us about different events over and over. It exploits the pg_notify() function within PERFORM because the output of the function is thrown away:

```
testdb=> DO $code$
DECLARE
  payload text;
BEGIN
  FOR i IN 1 .. 250000 LOOP
        payload := 'Event ' || i;
        PERFORM pg_notify( 'insert_table', payload );
  END LOOP;
END $code$ LANGUAGE plpgsql;
```

Listing 3: Notification of multiple unread events

After the execution of *Listing 3*, which might take up to three minutes, the queue status results are as follows:

```
testdb=# SELECT pg_notification_queue_usage();
 pg_notification_queue_usage
-----------------------------
         0.000508308410644531
```

As you can see, the queue is hardly being used at all because it is configured to handle a lot of undelivered events (8 GB by default).

An example of IPC between two database backends

In order to demonstrate how to really use the event mechanism, let's consider a simple real-world scenario. Each time a new music file (of mp3 type) is added to the `files` table, a notification must be issued. Subscribers to the event could, for instance, add the file to the playlist or suggest the file to the user as a possible new addition to their playlist.

Let's start with the notifications. The name of the channel will be `new_music_event` and the payload will contain the primary key of the new inserted file. To automate the notification, we could use a *trigger* to fire the event publishing over the channel, or we could use a rule. To keep things simple, this example will use a trigger, as shown in *Listing 4*. This trigger will fire before the completion of every `INSERT` or `UPDATE` against the `files` table when the new tuple has a `f_type` of `'mp3'`. The function executed, `f_tr_notify_new_music()`, will receive the channel name as an argument. Please note that, in order to make this trigger work, you have to disable other triggers that may clash with the one shown in *Listing 4*:

```
testdb=> CREATE TRIGGER tr_notify_new_music
BEFORE INSERT OR UPDATE ON files
FOR EACH ROW WHEN ( NEW.f_type = 'mp3' )
EXECUTE PROCEDURE f_tr_notify_new_music( 'new_music_event' );
```

Listing 4: A trigger to notify about the insertion of a new musical file

Listing 5 shows the `f_tr_notify_new_music()` function, which is quite straightforward. If the file type is `mp3`, it notifies the event. Note that the function could omit the redundant check against the `f_type` column, since the trigger in *Listing 4* already includes a `WHEN` condition that fires the function only for `'mp3'` tuples. Note that we are using the `pg_notify()` function through `PERFORM` (since the output of the function is discarded):

```
testdb=> CREATE OR REPLACE FUNCTION f_tr_notify_new_music()
RETURNS TRIGGER AS $code$
 BEGIN
 IF NEW.f_type = 'mp3' THEN
 RAISE DEBUG 'Notifying new primary key % over channel %', NEW.pk, TG_ARGV[
0 ];
 PERFORM pg_notify( TG_ARGV[ 0 ], NEW.pk::text );
 END IF;
 RETURN NEW;
 END $code$ LANGUAGE plpgsql;
```

Listing 5: The function that performs the notification

Let's see the previous code in action. *Listing 6* shows a possible notification within a single `psql` session:

```
testdb=> LISTEN new_music_event;
testdb=> INSERT INTO files( f_name, f_hash, f_type )
        VALUES( 'sad-but-true.mp3', 'abdde44fcc763212', 'mp3') ;
DEBUG:  Notifying new primary key 12 over channel new_music_event
INSERT 0 1

Asynchronous notification "new_music_event" with payload "12" received from
server
process with PID 806.
```

Listing 6: An example of a notification within the same session

Of course, notifying the same session that performs the insert is not really particularly exciting, or useful, so let's see the interaction between two different sessions. *Listing 7* shows the session that performs the insertion, while *Listing 8* shows another session that gets notified. As you can see in *Listings 7* and *8*, two different processes (identified by different PIDs) exchange an event with a payload that contains the primary key of the fresh tuple:

```
-- publisher session
testdb=> SELECT pg_backend_pid();
 pg_backend_pid
----------------
           806
```

```
testdb=> INSERT INTO files( f_name, f_hash, f_type )
                VALUES( 'wheels.mp3', '3456abdde44fcc763212', 'mp3') ;
```

Listing 7: A session that performs an insert

```
-- subscriber session
testdb=> LISTEN new_music_event;

Asynchronous notification "new_music_event" with payload "14" received from
server process with PID 806.
```

Listing 8: A session that subscribes to events

On top of this simple and powerful event mechanism, it is possible to build quite complex asynchronous notification scenarios.

An example of IPC between different applications

The event mechanism is available across the whole database. This means that it is possible to build clients that get notified about events or push events. In order to demonstrate how this is possible, let's build a client application that will get notified by new musical file events.

We'll start with a Perl example, shown in *Listing 9*. The program connects to the database and performs the LISTEN command, then does an infinite loop, invoking the special pg_notifies driver function. The pg_notifies function polls for a new event and returns an array reference with the element of the array set to the channel name, PID, and payload respectively. Since the payload is the primary key of the fresh musical file, it is possible to build a straightforward query to insert the new song into the playlist table:

```perl
#!env perl
use v5.20;
use DBI;

my $database_connection =
    DBI->connect( 'dbi:Pg:dbname=testdb host=localhost', 'luca', 'xxxx' )
    || die "\nCannot connect to database \n$!";

# subscribe to the channel
$database_connection->do( 'LISTEN new_music_event' );

while ( 1 ) {
    while ( my $event = $database_connection->func( 'pg_notifies' ) ){
        my ( $name, $pid, $payload ) = @$event;
        say "Received an event over $name from process $pid with payload
```

```
$payload";

        # add the new song to the playlist
        my $query = sprintf 'INSERT INTO playlist( p_name ) SELECT f_name
FROM files WHERE pk = %d' , $payload;
        $database_connection->do( $query );
        sleep 1;
    }
}
```

Listing 9: A Perl client that subscribes to events

When the trigger shown in *Listing 4* fires, a notification will be sent over the channel and the client application will be notified. If you execute the Perl application, the output will be similar to the following:

```
% perl 8_06.pl
Received an event over new_music_event from process 1925 with payload 16
```

As a result, a new entry will be added to the playlist table:

```
testdb=> SELECT * FROM playlist;
 pk |          p_name
----+------------------------
 10 | precious-illusions.mp3
```

The same application client can be developed in Java, where the notifications are handled by means of a special method, getNotifications(). This returns the events on a PostgreSQL connection. In the Java client, there is a little more work to do because of the stronger type system and casting, but the implementation is straightforward, as shown in *Listing 10*. As you can see, the first step is to subscribe to the channel. Again, this is done using an explicit statement that executes the LISTEN command. Then, an infinite loop is performed and the special PGNotification object is extracted from the connection. First, the connection is unwrapped, or transformed back to the actual PostgreSQL connection type. This allows us to use the special getNotifications() method on the connection. The connections are returned as an array of the PGNotification object, on which the getName() method returns the event name (the channel), getParameter(), the payload, and getPID(), which is the PID of the sender process. With this information, it is possible to construct the query that inserts the new musical file into the playlist table:

```
import org.postgresql.*;
class PlayListManager {
    public static void main( String argv[] )
        throws Exception {
        Class.forName( "org.postgresql.Driver" );
        String url = "jdbc:postgresql://localhost:5432/testdb";
```

```
        Connection databaseConnection = DriverManager.getConnection(
url,"luca", "xxxxx" );
        Statement listenCommand = databaseConnection.createStatement();
        listenCommand.execute( "LISTEN new_music_event" );
        listenCommand.close();

        while ( true ) {
            PGNotification notifications[] = databaseConnection
                .unwrap( org.postgresql.PGConnection.class )
                .getNotifications();

        if ( notifications == null || notifications.length == 0 )
            continue;

        for ( PGNotification event : notifications ){
            System.out.println( String.format( "Got event over %s from
process %d payload %s",         event.getName(), event.getPID(),
event.getParameter() ) );

            String query = String.format( "INSERT INTO playlist(
p_name) SELECT f_name FROM files WHERE pk = %d", Integer.parseInt(
event.getParameter() ) );

            Statement insert = databaseConnection.createStatement();
            insert.execute( query );
            insert.close();
        }
        Thread.sleep( 1000 );
    }
    }
}
```

Listing 10. A Java client that subscribes to events

With the client running, we can place a new file into the files table, as follows:

```
testdb=> INSERT INTO files( f_name, f_hash, f_type )
        VALUES ( 'take-a-picture.mp3', '365456abdde44fcc763212', 'mp3') ;
```

The client is notified as follows:

```
% java PlayListManager
Got event over new_music_event from process 1207 payload 21
```

The result in the playlist table is, as expected, the following:

```
testdb=> SELECT * FROM playlist
         WHERE p_name like '%picture%';
 pk |        p_name
----+--------------------
 11 | take-a-picture.mp3
```

Background Workers

Background Workers are processes that run under the monitoring of the cluster itself, which means they have a life cycle bound to the life cycle of the cluster itself. Background Workers are a special kind of process: they can plug in as extensions and can exploit PostgreSQL's internal features, most notably its shared memory (where the data resides at runtime).

We can use background workers to form the communication infrastructure in the publish-subscribe model of the logical replication introduced with PostgreSQL 10, even though background workers are actually older than that.

Background Workers are written in the C language, compiled against the PostgreSQL version, and loaded at runtime as shared libraries. Since these processes can access PostgreSQL's internal data structures, they represent both a powerful and possibly dangerous way to extend the cluster behavior.

A Background Worker can be started either when the cluster boots or when it is already running. In the former case, the *postmaster* process is the only responsible for starting the Background Worker, while in the latter case the Background Worker can be started by any regular background process running within the cluster.

Background Workers require a deep knowledge of the internal workflow of PostgreSQL, which is out of the scope of this book. However, this section will give you a taste of what it means to write a background worker. Luckily, PostgreSQL ships with a complete set of examples and tests, and more are available online.

Implementing a Background Worker

A Background Worker is usually implemented as a PostgreSQL module that registers the worker process. A Background Worker process is represented by a BackgroundWorker struct with the following definition:

```
typedef struct BackgroundWorker
{
```

```
       char          bgw_name[BGW_MAXLEN];
       int           bgw_flags;
       BgWorkerStartTime bgw_start_time;
       int           bgw_restart_time;         /* in seconds, or BGW_NEVER_RESTART
 */
       char          bgw_library_name[BGW_MAXLEN];
       char          bgw_function_name[BGW_MAXLEN];
       Datum         bgw_main_arg;
       char          bgw_extra[BGW_EXTRALEN];
       int           bgw_notify_pid;
 } BackgroundWorker;
```

The main fields of the `BackgroundWorker struct` are as follows:

- `bgw_name`: A textual name of the process used in logs, process listing, and so on.
- `bgw_flags`: A set of flags that can be set to one of the following options:
    - `BGWORKER_SHMEM_ACCESS`: This allows access to shared data, which might be shared buffers, locks, and other internal PostgreSQL structures.
    - `BGWORKER_BACKEND_DATABASE_CONNECTION`: This provides the ability to connect to a database and run transactions. Using this flag requires the `BGWORKER_SHMEM_ACCESS` flag to be set at the same time.
- `bgw_start_time`: Indicates when the cluster must start the background worker. The available choices are tied to the PostgreSQL boot cycle, with the following three available values:
    - `BgWorkerStart_PostmasterStart`: This starts the worker as soon as PostgreSQL has completed the boot process.
    - `BgWorkerStart_ConsistentState`: This starts the worker as soon as a hot standby server accepts read-only connections.
    - `BgWorkerStart_RecoveryFinished`: This starts the worker as soon as the cluster is in read-write normal operational mode. It is worth noting that `BgWorkerStart_RecoveryFinished` corresponds to `BgWorkerStart_ConsistentState` for a server that is not a hot standby node.
- `bgw_restart_time`: The amount of seconds PostgreSQL will wait before restarting a crashed worker.
- `bgw_function_name`: The name of the entry point function for the background worker. This function must accept a single argument of Datum type and must return a void value.

- `bgw_library_name`: The library name (the name of the shared library file to use in order to search for the worker function).
- `bgw_main_arg`: The single Datum parameter passed to `bgw_function_name`.
- `bgw_extra`: A pointer to extra data that is not passed to `bgw_function_name` as an argument, but can be accessed by that function.
- `bgw_notify_pid`: The PID of the parent process to be notified when the worker starts or ends. It can be zero if no process is to be signaled (notably, this is the case for the postmaster).

An example implementation of a Background Worker

In order to see a simple example of a Background Worker process, imagine we have the need to implement a *keep-alive* process: a process that will continuously log a specific message to indicate that it is still alive and running. In particular, such a process will log a textual message to a specific table after every set period of time to indicate that the process is still alive. In this section, we'll look at how to implement a background worker, how to schedule a task (a database update) with it, and how to interact with the database by means of SQL queries.

For simplicity, assume there is a log table with a message text field and an automatic timestamp field. Suppose the process must insert a tuple in the table every 10 seconds. This is what is going to be implemented in the following sections.

The module entry point

The `_PG_init()` method is the module entry name and therefore it is responsible for registering the Background Worker within the cluster. *Listing 3* shows the entry point implementation. As you can see, the only thing the function does is to initialize the worker struct (which is of the `BackgroundWorker` type) and, once finished, call the `RegisterBackgroundWorker()` function passing the just-populated `struct`. The cluster will then start the background worker according to the fields in the worker `struct`. It will execute a method called `worker_main` as the horsepower for the Background Worker:

```
void _PG_init(void) {
    BackgroundWorker worker;
    worker.bgw_flags         = BGWORKER_SHMEM_ACCESS   |
BGWORKER_BACKEND_DATABASE_CONNECTION;
    worker.bgw_start_time    = BgWorkerStart_RecoveryFinished;
```

```
    worker.bgw_restart_time   = BGW_NEVER_RESTART;
    snprintf( worker.bgw_name, BGW_MAXLEN, "counter worker" );
  snprintf( worker.bgw_function_name, BGW_MAXLEN, "worker_main" );
  snprintf( worker.bgw_library_name, BGW_MAXLEN, "count_worker" );
  worker.bgw_notify_pid   = 0;

  elog( INFO, "counter_worker::_PG_init registering worker [%s]",
worker.bgw_name );

    RegisterBackgroundWorker(&worker);
}
```

Listing 3: Background Worker entry point

Background Worker Main Function

Listing 4 shows the implementation of the Background Worker process. First of all, the worker creates a StringInfoData variable named queryStringData. This is an internal PostgreSQL type that holds a string (.data), its length (.len), and its possible maximum length (.maxlen). Then, a set of simple log_* variables are initialized with data about the table, including the schema, the username, and other information used to connect to the database in which the entries are to be registered.

When a Background Worker is started, its Posix signals are blocked, so that other processes cannot interrupt the Background Worker during this phase. This way, it can complete its initialization without being interrupted. However, if the worker needs to catch back signals, it has to re-enable the signals. First of all, it has to associate each signal with a handler using the pqsignal() internal function. This function accepts a Posix signal (such as SIGHUP) and a handler function to execute when the signal arrives (such as sighup_handler). Once the signal handlers are in place, it is possible to re-enable the signals by calling BackgroundWorkerUnblockSignals().

At this point, the initialization of the worker is almost done and it can establish a database connection via the BackgroundWorkerInitializeConnection() function. This can be thought of as the lightweight way of establishing a client connection to the database, but this time the connection is within the database itself.

Now that the worker is connected to the database, it runs an infinite loop, at least until it gets SIGTERM. In the loop, the worker sleeps for 10 seconds using a wait latch, a structure used to sleep with the guarantee that it will be resumed if the postmaster process (and therefore the cluster) dies. The rc variable is set every time the latch expires, which is when the worker wakes up. If the rc variable holds WL_POSTMASTER_DEATH, this means that the worker has been resumed because the cluster is dead and there is nothing more to do, so the process terminates with proc_exit(). Otherwise, the worker is resumed because the latch timeout has expired, so it can place a tuple in the log table. To do that, it exploits the **Server Provider Interface** (**SPI**) functions.

The SetCurrentStatementStartTimestamp() method initializes the transaction timestamp, and StartTransacionCommand() begins a real transaction. SPI_connect() call allows the process to issue queries against the database and within the transaction, while PushActiveSnapshot() enables the transaction to have a valid MVCC snapshot. All these functions are called in a defined order to allow the process to interact correctly with the database. The pgstat_report_activity() call is optional and allows statistical reporting about the process (it populates pg_stats and related information tables).

After all this setup, queryStringData is populated with the query (which might look as follows: INSERT INTO public.log(message) VALUES ('STILL ALIVE and counting 1')) via the appendStringInfo() method, which, as you can see, works in a similar way to sprintf(3).

 Before the query is built, queryStringData is reset via resetStringInfo() because it must be changed from the preceding loop value.

It is then time to execute the query via SPI_execute(), to which the query string is passed. The returning value, ret, should be SPI_OK_INSERT in the case of success, or a different value in the case of failure (PostgreSQL provides several SPI_OK values for every different statement and a few SPI_ERROR values for particular error conditions). The last block of code finishes the transaction. Note the CommitTransactionCommand() call and the change to pgstat_report_activity(), which means the process is listed as idle. Once the loop finishes, when SIGTERM has been caught, the process (worker) ends:

```
void worker_main( Datum main_arg ) {
    StringInfoData queryStringData;
    initStringInfo( &queryStringData );
    char *log_table_database = "testdb";
    char *log_table_schema   = "public";
    char *log_table_name     = "log";
```

```
   char *log_table_message  = "STILL ALIVE and counting!";
   char *log_username       = "luca";
   int  log_entry_counter   = 0;
   elog( DEBUG1, "starting counter_worker::worker_main" );

     pqsignal( SIGHUP,  sighup_handler );
     pqsignal( SIGTERM, sigterm_handler );
   sigterm_activated = false;
     BackgroundWorkerUnblockSignals();
     BackgroundWorkerInitializeConnection( log_table_database, log_username,
0 );

     while ( ! sigterm_activated ) {
         int    ret; int    rc;
         elog( DEBUG1, "counter_worker in main loop" );
         rc = WaitLatch( &MyProc->procLatch,
                                   WL_LATCH_SET | WL_TIMEOUT |
WL_POSTMASTER_DEATH,
                     10000L,
                     PG_WAIT_EXTENSION ); /* 10 seconds */
         ResetLatch( &MyProc->procLatch );
         if ( rc & WL_POSTMASTER_DEATH )
             proc_exit( 1 );

         SetCurrentStatementStartTimestamp();
         StartTransactionCommand();
         SPI_connect();
         PushActiveSnapshot( GetTransactionSnapshot() );
         pgstat_report_activity( STATE_RUNNING, queryStringData.data );

         resetStringInfo( &queryStringData );
         appendStringInfo( &queryStringData,
                     "INSERT INTO %s.%s( message ) "
                     "VALUES( '%s %d' ) ",
                     log_table_schema,
                     log_table_name,
                     log_table_message,
                     ++log_entry_counter );

         elog( DEBUG1, "counter_worker executing query [%s] by [%s]",
           queryStringData.data,
           log_username );
         ret = SPI_execute( queryStringData.data, /* query to execute */
                     false,                 /* not readonly query */
                     0 );                   /* no count limit */

         if ( ret != SPI_OK_INSERT )
             elog( FATAL, "counter_worker cannot execute query, error code
```

```
[%d]", ret );

        SPI_finish();
        PopActiveSnapshot();
        CommitTransactionCommand();
        pgstat_report_activity( STATE_IDLE, NULL );
    }
    proc_exit(0);
}
```

Listing 4: Background Worker implementation

Module Signal Handlers

The function to handle SIGTERM is shown in *Listing 5*. The only thing this does is to set the module global variable sigterm_activated, which makes the module loop of *Listing 4* end spontaneously:

```
static void sighup_handler( SIGNAL_ARGS ) {
    int    caught_errno = errno;
    if (MyProc)
        SetLatch(&MyProc->procLatch);

    errno = caught_errno;
}

static void sigterm_handler( SIGNAL_ARGS ) {
  sighup_handler( postgres_signal_arg );
  sigterm_activated = true;
}
```

Listing 5: Module signal handlers

Deploying and starting the Background Worker

In order to compile and deploy the module to the cluster, `Makefile` must be used. The simplest `Makefile` possible for this example is shown in *Listing 6*. The `makefile` instructs the PGXS build system to compile the `count_worker` module:

```
MODULES = count_worker
PG_CONFIG = pg_config
PGXS := $(shell $(PG_CONFIG) --pgxs)
include $(PGXXS)
```

Listing 6: The module Makefile

In order to deploy the module, it is therefore sufficient to run the following command:

```
% sudo make install
/bin/sh /opt/pg11/lib/postgresql/pgxs/src/makefiles/../../config/install-sh
-c -d '/opt/pg11/lib/postgresql' /usr/bin/install -c -m 755 count_worker.so
'/opt/pg11/lib/postgresql/'
```

The Background Worker must be enabled by setting the following in the `postgresql.conf` configuration file:

```
shared_preload_libraries = 'count_worker'
max_worker_processes = 8  # at least one worker!
```

Before restarting the cluster, create the `log` table so that the Background Worker can start its job:

```
testdb=> CREATE TABLE public.log( pk serial PRIMARY KEY, message text, ts
timestamp DEFAULT now() );
```

Finally, restart the server so that the Background Worker can be launched. In the server logs, assuming the minimal log level is at least `DEBUG1`, you will see messages from the Background Worker similar to the following:

```
2018-08-06 20:16:12.547 CEST [2451] DEBUG:   counter_worker in main loop
2018-08-06 20:16:22.613 CEST [2451] DEBUG:   counter_worker executing query
[INSERT INTO public.log( message ) VALUES( 'STILL ALIVE and counting! 3' )
] by [luca]
2018-08-06 20:16:22.614 CEST [2451] DEBUG:   counter_worker in main loop
2018-08-06 20:16:32.685 CEST [2451] DEBUG:   counter_worker executing query
[INSERT INTO public.log( message ) VALUES( 'STILL ALIVE and counting! 4' )
] by [luca]
```

These messages will be at intervals of 10 seconds. The `public.log` table will also be populated with a new record every 10 seconds:

```
testdb=> SELECT * FROM log LIMIT 5;
 pk |          message          |             ts
----+---------------------------+----------------------------
  1 | STILL ALIVE and counting! 1 | 2018-08-06 20:14:43.645351
  2 | STILL ALIVE and counting! 2 | 2018-08-06 20:14:53.65047
  3 | STILL ALIVE and counting! 3 | 2018-08-06 20:15:03.67338
  4 | STILL ALIVE and counting! 4 | 2018-08-06 20:15:13.748284
  5 | STILL ALIVE and counting! 5 | 2018-08-06 20:15:23.765497
```

Signaling the Background Worker

The process will be present in the system table under its custom name, `count_worker`:

```
% ps -auxw | grep worker
postgres 2451   0.0  4.3 165264 21344  -  Ss  20:16    0:00.02 postgres:
counter worker    (postgres)
```

It is therefore possible to send a `SIGTERM` signal to the process. To stop the worker from running, run the following command:

```
% sudo kill -s TERM 2451
```

In the server logs, a message will appear to indicate that the background process has been removed:

```
2018-08-06 20:21:35.026 CEST [2443] DEBUG: unregistering background worker
"counter worker"
```

Summary

PostgreSQL provides several facilities to interact with processes, either internal or external to the server. One important facility is the IPC layer built on top of events and channels, which allows applications and database connections to exchange information through asynchronous events. Another important feature is the Background Worker layer, which enables developers to plug their own specific custom processes into the server.

In the next chapter, we will learn how to add a custom data type to the already rich set provided to you by PostgreSQL.

References

- The PostgreSQL official documentation related to NOTIFY is available at: `https:/ /www.postgresql.org/docs/11/static/sql-notify.html`
- The PostgreSQL official documentation related to LISTEN is available at: `https:/ /www.postgresql.org/docs/11/static/sql-listen.html`
- The PostgreSQL Java Database Connectivity Driver official documentation about JDBC Listen/Notify is available at: `https://jdbc.postgresql.org/ documentation/81/listennotify.html`
- The PostgreSQL official documentation related to Background Workers is available at: `https://www.postgresql.org/docs/11/static/bgworker.html`

10
Custom Data Types

PostgreSQL allows you to create your own data types that are specific data abstractions you can use in your tables, functions, and other database objects.

While PostgreSQL comes with a very rich set of built-in data types, being able to create and customize your own types makes the database more flexible and able to handle very special cases.

This chapter will show you the basic concepts of creating, using, and managing custom data types. However, before you rush into creating your own custom data type, please consider reading the official documentation and searching for the available data types.

In the following sections, we will cover the following topics:

- Creating an enumerated data type
- Creating a composite data type
- Creating your own basic data type

Custom data types

Each custom data type must have a unique name that can be fully qualified if the type belongs to a specific schema, otherwise the type will be created in the current schema.

Data types are created by means of the CREATE TYPE command, as you will see in detail in the following sections. Each data type belongs to the user that creates it. It is possible to drop a type with the DROP TYPE command, as well as to change the type definition via ALTER TYPE. However, changes are limited to the specific data type (as you will see in detail in the next sections).

Available custom data types can be inspected with the \dT (describe types) psql command. Types are handled in the pg_type system catalog, which provides the basic information about the type (for instance, its name, size, and ownership), while specific implementation details can be handled in separated tables. It is worth noting that the pg_type.typtype column contains a letter that indicates the specific implementation of a custom data type (for instance, 'e' for enumerations and 'c' for composite).

PostgreSQL allows the creation of the following data types:

- Composite types
- Basic types
- Range types

In the following sections, only the enumerations, composite, and basic data types will be shown. It is worth noting that creating new types requires a deep knowledge about the database and its internal mechanics, as most of the customizations are implemented in the C language.

Enumerations

Enumerations are probably the simplest data type you can create; they handle a specific set of allowed values and nothing more. In PostgreSQL, enumerations behave similarly to the enum type of many other programming languages such as C or Java.

An enumeration is defined by adding text labels to the type. Each label represents one, and only one, value. There are a few rules to keep in mind when creating an enumeration. These are as follows:

1. Labels are case-sensitive and can include spaces
2. The order in which labels are added to the data type also represents the order of comparison between different labels (for example, the first label is *less than* the last one)
3. Usually, a label cannot be longer than 63 bytes (for example, the internal NAMEDATLEN value)
4. A label cannot be removed once it has been added

Creating an enumeration

In order to see how to create and use an enumerated type, let's implement a type named t_media_file_type that must enumerate available file types (such as audio and text). The implementation of this data type is shown in *Listing 1*; the type is marked with the AS ENUM property that makes PostgreSQL aware that the type is an enumeration. Allowed values are specified as a text list of labels:

```
testdb=> CREATE TYPE t_media_file_type
AS ENUM ( 'audio', 'image', 'text' );
```

Listing 1: A file type enumeration

The t_media_file_type represents an improved version of the f_type column, which at the moment handles the extension of the file (see previous chapters). It is therefore possible to add a new column to the files table to handle the custom enumeration, as shown in *Listing 2*. As you can see, the table is enriched by the f_media_type column with the t_media_file_type data type, whose value defaults to the 'text' enumeration label (of course, the default value is optional):

```
testdb=> ALTER TABLE files
ADD COLUMN f_media_type t_media_file_type
DEFAULT 'text';
```

Listing 2: Adding the enumeration as a column to the files table

It is then possible to update the files table in order to make the new column reflect the file type effectively. As an example, you can issue an UPDATE statement as shown in *Listing 3* (please note the need to cast the text string returned by CASE into the appropriate enumerated type):

```
testdb=> UPDATE files SET f_media_type = CASE f_type
                    WHEN 'png' THEN 'image'
                    WHEN 'mp3' THEN 'audio'
                    ELSE 'text'
                    END::t_media_file_type;
```

Listing 3: Updating the files table using the enumerated values

Querying the enumerated data type works similarly to using a text value. For instance, as shown in *Listing 4*, you can get all the files in a media type range by specifying the labels you are interested in:

```
testdb=> SELECT f_name, f_type, f_media_type
               FROM files  WHERE f_media_type IN ( 'audio', 'image' );

    f_name     | f_type | f_media_type
---------------+--------+--------------
 picture1.png  | png    | image
 picture2.png  | png    | image
 picture3.png  | png    | image
 audio1.mp3    | mp3    | audio
 audio2.mp3    | mp3    | audio
 audio3.mp3    | mp3    | audio
```

Listing 4: Querying the enumeration data type

One rule about enumerations is that order matters: comparison operators work by comparing the order in which labels have been added to the enumeration. Since in the enumeration of *Listing 1* the 'text' label is the latest, it is also the *greatest*, with the 'audio' label being the *smallest* and the 'image' one being in the middle. In other words, a query like the one shown in *Listing 5* will select any label smaller than 'text' and greater than 'audio'. This results in 'image':

```
testdb=> SELECT f_name, f_type, f_media_type
        FROM files  WHERE f_media_type > 'audio' AND f_media_type < 'text';
    f_name     | f_type | f_media_type
---------------+--------+--------------
 picture1.png  | png    | image
 picture2.png  | png    | image
 picture3.png  | png    | image
```

Listing 5: Comparison among enumeration labels

Type safety

An enumerated type allows only types that have been explicitly labeled, meaning that executing a statement like the following will produce an error since the 'mpeg-3' label has not been created in the enumeration:

```
testdb=> UPDATE files SET f_media_type = 'mpeg-3'
        WHERE f_type = 'mp3';

ERROR:  invalid input value for enum t_media_file_type: "mpeg-3"
LINE 2: SET f_media_type = 'mpeg-3' WHERE f_type = 'mp3';
```

Adding values to an existing enumeration

It is possible to add new values to an existing enumeration by means of the ALTER TYPE ADD VALUE command. The command accepts a few options such as IF NOT EXIST that will perform the addition only if the enumerated value is not already a label within the enumeration, and the BEFORE or AFTER options which allow for the insertion of the new value between other values (otherwise it will be added last). In particular, the last two options allow you to control how comparison among values is performed.

In order to demonstrate the addition of a new value, let's extend the previously created t_media_file_type enumeration with the 'pdf' file type. Since such a type can be thought of more as an image type than a textual one, let's add it just after the 'image' type. All of this is expressed by the command in *Listing 6*, where the new 'pdf' type is added AFTER the 'image' one:

```
testdb=> ALTER TYPE t_media_file_type
ADD VALUE
IF NOT EXISTS   -- optional
'pdf'           -- the new label
AFTER 'image';  -- optional
```

Listing 6: Adding a new value to an existing enumeration

In order to use the new value, there is a need to update the table again, for example, with a query like the following:

```
testdb=> UPDATE files SET f_media_type = 'pdf'  WHERE f_type = 'pdf';
```

As a result, executing a query with a comparison like the one in *Listing 5* will provide the output shown in *Listing 7*. As you can see, both 'pdf' and 'image' are now selected since such values are now within the enumeration head ('audio') and tail ('text'):

```
testdb => SELECT f_name, f_type, f_media_type
       FROM files   WHERE f_media_type > 'audio'  AND f_media_type <
'text';
     f_name    | f_type | f_media_type
--------------+--------+--------------
 picture1.png | png    | image
```

```
picture2.png | png     | image
picture3.png | png     | image
chapter5.pdf | pdf     | pdf
```

Listing 7: Comparison among enumeration labels (with a new value)

Where is my enumeration?

Enumerations are stored in the special `pg_enum` catalog with one row per label, which has the following main columns:

- `enumlabel` contains the text label of the enumeration
- `enumsortorder` is a real value that represents the ascending sort order of the enumerated labels

It is possible to extract the generic type information (such as the name) from the `pg_type` catalog and join such information with the `pg_enum` information to get a dump of the enumeration:

```
testdb=> SELECT typname AS enum_name,
               enumlabel AS label,
               enumsortorder AS ordering
        FROM pg_type JOIN pg_enum
             ON pg_type.oid = pg_enum.enumtypid
        WHERE typname = 't_media_file_type'::name
        AND    typtype = 'e'
        ORDER BY 3 ASC;

       enum_name       | label | ordering
-----------------------+-------+----------
 t_media_file_type | audio |        1
 t_media_file_type | image |        2
 t_media_file_type | pdf   |      2.5
 t_media_file_type | text  |        3
```

As you can see, all the labels are listed from the *smallest* (the one with the min `ordering` value) to the highest. Please note that the added `'pdf'` label has been assigned a value between the one of `'text'` and `'image'` since it has been added `BEFORE` `'text'` (see the previous section, *Adding values to an existing enumeration*).

Changing an existing label

There is no specific command to update an enumeration label, even though it is possible, as an administrator, to modify the pg_enum catalog. This, however, is discouraged since it could impact other running queries and applications.

The following is an example of how to update the 'pdf' label to something more verbose:

```
testdb=# UPDATE pg_enum SET enumlabel = 'PDF and PDF/A' WHERE enumlabel =
'pdf' AND enumtypid = ( SELECT oid FROM pg_type
 WHERE typname = 't_media_file_type'::name );
```

Similarly, you can move labels up and down the comparison chain by modifying the enumsortorder value but, again, this is not a standard practice.

Composite types

A composite type is very similar to a record or a rowtype type without having to belong to a table. This is a row made up of other types (columns) with no specific storage table behind. A composite type can be built on top of existing built-in and custom data types, and of course can be used as an argument or return value to a function, as well as a column of a table.

Creating a composite type

In order to demonstrate how to use a composite data type, let's imagine building a type that provides information about a file origin on a version control repository. Such a type will include the commit hash, the branch, and the URI for the repository. The implementation of this new composite type, named t_repository, is shown in *Listing 8*. As you can see here, the implementation is similar to the creation of a regular table:

```
testdb=> CREATE TYPE t_repository
AS ( repo_protocol text,  repo_url      text,
   repo_branch   text,  repo_commit   text );
```

Listing 8: A composite type that represents a version control repository

Before applying the composite type to a table, let's see how it can already be used by functions. *Listing 9* shows a simple function implementation where a text URL is passed as argument and the `t_repository` composite type is returned. As you can see, the composite type is managed as a `record` or `rowtype` type, meaning that individual fields are accessed via the *dot notation*:

```
testdb=> CREATE OR REPLACE FUNCTION
f_url_to_repository( url text, branch text DEFAULT 'master' )
RETURNS t_repository  AS  $code$
  DECLARE
    repo t_repository;
    parts text[];
  BEGIN
    -- extract URL information
    parts := string_to_array( url, '://' );
    repo.repo_protocol := parts[ 1 ];
    -- extract all is before the commit part
    parts := string_to_array( parts[ 2 ], '/commit' );
    repo.repo_url := parts[ 1 ];
    -- if we have a commit, set also the branch
    IF parts[ 2 ] IS NOT NULL AND length( parts[ 2 ] ) > 0 THEN
        repo.repo_commit := parts[ 2 ];
        repo.repo_branch := branch;
    END IF;
    RETURN repo;
  END   $code$ LANGUAGE plpgsql STRICT;

testdb=> SELECT f_url_to_repository(
'https://github.com/fluca1978/fluca1978-pg-utils/commit/bd58bc3203326c63111
80cf9177420c6d88d38af' );
                                      f_url_to_repository
----------------------------------------------------------------------------
-----------------------
 (https,github.com/fluca1978/fluca1978-pg-
utils,master,/bd58bc3203326c6311180cf9177420c6d88d38af)
```

Listing 9: A function that returns the composite type

The function shown in *Listing 9* is really simple and does not perform any advanced checks on the input arguments; it has been shown only to demonstrate that functions can handle composite types in an easy way.

It is now possible to enrich the `files` table with a `t_repository` column that will hold information about the optional repository for each file:

```
testdb=> ALTER TABLE files  ADD COLUMN f_repo t_repository;
```

Composite types are handled in write statements (such as INSERT) by wrapping the values into parentheses, while in read statements (such as SELECT) this is done by wrapping the type name in parentheses and using the dot notation.

As an example, *Listing 10* shows both an UPDATE of a tuple to include the repository information, as well as a couple of queries to get back the results:

```
testdb=> UPDATE files
   SET f_repo = ( 'git',  '~/git/packt',
'14b8f225d4e6462022657d7285bb77ef', 'master' )
    WHERE f_name = 'chapter3.org';

testdb=> SELECT f_name,
  (f_repo).repo_url, (f_repo).repo_commit
 FROM files WHERE f_name = 'chapter3.org';

    f_name     |   repo_url   |  repo_commit
--------------+-------------+-------------
 chapter3.org | ~/git/packt | master


testdb=> SELECT f_name,
  (f_repo).repo_url, (f_repo).repo_commit
 FROM files WHERE (f_repo).repo_protocol IS NOT NULL;

    f_name     |   repo_url   |  repo_commit
--------------+-------------+-------------
 chapter3.org | ~/git/packt | master
```

Listing 10: Handling composite types in statements

It is also possible to reference exactly one field of the composite type by means of the dotted notation without surrounding parentheses, as shown in *Listing 11*:

```
testdb=> UPDATE files
SET  f_repo.repo_protocol = 'file',  f_repo.repo_url = '/packt/code/files/'
WHERE f_type = 'txt';
```

Listing 11: Referencing only a part of a composite type

Adding or removing attributes to composite types

It is possible to add or remove attributes to a composite type by means of the `ALTER TYPE ADD ATTRIBUTE` and `ALTER TYPE DROP ATTRIBUTE` commands respectively. This is really similar to the way a new column is added to or removed from a table.

As a simple example, consider the need to add a new `repo_sync` attribute that indicates whether or not the checkout is in sync with the repository or not. This change is shown in *Listing 12*:

```
testdb=> ALTER TYPE t_repository ADD ATTRIBUTE repo_sync boolean;
```

Listing 12: Adding a new attribute

It is also possible to change the data type of an attribute via the `ALTER TYPE ALTER ATTRIBUTE` command, but the composite data type must be in use.

Type safety

A composite data type will only accept values that can be converted to the right type for the attribute. As an example, if you try to place a wrong data type into a field, PostgreSQL will raise an error:

```
testdb=> UPDATE files SET f_repo.repo_sync = now();

ERROR:  subfield "repo_sync" is of type boolean but expression is of type
timestamp with time zone
LINE 2: SET f_repo.repo_sync = now()
                 ^
HINT:  You will need to rewrite or cast the expression.
```

As you can see, `UPDATE` is prevented because the `repo_sync` field of the `t_repository` type is a Boolean and a `timestamp` cannot be cast automatically to a Boolean value.

Where is my composite type?

A composite type is pretty much managed as a regular relation (such as a table), and you can find references to this in `pg_class`, `pg_attribute` (columns and attributes), and, of course, `pg_type` catalogs. In order to extract basic information about a composite type, the query shown in *Listing 13* joins these three catalogs and produces the attribute names and types for the `t_repository` type.

Please note the usage of the `format_type()` special function to get a human-readable representation of each attribute type:

```
testdb=> SELECT    a.attname AS attribute_name
  , format_type( a.atttypid, a.atttypmod ) AS attribute_type
  FROM pg_attribute a   JOIN pg_class c ON c.oid = a.attrelid
      JOIN pg_type t ON   t.oid = c.reltype   WHERE t.typname =
't_repository'::name   AND    t.typtype = 'c'   AND    c.relkind = t.typtype;


 attribute_name | attribute_type
----------------+----------------
 repo_protocol  | text
 repo_url       | text
 repo_branch    | text
 repo_commit    | text
 repo_sync      | boolean
```

Listing 13: Querying the system catalog to get back the composite type basic information

Basic types

A basic type, also known as a scalar type, can be created only by a superuser and at least requires the definition of two functions to handle type transformation. These data types must have an implementation contained in a PostgreSQL module, written in the C language. The details about how a PostgreSQL module works, as well as its internal types and facilities, are out of the scope of this book, so in the following only the basic concepts will be explained.

A basic type requires at least two functions:

- An input function, used to convert a textual representation of the type into PostgreSQL data
- An output function, used to convert PostgreSQL data into a textual form

In order to better clarify the use of such functions, consider the following simple case:

```
testdb=> SELECT '1'::int + '2'::int;
 ?column?
----------
    3
```

The input function is invoked to convert the string `'1'` into an integer value with the same value, meaning that the PostgreSQL will convert the string into its internal representation for the int type. The same happens for the value `'2'`, where the input functions accept the string and return the integer value. Then PostgreSQL executes the sum between the two integer values (not the strings) and the resultant 3 integer value is converted into a textual form via the output function. The result of SELECT is therefore the output function applied to the sum result integer value.

While the input and output functions are mandatory, a basic type can be aggressively customized with other properties such as binary functions (for internal binary conversion), analyze functions, and modifiers.

One important property of a basic type is its internal representation size: PostgreSQL needs to know how big a single value of the custom type is in order to be able to pass it around. The size of a type can be either of the following:

- Fixed, meaning that each value will have a well-established size
- Variable, meaning that each value will have its own size

An example of fixed-size types are int, bigint, and smallint, while an example of a variable-size type is the text type.

There are other important properties tied to the size of the type. A type can be used by value or by reference, and only fixed-size types belong to the first category. A type used by value is a small type that is passed around the internal functions by value, while a type used by reference is moved around by means of pointers to its in-memory value. It is worth noting that only small types can be used by value, and in particular they must have a size smaller than or equal to the size of the PostgreSQL Datum variable (usually four bytes).

Lastly, it is a good habit to specify the *alignment* of the type with respect to byte boundaries (one, two, four, and eight bytes): this property defines how the storage must align the internal binary representation of the custom type.

Basic type example – image resolution

In order to demonstrate the workflow for creating a new basic type, assume there is the need to implement an `Image Resolution` type that handles the dimensions of an image (in pixels) and its current resolution (in points per inch).

The user must be able to input the basic values for an image resolution and get back a formal representation of the type. In addition, they must be able to cast values into the image resolution type. The following subsections show how to implement this simple basic type.

Defining the textual representation

The first step is about deciding how to represent the new data type as text—that is, as output—and, on the other hand, how to convert text into the data type. For the specific data type, we are going to provide a representation made by the < H x V @ D dpi> pattern, where H and V are the horizontal and vertical size (in pixels) and D is the resolution in point per inch. The brackets and the other symbols are part of the textual representation. This means that, each time the data type needs to be printed out, it will be displayed with the previous pattern. On the other hand, each time the pattern is used, the server will be able to convert such text form into a type value.

However, the pattern requires too much typing from the user in order to express a value, so as input a short form of H V D will also be accepted. This means that, as a user, you will be able to specify the value as both '<123 x 456 @ 789 dpi' and '123 456 789'.

The two previous patterns are implemented by means of a couple of C macros shown here:

```
#define TEXT_PATTERN    "<%d x %d @ %d dpi>"
#define TEXT_PATTERN_IN "%d %d %d"
```

Listing 14: Macros to define type textual representation

Defining the basic type and helper functions

The `ImgRes` basic type is defined by means of an equally named C structure show in *Listing 15*. The type is really simple and defines three separated fields for handling the image size and resolution:

```
typedef struct ImgRes {
  unsigned int h_px;              /* horizontal pixels */
  unsigned int v_px;              /* vertical pixels */
```

```
    unsigned int dpi;              /* resolution */
} ImgRes;
```

Listing 15: Type implementation

The `ImgRes` structure is made by three integer variables, and since each variable occupies four bytes, the total size of the custom type is 12 bytes. In order to make things clean, the type will be 16 bytes in size and aligned to a `double` (eight bytes). Since the size is in any case larger than that of a `Datum`, the type will be used by reference. All these considerations will help you in defining the custom data type later on.

In order to keep the code clean, it is possible to define a couple of *helper* functions, the following in particular:

- `new_ImgRes()` will allocate memory for a new `ImgRes` object using the `palloc()` PostgreSQL memory allocator
- `to_string()` will convert an `ImgRes` object into a string representation using the output pattern described in the previous section, using the PostgreSQL `sprintf(3)` replacement named `psprintf()`

Both functions are shown in *Listing 16*:

```
ImgRes* new_ImgRes() {
  ImgRes* new_object = (ImgRes*) palloc( sizeof( ImgRes ) );
  new_object->h_px = 300;
  new_object->v_px = 300;
  new_object->dpi = 96;
  return new_object;
}

char* to_string( ImgRes* object ){
  return psprintf( TEXT_PATTERN,
  object->h_px, object->v_px, object->dpi );
}
```

Listing 16: Helper functions to create a new type instance and convert it to its textual representation

Defining the input and output functions

It is now time to define the input and output functions that PostgreSQL is going to use to convert a type value into a string representation and vice versa.

Both functions have a similar prototype:

- They return a `Datum`, an opaque type used by PostgreSQL
- They accept `PG_FUNCTION_ARGS` arguments using a macro that defines the type of the function's arguments
- They are declared using a `PG_FUNCTION_INFO_V1` macro that handles the type declaration for the function

Every C module function must follow these simple rules to be PostgreSQL-usable. The `PG_FUNCTION_ARGS` macro provides an argument named `fcinfo`, which is a structure containing effective function arguments. Such arguments are usually extracted from the structure by means of C macros such as `PG_GETARG_POINTER`. Similarly, functions do return values by means of special C macros such as `PG_RETURN_POINTER`, `PG_RETURN_INT32`, and `PG_RETURN_BOOL`.

Having cleared that, the input function is shown in *Listing 17*. As you can see, the function extracts from its arguments the string representation and, using `sscanf(3)`, tries to match the text pattern to the type. If the pattern does not match, another attempt is made with the *simplified* pattern. In case of another failure, the function emits an error.

Otherwise, if any of the two patterns did succeed, the function can return the pointer to the initialized data structure via `PG_RETURN_POINTER`:

```
PG_FUNCTION_INFO_V1( imgres_input_function );
Datum imgres_input_function( PG_FUNCTION_ARGS ) {
  /* get the textual represntation */
    char     *input_string = PG_GETARG_CSTRING(0);
  /* create a new object */
  ImgRes *object       = new_ImgRes();
  /* try to convert the text into an object */
  int matches = sscanf( input_string,
                        TEXT_PATTERN,
                        &object->h_px,
                        &object->v_px,
                        &object->dpi );
    if ( matches != 3 )
    matches = sscanf( input_string,
                      TEXT_PATTERN_IN,
                      &object->h_px,
                      &object->v_px,
                      &object->dpi );
  if ( matches != 3 )
      ereport(ERROR,
              (errcode(ERRCODE_INVALID_TEXT_REPRESENTATION),
               errmsg("invalid input syntax for imgres: \"%s\"",
```

```
input_string ) ) );
    PG_RETURN_POINTER( object );
}
```

Listing 17: ImgRes input function

The output function is even shorter, since it can exploit the helper function previously defined in `to_string()`. As you can see from *Listing 18*, the function simply extracts the `ImgRes` value from its arguments and returns the string representation of it as a PostgreSQL `cstring` via a `PG_RETURN_CSTRING` macro:

```
PG_FUNCTION_INFO_V1( imgres_output_function );

Datum imgres_output_function( PG_FUNCTION_ARGS ) {
   /* get the object */
   ImgRes *object = (ImgRes*) PG_GETARG_POINTER(0);
     PG_RETURN_CSTRING( to_string( object ) );
}
```

Listing 18: ImgRes output function

The Makefile

Having a `Makefile` for a simple code such as the previous snippet is not mandatory, but since PostgreSQL already provides the PGXS build infrastructure, it is possible to write a short `Makefile` as shown in *Listing 19* to compile and install the module:

```
MODULES = imgres
PG_CONFIG = pg_config
PGXS := $(shell $(PG_CONFIG) --pgxs)
include $(PGXS)
```

Listing 19: Makefile for the ImgRes basic type module

With all the pieces in place, it is possible to compile the file and deploy to the server using a command similar to the following:

```
% sudo -u postgres make clean install
...
/usr/bin/install -c -m 755  imgres.so '/opt/pg11/lib/postgresql/'
```

Creating the glue code

The C functions and the data type are not yet visible from a PostgreSQL perspective, so there is the need to create the SQL type and the functions that will exploit the C code. Since to create the SQL type there is the need to specify the functions, and the functions must handle the type, to avoid the recursion the first step is to create a *placeholder* (also known as a *shell type*) for the type so that its name appears in the system catalog. PostgreSQL allows you to create a placeholder by issuing a simple CREATE TYPE command:

```
testdb=# CREATE TYPE imgres;
```

It is now possible to define the input and output functions that will return and accept the previous `imgres` type respectively. As shown in *Listing 20*, those functions have the very same name as the C counterparts and reference the compiled `imgres.so` file where such functions can be found:

```
testdb=> CREATE OR REPLACE FUNCTION
imgres_input_function( cstring )
RETURNS imgres AS 'imgres.so' LANGUAGE C IMMUTABLE STRICT;

testdb=> CREATE OR REPLACE FUNCTION
imgres_output_function( imgres )
RETURNS cstring AS 'imgres.so' LANGUAGE C IMMUTABLE STRICT;
```

Listing 20: Input and output functions

With the available functions, it is now possible to specify how the type must be implemented issuing another CREATE TYPE and specifying this time the input and output function properties, as shown in the following code snippet:

```
testdb=> CREATE TYPE imgres (
  input           = imgres_input_function,
  output          = imgres_output_function,
  internallength = 16,    alignment      = double );
```

Listing 21: Type redefinition

Please note that in *Listing 21* the size and alignment of the type have also been specified in order to make its redefinition as complete as possible.

It is now time to test the new created type. *Listing 22* shows how the two text patterns are used to convert a string into the type:

```
testdb=# SELECT '600 600 500'::imgres,  '<480x480@150dpi>'::imgres;
       imgres | imgres
----------------------+----------------------
 <600 x 600 @ 500 dpi> | <480 x 480 @ 150 dpi>
```

Listing 22: Using the new type

It is also possible to add operators related to the new data type so that computations between such types will be possible. However, this is out of the scope of this book.

Summary

PostgreSQL is very flexible even in the definition of user-specific data types. In fact, while the database comes with a very rich set of built-in types, users can implement their own on top of existing ones or even by writing a server-internal implementation.

Of course, before implementing a data type, you should carefully analyze your needs and search for an already implemented type that can handle your data requirements.

References

- For the PostgreSQL CREATE TYPE command, official documentation is available at: https://www.postgresql.org/docs/11/static/sql-createtype.html
- For the PostgreSQL C Language Functions, official documentation is available at: https://www.postgresql.org/docs/11/static/xfunc-c.html

Other Books You May Enjoy

If you enjoyed this book, you may be interested in these other books by Packt:

Learning PostgreSQL 10 - Second Edition
Salahaldin Juba, Andrey Volkov

ISBN: 978-1-78839-201-3

- Understand the fundamentals of relational databases, relational algebra, and data modeling
- Install a PostgreSQL cluster, create a database, and implement your data model
- Create tables and views, define indexes, and implement triggers, stored procedures, and other schema objects
- Use the Structured Query Language (SQL) to manipulate data in the database
- Implement business logic on the server side with triggers and stored procedures using PL/pgSQL
- Make use of advanced data types supported by PostgreSQL 10: arrays, hstore, JSONB, and others
- Develop OLAP database solutions using the most recent features of PostgreSQL 10
- Connect your Python applications to a PostgreSQL database and work with data efficiently
- Test your database code, find bottlenecks, improve performance, and enhance the reliability of database applications

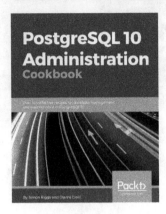

PostgreSQL 10 Administration Cookbook
Simon Riggs, Gianni Ciolli

ISBN: 978-1-78847-492-4

- Get to grips with the newly released PostgreSQL 10 features to improve database performance and reliability
- Manage open source PostgreSQL versions 10 on various platforms.
- Explore best practices for planning and designing live databases
- Select and implement robust backup and recovery techniques in PostgreSQL 10
- Explore concise and clear guidance on replication and high availability
- Discover advanced technical tips for experienced users

Leave a review - let other readers know what you think

Please share your thoughts on this book with others by leaving a review on the site that you bought it from. If you purchased the book from Amazon, please leave us an honest review on this book's Amazon page. This is vital so that other potential readers can see and use your unbiased opinion to make purchasing decisions, we can understand what our customers think about our products, and our authors can see your feedback on the title that they have worked with Packt to create. It will only take a few minutes of your time, but is valuable to other potential customers, our authors, and Packt. Thank you!

Index

executing 55, 58, 59

E

enumeration
  about 224
  creating 225
  existing label, changing 229
  storing 228
  type safety 226
  values, adding 227
error handling 50, 53
event trigger
  example, in foreign languages 165
  PL/Java event trigger 166
  PL/Perl event trigger 165
exception handling 50, 53
extension management
  about 187
  extension, creating 187
  extension, installation 188
  extension, removing 187
extension
  about 183
  backups 194
  control file 185
  creating 189
  data 194
  improved version, creating 192
  preceding version, installing 193
  relocatable extension 186
  scratch, initiating 189
  script file 186

F

FOUND global variable 61
functions
  about 68, 94, 96
  aggregate functions 66
  argument list 70, 73, 75
  compile problem detection 100
  costs 91
  declaration 66
  immutability 88, 91
  implementation 66
  moving, to other schemas 92

normal functions 66
permissions 98
return types 70
runtime problem detection 100
tag insertion function 98
temporary function 93
using 65
values, returning to caller 77, 79, 81, 83, 86, 87
window functions 66

I

insert statement 16, 17
Inter-Process Communication (IPC)
  about 204
  asynchronous events 204
  channels 207
  event queues 207
  event special functions 206
  event, limitations 205
  example, between database backends 208
  example, between different applications 210
  single process example 206
Internet Relay Chat (IRC) 9
iterations 44, 46, 48, 50

J

Java DataBase Connectivity (JDBC) 130

M

mandatory query string 55
modified data
  obtaining, with RETURNING statement 18, 20

N

nesting transactions 109

O

Object Relational Mappers (ORMs) 16
object
  adding, to existing extension 195

P

PGXN client
  reference link 198